MW01194343

THE CHURCH EVENT

THE CHURCH EVENT

CALL AND CHALLENGE OF A CHURCH PROTESTANT

VÍTOR WESTHELLE

FORTRESS PRESS
MINNEAPOLIS

THE CHURCH EVENT
Call and Challenge of a Church Protestant

Copyright © 2010 Fortress Press, an imprint of Augsburg Fortress. All rights reserved. Except for brief quotations in critical articles or reviews, no part of this book may be reproduced in any manner without prior written permission from the publisher. Visit http://www.augsburg-fortress.org/copyrights/ or write to Permissions, Augsburg Fortress, Box 1209, Minneapolis, MN 55440.

Scripture quotations are from the New Revised Standard Version Bible, copyright © 1989 Division of Christian Education of the National Council of the Churches of Christ in the United States of America. Used by permission. All rights reserved.

Cover design: Paul Boehnke
Book design and typesetting: Christy Barker

Library of Congress Cataloging-in-Publication Data
Westhelle, Vítor, 1952–
   The church event : call and challenge of a church Protestant / Vítor Westhelle.
      p. cm.
   Includes bibliographical references (p.   ) and index.
   ISBN 978-0-8006-6332-2 (alk. paper)
   1. Church. 2. Protestantism. 3. Church–Unity. I. Title.
   BV600.3.W48 2010
   262'.7–dc22
                                 2009035379

The paper used in this publication meets the minimum requirements of American National Standard for Information Sciences–Permanence of Paper for Printed Library Materials, ANSI Z329.48-1984.

Manufactured in the U.S.A.

14   13   12   11   10   1   2   3   4   5   6   7   8   9   10

CONTENTS

ABBREVIATIONS

AC	Augsburg Confession (1530)
CT	*Cahiers Théologiques*
CTM	*Currents in Theology and Mission*
DBWE	Dietrich Bonhoeffer Works
DTS	Department of Theology and Studies
ET	*Evangelische Theologie*
ISEDET	Instituto Universitario ISEDET
JR	*Journal of Religion*
LW	*Luther's Works*, American Edition. Edited by Jaroslav Pelikan and Helmut Lehman. Saint Louis: Concordia; Philadelphia: Muhlenberg Press and Fortress Press, 1955–1986
LWF	Lutheran World Federation
NRSV	New Revised Standard Version
SJT	*Scottish Journal of Theology*
TT	*Theology Today*
WA	Weimar edition of *Luther's Works. D. Martin Luthers Werke: Kritische Gesamtausgabe*. Weimar: Hermann Böhlaus Nachfolger
WA Br	Luther's letters. WA Briefwechsel. Weimar: Hermann Böhlaus Nachfolger
WA TR	Luther's *Table Talk*. WA Tischreden. Weimar: Hermann Böhlaus Nachfolger
WCC	World Council of Churches
WW	*Word and World*

INTRODUCTION

Be still, my heart, these great trees are prayers.
Rabindranath Tagore

A study of the church done from a staunch ecclesiological standpoint is akin to a self-dissectional forensic investigation. This requires special inquest skills, for the clues that point to a dysfunction might be hidden in the body under examination. As the coroner's[1] investigations aid in the solving of the mystery of what plagues the body under examination, my inquiry will address the ecclesiological disputes that have assailed the church and are symptoms of its infirmities. It is a difficult task to dissect one's own flesh, as it reveals the entrails where diseases abide. The self-assured among coroners will insist that the procedure is a minor biopsy that reveals no malignity; others, however, will find evidence of terminal necrosis. Yet because the specimen on the autopsy table is not a cadaver but a body throbbing with life, whose vigor is precisely not being subjected to examination, the procedure misses the point: the living body. In other words, a discourse about the church, even such as this, is not a church event. Representing the church by ecclesiological discourse congeals in a given figure the fluidity of presence.

What has been penned in the leaves of this book, while demonstrating the inevitable ecclesiological predicament of representation, is also, and more importantly, an earnest search to detect, even if by *via negativa*, signs of the

---

1. The word *coroner* has its origin in England and comes from "keep the pleas of the Crown," or in Latin *custos placitorum coronas*, and implies a role where the coroner's inquisition and verdict play an important part in the carrying out of justice.

living church in the liminal and adjacent spaces where the church finds itself alive. Church is an event that takes place. This is certainly a counterintuitive assertion, for two reasons. First, it is so because what takes place leaves registered the evidence of its permanence; thus it is not an event that then fades into a background from which it will not be retrieved. Another analogy may be helpful. In the study of micro-atomic particles, the physicist Werner Heisenberg proposed what is called the uncertainty principle. According to this principle, in the observation of the behavior of these particles, the physicist can establish either the position in which a particle is detected or the momentum or velocity with which it is traveling, but never the two—position and momentum—simultaneously; the more precisely one is defined, the less certain the other is. A similar uncertainty principle is at work in the study of the church. We can either locate the church spatially (or represent this location) or detect its motions and trace the events by which it is defined, but the two—representable location and event—cannot be determined simultaneously even as both are ecclesial experiences inscribed in the life of the church. This is so because the spaces in which the church takes place are liminal spaces, defined only by the evanescent transit they register in connecting other and more stable spaces.

Second, the assertion that the church event takes place in liminal spaces is also strange because liminal spaces are spaces where danger lurks. Nonetheless, it is on this dangerous playground that freedom germinates and the church has its roots; and there and there alone, precisely in the adjacency of danger, it is at ease. John of Patmos vividly depicts this space: "And I saw what appeared to be a sea of glass mixed with fire, and those who had conquered the beast and its image and the number of its name, standing beside the sea of glass with harps of God" (Rev. 15:2). But what requires a thorough examination are the mechanisms through which, in search for more solid ground, the church circumvents the spaces of adjacency and creates one or more representations of itself that are stable or at least aim at being stable. Representation works; it offers a stable image of unstable appearances. But in them the church discovers itself also in captivity.

This captivity is twofold, confining all conversation about church either to its inner institutional formation or to its integration into the politico-cultural order of the day, resulting in either an unapologetic exclusivism or an inclusivism that blurs distinctiveness. The various denominations—be it Roman Catholicism with its robust magisterium; Eastern Orthodoxy with its elaborate liturgy, the centrality of its episcopacy, and stout theological backing from the early Greek fathers; Pentecostalism with its charismatic spontaneity and its financial and organizational strength; or mainline Protestantism with its congregationalism, confessionalist verve, and ecumenical endeavors—all articulate their teachings about the church and its ministry based on what they regard as the unassailable core of their tradition. These churches either ground these teachings in their own resources, thus being their own public, or else draw them from the surrounding public arena in which they find themselves immersed.

Historically, so far, we have remained true to our mammalian trait of territoriality,[2] since, with few exceptions, almost all of church-talk has been a territorial dispute shifting from fighting over borders to signing truce treaties. This territorialization of the ecclesiological discourse is mitigated only by eschatological provisos, which are regularly claimed as a promise yet to be fulfilled, its verification remitted to the "second coming," an unending temporal deferred eschatology, which becomes the inaccessible verification of the territorial truth.[3] The creedal definition of the church as being one, holy, catholic, and apostolic is commonly dispatched to such an unattainable eschatological horizon. Yet such eschatological deferment functions only as a perfunctory gesture to account for deficits in the conceptual effort to ground the church's identity. The combination of territorialization with eschatological deferment has been the foundation and the relentless aim of apologetic ecclesiology. The eschatological proviso works as a veil for the defense of the territorial church. What we find is an inverse relation between the two: if the function of the church is to proclaim the kingdom until it comes, its coming means that the territorial church will be no more. This relation leads to the paradoxical affirmation that while the church "proclaims" the kingdom, it needs to claim its own institutional reality, protecting itself from this very coming.[4] If an institution is created to address and solve a problem, self-interest and base instinct of self-preservation dictate that its first function is to ensure that the problem is not solved.

H. Richard Niebuhr, in *Social Sources of Denominationalism*, denounced with prophetic incisiveness the situation in which the churches found themselves in his time, a situation that does not seem to have changed in any substantial way:

> Denominationalism in the Christian church is such an unacknowledged hypocrisy. . . . It represents the accommodation of Christianity to the caste-system of human society. . . . The division of the churches closely

---

2. Territoriality is a characteristic feature of mammals, the order to which human beings belong, where one's space or territory is guarded at all costs.

3. Laurel C. Schneider, *Beyond Monotheism: A Theology of Multiplicity* (London: Routledge, 2008), describes this deferment as the "logic of the One" that works within this eschatological horizon and asks rhetorically, "What will happen to the horizon of Christian thought if the One—even as an eschatological hope that disciplines the many in the now—is not one?" (89).

4. A parallel criticism that draws on the theologies of Karl Barth and Martin Luther can be found in Matthew Myers Bolton, *God against Religion: Rethinking Christian Theology through Worship* (Grand Rapids: Eerdmans, 2008).

follows the division of men into the castes of national, racial, and economic groups. It draws the color line in the church of God; . . . it seats the rich and poor apart at the table of the Lord, where the fortunate may enjoy the bounty they have provided while the other feed upon the crusts their poverty affords.[5]

Niebuhr decries the contradiction between the territorial principle of denominationalism and the values of the kingdom, even as the church under this condition "often regards itself as a Christian achievement and glorifies its martyrs as bearers of the Cross."[6]

Territories are demarcated by borders, institutions by the limits of their mandate and their resources, and societies by their margins, as bodies have their limits defined by their skin. These limits, margins, or borders are places delimited by their proximity to other places with which they are also bound by vicinity. While the church proclaims a kingdom that is not of this world, it is this border that appears as its antithesis, as a possible port of entry to this other reality. And it does not matter whether the kingdom comes from outside, invading the protective skin, or whether the church is thought to be the very kingdom in a state of germination. The result is the same: the incoming or the blossoming of the kingdom spells doom to the church frontier. It will bring the limit to an end and the church will be no more. And this end is at the same time the church's goal (*telos*) and its consummation (*eschaton*).

Territorial principles are deduced from the unsettling etymology of the word *territory*. It derives both from *earth* (*terra*) and from *terrere* (to frighten).[7] If in one sense it defines the space of belonging, it also simultaneously indicates that which frightens off the one who does not belong or is excluded. The book of Acts is regarded as the first book on the history of the Christian church. However, the word *church* (*ekklēsia*) appears only in chapter 5, where the story is told of two new members of the church, Ananias and Sapphira, who hid part of their resources to avoid sharing it with the whole congregation. By divine intervention they were struck dead. The word *church* is first registered in this verse that closes the pericope: "And great fear (*fobos megas*) seized the whole church (*holēn tēn ekklēsian*) and all who heard of these things" (Acts 5:11). The church is presented here as a threshold that offers an entrance to a community that is a reassuring home on unstable ground but is also a fatal exit for those who betray the solidarity it demands.

---

5. H. Richard Niebuhr, *The Social Sources of Denominationalism* (New York: Henry Holt, 1929), 6. In his description of denominationalism, Niebuhr includes what today would be regarded as nondenominational churches as well as the Roman Catholic Church.

6. Ibid.

7. Homi K. Bhabha, *The Location of Culture* (New York: Routledge, 1994), 99–100.

Belonging and fear are the opposing poles that define the borders, limits, and margins of a territory; they define what is proper and what is alien. Those who inhabit margins, the marginalized, belong to them—insofar as they do not have another option—and also stand frightened on this infirm ground. Church happens here, and in the midst of danger there is an overwhelming experience of ease. Yet the shaky ground and the impossibility of holding to an assurance of permanence and security propel us to safer ground. This ground that lies in the vicinity of the church event and offers to it a tempting stability is attained by a process unfolded in two steps. First, a genealogy needs to be established that provides a sense of permanence and an identity. In construing this identity, one needs to define a given genealogy, a lineage, an ancestry that tells whether one belongs there or not. Second, these genealogies then need to be re-presented, transposed to the present since they belong to an elected past. An image that conveys this twofold process of according a sense of belonging is the identity card. One establishes one's identity by retelling stories, identifying sources, and evoking symbols and metaphors that will serve as emblems for such identity. While origins are fluid and the memory of them is always selective, the images we elect to stand for them easily harden, like a piece of pottery fired in the oven of history.

Such images are varied and plentiful, but some are more easily recognizable than others. Roman Catholicism, for example, appeals to Matthew 16, Peter's reception of the office of the keys for the administration of the household of God built upon the rock called Peter (vv. 18–19). The rock upon which a house is built and the keys that give access to heaven and earth are indeed a powerful image. Protestants in general and Eastern Orthodox Christians[8] as well gravitate toward the Pentecost account of Acts 2 to establish the genesis of the church, suggesting that from its inception it is constituted by a public meeting in which people of different nations, cultures, and languages are participatory members, able to communicate among themselves and with God through tongues of fire in a language that bridges human divisions. But the images pertaining to the church's genealogy in theological discourse precede those generated by the New Testament as the rock (*kephas* in Aramaic; *petra* in Greek) and the tongues of fire. I am interested in pursuing these other metaphors, not in order to provide an alternative, but for the sake of destabilizing an ecclesiological discourse that has been held captive by images of the church that reflect and reinforce modes of church representation tied to territorial allegiances. Other images and models of the church might eventually fall into place

---

8. See, e.g., Sergius Bulgakov, *The Bride of the Lamb* (Grand Rapids: Eerdmans, 2002), 423: "[T]here is always a place in the world for the Holy Spirit's descent and presence. This place is the incarnate Son Himself, the world as the body of Christ, which, in the Pentecost, also becomes the temple of the Holy Spirit."

as well in the course of my perusal. But the reason for employing this modus operandi of alternating images is pertinent. I am seeking to avoid stabilization and reification within a single motif, for when that happens the medium, the image, becomes the message, in the apt expression of Marshall McLuhan. Representations work, and they work only too well; they hold us captive to and captivated by ideals! To use a Platonic notion in its reverse, the body of the church is imprisoned by its soul.[9]

To exemplify how this destabilizing works, consider two further images as alternative root metaphors that disturb the tranquil realm of domesticated representations we have of the church and how it liberates its body. One comes from the *Shepherd of Hermas*, where the church is an "old woman." The other is from Luther, who used the "tree" to stand for the church, placing it in a landscape in which church cannot be conceived on its own or conceptualized by itself apart from other dimensions of everyday life. Neither the author of the *Shepherd of Hermas* nor Luther allowed the metaphor to exhaust the meaning or subsume it under the political and economic regime of the day.

HERMAS AND LUTHER

In the *Shepherd of Hermas*, a very popular second-century book regarded in some areas as canonical even at a time when the canon was still in process of reception,[10] we have this description of a vision of the church:[11] Hermas is carried by the Spirit to a place in the countryside where an old woman appears to him. She is walking and reading a book. She approaches and gives the book to Hermas, asking him to pass it on to the "elect of God." Then a revelation is given to him. A young man appears to him and asks Hermas: "Who do you think that old woman is from whom you received the book?" Hermas responds that she is "The Sibyl," a legendary female seer and prophet from several cults of classical antiquity and even regarded by Celsus as the object of Christian belief and cult.[12] The young man says: "You are in a mistake, it is not the Sibyl." "Who is it, then?" asks Hermas. "It is the church," says the young man. Hermas, living in a time when the Christian church was barely coming into existence, asks the obvious question: "Why then is she an old woman?" And the response

---

9. Foucault describes this inversion of the Platonic formula as a feature of modernity in which "the soul is the prison of the body." Michel Foucault, *Discipline and Punish* (trans. Alan Sheridan; New York: Vintage, 1979), 30.

10. Irenaeus, *Against Heresy* 4.20.2., in *Ante-Nicene Fathers*, vol. 1 (ed. Alexander Roberts and James Donaldson; repr., Peabody, Mass.: Hendrickson, 1994), 488.

11. *Ante-Nicene Fathers*, vol. 2 (ed. Alexander Roberts and James Donaldson; repr., Peabody, Mass.: Hendrickson, 1994), 11–12 ("Second Vision"). All the quotations from the dialogue that follow are from this passage.

12. See Origen, *Against Celsus* (Cambridge: Cambridge University Press, 1965), 5, chap. 61.

is thus: "Because she was created first of all. On this account is she old. And for her sake was the world made."

This vision would not have surprised Luther. In his *Lectures on Genesis* he explains the establishment of the day of Sabbath as "intended for the worship of God. . . [in] which God speaks with us through His Word and we, in turn, speak with Him through prayer and faith." This is God's first instituted order. As in the vision of Hermas, the human, says Luther, "was specially created for the knowledge and worship of God. . . . This is the real purpose of the seventh day: that the Word of God be preached and heard."[13] And in addition, God built for Adam "as it were, a temple: . . . the tree of the knowledge of good and evil was Adam's church, altar and pulpit . . . somewhat like a chapel in which there were many trees of the same variety, namely, the trees of the knowledge of good and evil."[14] Following Hermas, in Luther's view also the "church was established first."[15] This is indeed a radically catholic view of the church; it includes all humans insofar as all are descendents of Adam, "who would have gathered on the Sabbath day"[16] in Eden, where trees were planted in large number.

Thus the Reformer articulated his interpretation that there were several trees of life and also several trees of the knowledge of good and evil. His insistence that this interpretation "does not appear at all preposterous"[17] is indeed intriguing and revealing. Henceforth I surmise that it is no more preposterous to imply that this multiplicity prefigures, in Luther's mind, the diversity of religions and their different forms of worship. This interpretation is at least consistent with Luther's and the Reformation's conception of the multicentered character of the church, if not the plurality of world religions. This is a unique view of the universality of the church. In this view every tree of life offers sustenance for different communities, and every tree of the knowledge of good and evil is a place of worship and discernment. To each tribe its scribe; to each tree its creed.

The epigraph to this introduction is an injunction from Rabindranath Tagore, the Nobel Laureate poet and educator, from early-twentieth-century India: "Be still, my heart, these great trees are prayers." There is an amazing resonance between the poet's words from one hundred years ago and the Reformer's lectures from five hundred years past. In fact, all of nature is itself a lesson on law and gospel. The tree of good and evil is the place not only of worship but also of condemnation: "Not only in the churches, therefore, we hear ourselves charged

---

13. *Lectures on Genesis, LW* 1:80f.

14. Ibid., 94f.

15. Ibid., 104. Note that being *established* first is, for Luther, not being *created* first; a creation and a mandate are different things. This is a distinction that the *Shepherd of Hermas* does not make.

16. Ibid., 105. The Lutheran *simul* works here too. For him the trees of knowledge that condemn are also the trees of life that nourish and bring vigor (ibid., 92f.).

17. Ibid., 95.

with sin. All the fields, yes, almost the entire creation is full of such sermons."[18] We can trace the motif and go back a further two millennia and hear the hopeful verses of a prophet announcing the end of the Babylonian exile:

> . . . the trees of the field shall clap their hands.
> Instead of the thorn shall come up the cypress;
>> instead of the brier shall come up the myrtle;
> and it shall be to the LORD for a memorial,
>> for an everlasting sign that shall not be cut off.
>
> (Isaiah 55:12-13)

Further exploring this metaphor of the tree, we find it used across cultures to represent symbolically that which connects us to nature and the divine. We encounter it in African traditional folklore as the tree that represents the space in which mediation and reconciliation can happen.[19] Or take the poem "Hope" by French poet Charles Péguy:

> I am says God, Lord of the Three Virtues.
> Faith [metonym for the church] is a great tree, an oak rooted in the heart
>> of France
> And under the wings of that tree, Charity, my daughter Charity shelters
>> all the woes of the world.
> And my little hope is nothing but a bud that little earnest of a bud which
>> shows itself at the beginning of April.[20]

Finally, I need to mention the image of the tree evoked by the book of Revelation, which describes the New Jerusalem as being crossed by the river of life, and at the banks of the river is the tree of life "producing its fruits each month; and the leaves of the tree are for the healing of the nations" (Rev. 22:2). The New Jerusalem has trees for nourishment and healing but has no temple (21:22), no institution that holds its center; it has only this living entity, a tree at the margins of the river of life.

This virtually universal, not to mention ecologically evocative, image of the church, the church of Adam and all of his descendants, stands in sharp contrast to another of Luther's major themes: his enraged words against his own church. After all, he was the pivot of the Protestant schism in Western

---

18. *LW* 1:209.

19. See Thomas G. Christensen, "The Gbaya Naming of Jesus: An Inquiry into the Contextualization of Soteriological Themes among the Gbaya of Cameroon" (Ph.D. diss., Lutheran School of Theology at Chicago, 1984).

20. Charles Péguy, "Hope," in *Men and Saints* (New York: Pantheon, 1944), 237.

Christianity, calling the church nothing less than the *magna peccatrix*, the great sinner or whore. As corrupted as the churches may be, they remain as places in which the law that condemns is pronounced, even against the church itself, and the word of salvation and liberation is proclaimed.

The tree or trees metaphor of the church on which Luther dwells extensively in his *Lectures on Genesis* is exceedingly rich in its imagery. However, we can understand its role in Luther's theology and the suggestive plays with the metaphor only by looking at the way he places it in relation to two other institutions mandated by God, which flank the church. Being the first institution established by divine mandate, the church stands in proximity to the household, which for Luther's medieval mind encompassed all that pertained to the *oeconomia*, the rule of the house, from biological reproduction to the production of the means for the sustenance of life (i.e., labor), the economy in the modern sense of the word. The other institution is politics (*politia*), including everything from the state administration to courts, guilds, and associations (*societatis*) that would roughly correspond to what we would call the state and civil society. The church, or to stay with the symbolic image of Luther, the tree in the garden, is what provides a place of respite where people can sojourn while moving in between the two distinct spaces—the space of the house where nourishment is produced and provided but life is regimented by hierarchy, and the public space of the city where the practice of governance is exercised but demands a constant struggle to fence a space for oneself. To use another set of metaphors (which for Luther are in fact metonymies), the church's location is the space between the house and the street. This was his challenge, to find images for the church that convey not only its marginal existence, but its centrality to the life of those who inhabit these margins, this space between spaces, where economic efficiency comes to a halt and political strategies are subverted.

The theological reflection I present in the following pages develops its argument in two parts. The first section (chaps. 1–5) presents the parameters for the formation, inception, and construal of the ecclesiological disputes locating the basic issues at stake both in the multifaceted ecclesiological debates throughout history and in the global presence of communities that pledge allegiance to the message of Jesus Christ. The second part (chaps. 6–10) offers a language for reconstructing the debate without falling into some of the linguistic traps of the past disputes that are clarified in the first part. The problem of church and eschatology is the guiding thread throughout the whole book. It is thus an essay on the church and its end, in the double sense of limit (or termination), and of goal. The unraveling of what church *representation* means offers the key to open deadlocks of historical disputes and will be elaborated in the first part, while the second part is construed around the notion of *adjacency*, being at ease in the frightening borders of the representations of church that hold it captive.

The argument I propose is succinct: The ecclesiological problem is situated within the tension of two forms of institutional representation. Each of these has its merit and internal consistency but is only marginally related to what constitutes the church as such. Hence the question is not framed by the polarities as in mystical communion versus institution, charism versus power, dogmatic pontifications versus sociological analysis, *kairos* versus *topos*. The problem is to locate the church as it delineates different institutional claims, distinct justifications of its power, divergent social formations, and the spaces it claims to regiment. The situation is similar to the performance of a play: although the play cannot happen without the dexterity of the actors, the text of the play, or the building of the stage, the performance itself is nonetheless sui generis. The performance is not reducible or accounted for even if all the previous components are added up. Whatever form of representation ecclesial communities choose to reenact, that choice will always be a given ground, a presupposed infrastructure, but will never induce the blossoming of the church as such. To use a more blunt but fitting image, the living church is to the forms of its self-representation what a parasite is to its host; the orchid[21] that blooms would not have a "presence" but for the tree that hosts it, yet it does not blossom because of the tree. In theological jargon, the host is the law, but the bud and its blossoming are the gospel.

---

21. The orchid is an epiphyte, a plant parasite that grows on another plant, usually a tree. Orchids anchor themselves to the host plant so as to expose themselves to light, air, and moisture. Most orchids derive only support and not nourishment from their host.

CHURCH PROFILES

1

AND THE SO-CALLED ECCLESIOLOGICAL DEFICIT OF PROTESTANTISM

> *We need a bit of negative ecclesiology, church theology in a minor key,*
> *in order to do away with centuries-long ecclesiocentrism*
> *of the empirical phenomenon of "Christian religion": for the sake of God,*
> *for the sake of Jesus the Christ and for the sake of humanity.*
> Edward Schillebeeckx

ON THE CHURCH ECUMENICAL

Whether we like to admit it or not, ecclesiology, the doctrine of the church, has always been a touch-me-not and yet forget-me-not subject. What is it that makes this doctrine a touchy and tetchy subject at the same time? My argument is that it has to do with the question of how the church's identity is shaped, and that has always been a topic of dispute, even if it is not always discerned. But why? Because this identity is what gives the church its proper characteristics and defines its contours over and against what it does not stand for. But institutional identities are malleable; they wither or bloom due to a complex array of circumstances in the negotiation of what constitutes the unity of the church. The modern ecumenical movement serves as an exemplary case study of how the waxing and waning of forming identity and defining unity are displayed.

Protestant ecclesiology, which for some of its detractors is a contradiction in terms, is finding its identity far beyond the historically recognized mainstream Protestant churches, and well beyond its traditional geographic territories—central and northern Europe and North America. This worldwide Protestant phenomenon is in many respects faithful to the spirit of the Reformation of the sixteenth century. As was the case with the Reformation, a variety of Protestants still search for the unity of the church but without surrendering freedom and pluralism. Ecumenism is celebrated, but it is not a value of itself.

Serious criticisms have been raised with respect to the ecumenism of theological consensus, visible unity, or ecclesial approximation from the "underside of history" (in the apt expression of Gustavo Gutiérrez),[1] that is, from the subaltern nations of the world. But simultaneously, some of the most vigorous ecumenical accomplishments have taken place within the same context. I refer not only to cooperation in social action. Ecclesial practice and ministry have also been affected by such an ecumenism, notwithstanding lack of agreement at the doctrinal level. In Latin America, for example, Presbyterians, Roman Catholics, Methodists, Episcopalians, and Lutherans have not reached a doctrinal agreement over the Eucharist, but they often celebrate it together at the grassroots level without official sanction or even against it. Such celebrations are possible only under certain social and political conditions, which provide the context that justifies them. No confessional agreements regulate them. Nor do doctrinal differences prevent them, either in practice or in theological interpretations.

Such ecumenical accomplishments are extremely circumstantial. It is the circumstances that determine their power and also their limitations in defining a stable unity and identity for the church. The criticism of both ecumenism and ecumenical accomplishments themselves is framed by social, political, and economic relations, and by the conflicts and contradictions manifested in given historical junctures. And they simultaneously affect both the inner unity of an ecclesial institution and the relation among ecclesial bodies in practice and theory.[2] How are we to understand this phenomenon?

Camilo Torres, the Colombian priest who died as a guerrilla fighter in 1968, raised the problem and suggested an answer:

> I have given up the duties and privileges of the clergy, but I have not ceased to be a priest. I believe that I have given myself to the revolution out of love for my fellow man. I have ceased to say Mass to practice love for my fellow man in the temporal, economic, and social spheres. When my fellow man has nothing against me, when he has carried out the revolution, then I will return to offering Mass, God permitting.[3]

He continues his commentary, reiterating Matthew 5:23-24: "So when you are offering your gift at the altar, if you remember that your brother or sister has something against you, leave your gift there before the altar and go; first be reconciled to your brother or sister and then come and offer your gift." His criticism is clear. To celebrate communion in a context of social injustice is

1. Gustavo Gutiérrez, "Theology from the Underside of History," in idem, *The Power of the Poor in History: Selected Writings* (trans. R. R. Barr; London: SCM, 1983), 169–221.

2. See Julio de Santa Ana, *Ecumenismo e Libertação* (Petropolis: Vozes, 1987), 116–21; and Gerhard Tiel, "O Processo Conciliar de Mutuo Compromisso (Pacto) para Justiça, Paz e Integridade da Criação," *Estudos Teológicos* 2, no. 28 (1988): 164–69.

3. Camilo Torres, *Revolutionary Priest* (ed. John Gerassi; New York: Vintage, 1971), 368.

hypocritical. Hence he also censured the church for permitting it and thus veiling in a pretense of unity a conflict that grows out of an unjust situation. This has been the suspicion behind ecumenical efforts. Meanwhile, accomplishments in ecumenical endeavors are celebrated in the context of the struggle for justice.

A few years ago the General Secretary of the World Council of Churches, Konrad Raiser, raised a similar issue in a poignant manner, calling attention to the patriarchal implications of the quest for unity:

> The notion of unity is part of a pattern of mind which has entered Christian thinking and practice through its inculturation in the classical Greco-Roman world. . . . The orientation of thinking and practice towards achieving and maintaining unity almost inevitably leads to hierarchical systems of order. . . . In view of this questionable ancestry of the key notion of "unity," it is surprising that the question has been so seldom asked as to whether it is a suitable concept to express the ecumenical vision.[4]

The stronger the emphasis on unity, the more robust and domineering the church will be. New Testament scholar Barbara Rossing has shown that the very word *oikoumenē* is now associated often with tolerance, although in the New Testament it has always a pejorative connotation and is coextensive with the Roman Empire and has been implicated in the equation of unity and totality. Noting the irony that most of the critics of the "imperial ecclesiology" of *oikoumenē* are within the ecumenical movement, she asks, "[I]s an ecumenical understanding of the church and *oikoumenē* inevitably imperial, because it pursues globalized unity at the expense of local community?" And she answers, "Any attempt to reclaim or redefine the word *oikoumenē* for the agenda of ecumenism must begin by repudiating the imperial trajectory of the word, including the church's own imperial legacy."[5]

Enrique Dussel carries this reflection even further, suggesting that the problem is not simply that the overcoming of social divisions makes true unity possible, but that the very search for unity necessarily suppresses difference. And this "difference" has an ontological (not merely social or economic) status.

---

4. "Ecumenism in Search of a New Vision," in *The Ecumenical Movement: An Anthology of Texts and Voices* (ed. Michael Kinnamon and Brian E. Cope; Geneva: WCC, and Grand Rapids: Eerdmans, 1997), 73. Thanks to Barbara Rossing for pointing me to this text.

5. Barbara Rossing, "(Re)claiming *Oikoumenē*? Empire, Ecumenism and the Discipleship of Equals," in *Walk in the Ways of Wisdom: Essays in Honor of Elisabeth Schüssler Fiorenza* (ed. Shelly Matthews, Cynthia Briggs Kittredge, and Melanie Johnson-Debaufre; New York: Trinity Press International, 2003), 82–84.

Ecumene is the same as "totality," a highly abstract technical term; "totality" obviously comes from "total"; we say: "the totality of meaning" of
my day-to-day world, because everything in that world has meaning.
What is in my world makes sense for me but it would not necessarily
do so for another. . . . [T]herefore whoever understands the meaning of
all that takes place there has to be in the center of the world. One in the
periphery of the world does not know what it is all about.[6]

Dussel does not recognize either economic or social justice as a condition for a
possible unity, for such unity already suppresses otherness or vilifies it. Therefore, the very search for unity as such—and therefore for identity—is already
fraught with the spirit of domination and intolerance. However, the criticism
of a possible total unity is not the total criticism of a possible unity. Herein
rests the problem: What are the conditions for a possible unity, and not for a
unity of all that is possible? Or is *unity* even the right word to describe a mark
of the church?

The ecumenical movement, after it was instituted under the guidance of
the World Council of Churches in 1948, reached the turn of the millennium in
what has been dubbed as the ecumenical winter. After going from the 1960s
through the 1980s with exuberance, conducting a "conciliar process" and defining the basic convergent outline of an ecumenical and pluralist conversation,
it encountered in the last couple of decades a reaction that hit the core of its
ecumenical project and liberal proclivities. The conciliar process catalyzed by
the "Justice, Peace, and Integrity of Creation" program all but disappeared
from ecclesial circles. The fragmented identity of confessions and denominations makes its return, privileging bilateral agreements for mutual church
cooperation. The return to the question of confessional identity obfuscates
earlier efforts in search of a post-denominational landscape of the Christian
church. After all the openings offered by the Second Vatican Council in the
wake of Pope John XXIII's call for an *aggiornamento* (bringing the church up to
date), the Roman Catholic Church similarly experienced a process of defining
its own uniqueness. Shortly after signing with the Lutheran World Federation
a "Joint Declaration on the Doctrine of Justification,"[7] the Sacred Congregation for the Doctrine of the Faith in 2000 issued the declaration "Dominus

---

6. Enrique Dussel, *Ethics and the Theology of Liberation* (Maryknoll, N.Y.: Orbis, 1978), 4–5.
Laurel C. Schneider, *Beyond Monotheism: A Theology of Multiplicity* (London: Routledge, 2008),
explores at length the connection between the search for unity or the "logic of the One" in
the Christian church from Constantine through the twenty-first century, which has grounded
its imperial enterprise throughout history.

7. The Joint Declaration on the Doctrine of Justification was signed by the Lutheran World
Federation and the Catholic Church in Augsburg, Germany, October 31, 1999.

Iesus," denying Protestant communities the title of "church" for not keeping the historical episcopate and a "valid Eucharist."[8] This same position is repeated emphatically in a 2007 document by the same Sacred Congregation.[9] Thus a process of re-Romanization of the Catholic Church is proceeding in tandem with the "ecumenical winter."[10]

If this looks like a gloomy scenario to mark the end of a century with so many ecumenical achievements, there is another side to the picture. An impressive ecumenical convergence of historical churches in the Protestant tradition, and also with the Church of Rome, culminated in the landmark bilateral (sometimes plurilateral) agreements. Porvoo (1993), between Scandinavian Lutherans and the Church of England; Leuenberg (1973), between European Lutherans and Reformed; Call to Common Mission (1999), between Lutherans and Episcopalians in the United States; Formula of Common Agreement (1997), between Reformed churches and Lutherans in the United States; and the Joint Declaration on the Doctrine of Justification (1999), between the Vatican and the Lutheran World Federation, are a few examples that have been celebrated as accomplishments outside of the direct purview of worldwide ecumenical organizations such as the WCC. That these agreements have been by and large restricted to the North Atlantic world and among churches of traditional standing is in itself an indication of the problem, because most of these institutional accomplishments bypass the places in the world where Christianity has shown its most dynamic power over the last century. The ecumenical agenda as far as institutional accomplishments are concerned was set by the northern hemisphere of our planet with the undoubtedly earnest intention of encompassing the whole globe. But the south seems to have had other ideas.

The Pentecostal and charismatic movement, whose numerical size is notably substantial and its complexity defiant of typologies,[11] reconfigures the map

---

8. "The Churches which, while not existing in perfect communion with the Catholic Church, remain united to her by means of the closest bonds, that is, by apostolic succession and a valid Eucharist, are true particular Churches. . . . [T]he ecclesial communities which have not preserved the valid Episcopate and the genuine and integral substance of the Eucharistic mystery, are not Churches in the proper sense." "Dominus Iesus," subtitled "On the Unicity and Salvific Universality of Jesus Christ and the Church," was approved by Pope John Paul II and published on August 6, 2000. By "valid Eucharist" what is meant is the doctrine of transubstantiation. See M. Welker, *What Happens in Holy Communion* (Grand Rapids: Eerdmans, 2000), 31.

9. "Responses to Some Questions regarding Certain Aspects of the Doctrine of the Church," written by William Cardinal Levada, head of the Roman Catholic Congregation for the Doctrine of the Faith, on July 10, 2007.

10. Riolando Azzi, "A Romanização da Igreja a Partir da República (1889)," in *Inculturação e Libertação* (ed. Carlos Barndão et al.; São Paulo: Paulinas, 1986), 105–16.

11. Michael Welker, *God the Spirit* (trans. John F. Hoffmeyer; Minneapolis: Fortress Press, 1994), 7–14; Veli-Matti Karkkainen, *An Introduction to Ecclesiology: Ecumenical, Historical and Global Perspectives* (Downers Grove, Ill.: InterVarsity, 2002), 68–78.

of what has been considered normative as far Christianity is concerned.[12] Contrary to the confessional resistance to ecumenical efforts of historical or traditional churches, be they of Roman, Orthodox, or Protestant persuasion, these "new" ecclesial expressions of the Christian faith have shown a vitality that not only dodges confessional disputes but also locates the focus of the Christian expressions of the church in territories that since Constantine have been geographically marginal or regarded only as mission fields. During the last hundred years the location of the majority of Christians has moved to the south and the east of the planet to Africa, Asia, and Latin America. With the increase in their numbers in the south and the east of the planet, there has been also a corresponding and substantial increase in their hold of world Christianity.

In his seminal work that opens the history of modern Protestant theology, *The Christian Faith*, Friedrich Schleiermacher, reflecting on the missionary work in distant lands, discusses the impossibility of new heresies appearing in Christianity. For him,

> new heresies no longer arise, now that the church recruits itself out of its own resources; and the influence of alien faiths on the frontier and in the mission-field of the Church must be reckoned at zero.[13]

And then the great Berliner adds condescendingly:

> [T]here may long remain in the piety of the new converts a great deal which has crept in from their religious affections of former times, and which, if it came to clear consciousness and were expressed as doctrine, would be recognized as heretical.[14]

But he is quick to dismiss any serious threat coming from that direction.

This confidence was expressed less than two centuries ago. At the turn of the millennium the missionary fringes of the still-robust churches of Europe and North America have not only gained in number, surpassing the "mother" churches, but have been facing new challenges to church and doctrine that Schleiermacher could not have dreamed of. This new majority, as mentioned earlier, is now found, particularly in Asia and parts of Africa, in places where Christians are minorities surrounded by other religions. The old certainties,

---

12. Philip Jenkins, *The Next Christendom: The Coming of Global Christianity* (New York: Oxford University Press, 2002), 57–60.

13. Friedrich Schleiermacher, *The Christian Faith* (Edinburgh: T&T Clark, 1989), 96 (*Der christliche Glaube* [2 vols.; Berlin: de Gruyter, 1960], 1:128).

14. Ibid.

built on centuries of debate over doctrines, were, from the fourth century, the resolutions of domestic quarrels within the Christian "house." One such example is the dispute with Arianism regarding the *homoousios* versus *homoiousios*. While the former was about the Son being of the same essence of the Father, the latter affirmed the similarity of the two persons but not identity of the essence. The Arian controversy, among others that were crucial in the weaving of the early church, has recently met contemporary counterparts exemplified by the engagement with and response to the new challenges in the encounter of the Christian with the living faith of her Buddhist, Muslim, or Hindu neighbor. And this phenomenon is largely due to the inheritance of the Enlightenment that shook the foundations out of which the "church recruits itself," to use Schleiermacher's expression.

THE NEW CHALLENGES TO THE CHURCH IN WORLD CHRISTIANITY

The Enlightenment pulverized the basic grounding certainties of the Christian faith: that the prophecies of the Old Testament were fulfilled in Christ, that the miracle accounts are historically reliable, and that the permanence and expansion of the Christian church are evidence of its truthfulness.[15] In its aftermath, Christian theology has been able to find new foundations to regain the certainty that was shaken. The search for these foundations has taken many shapes, which began with Schleiermacher's "feeling of absolute dependence." A number of other rational, historical, empirical, or psychological groundings have been suggested. Alfred N. Whitehead expressed this quest for a foundation by saying that Christianity is a religion in search of metaphysics,[16] an unshakable ground on which to built its edifice. Others evaded the challenge of the Enlightenment and clung to the inerrancy of the scriptures no matter what objection could be raised. Still others find the unbroken tradition of institutional and liturgical practices to be a self-evident guarantor of truth and certainty in a time of deep uncertainties.

Reflecting on this uncertainty, Reinhard Hütter, in his authoritative study of Protestant ecclesiology, celebrates the ecclesiological accomplishments of two leading contemporary theologians, George Lindbeck and Oswald Bayer. Even as he regards their proposals as offering a "constructive point of departure for

---

15. See Herman Samuel Reimarus, "Fragmente," in *Lessings Werke* (Berlin: G. Hempel, 1879); and Gotthold E. Lessing, "On the Proof of the Spirit and of Power," in *Lessing's Theological Writings* (trans. Henry Chadwick; Palo Alto, Calif.: Stanford University Press, 1956), 51.

16. Alfred N. Whitehead, *Religion in the Making: Lowell Lectures 1926* (New York: Macmillan, 1926), 50.

understanding how theology can be conceived as a distinct church practice," for him they still "exhibit an ecclesiological deficit and specially an inadequate ecclesiological anchoring of church doctrine."[17] This is the basic concern that has been raised to modern foundationalist approaches that "anchor" its theology in something other than church doctrine. Lindbeck and Bayer, Hütter claims, "exhibit a thoroughgoing fundamental pneumatological and ecclesiological deficit."[18] Such a deficit will remain "as long as theology's relationship to church doctrine remains undefined," and turns it into "an inherently unstable undertaking."[19] This modern dénouement might indeed have revealed an ecclesial deficit and a theological instability as far as Western societies are concerned. However, it can also be seen as a denouncement of the impending end of the hegemony of the Christian ecclesiological discourse in these societies, where it flourished and was acculturated for almost two millennia.

Sociologist of religion Peter Berger, some time ago in an article in the *Christian Century*, wrote:

> In the course of my career as a sociologist of religion I made one big mistake . . . which I shared with almost everyone who worked in this area in the 1950s and '60s; [it] was to believe that modernity necessarily leads to a decline in religion.[20]

The argument of Berger is that modern pluralism and relativism erode values and beliefs that once were taken for granted as being self-validated. This process, however, does not necessarily lead to secularization and the elimination of all values and beliefs as he formerly believed. On the contrary, by introducing incredulity, doubt, and uncertainty, modernity has even multiplied these values and beliefs in the search for new certainties, thus generating, on the one hand, fundamentalism and totalitarian beliefs and ideologies, and, on the other, a radical relativism that easily slides into nihilism. Between these two extremes there is a pendulum movement characteristic of modernity itself. The religious phenomenon, however, does not pertain only to either of these extreme options, absolutism or nihilism; it is also situated in the middle of this spectrum where certainties are weak and coexist with doubts in institutions that are fragile and malleable. This is the case with most of the mainstream

17. Reinhard Hütter, *Suffering Divine Things: Theology as Church Practice* (Grand Rapids: Eerdmans, 1997), 94.

18. Ibid., 26.

19. Ibid., 26f.

20. Peter Berger, "Protestantism and the Quest for Certainty," *Christian Century* (August 26–September 2, 1998): 782.

Protestant churches characterized by some liberal persuasions within stable and affluent societies.

By focusing on the experience of these "weak" churches, to use the expression of Berger, analysts were inclined to establish a strict correlation between modern reflexivity[21] and the malleable or "weak" nature of these churches. In other words, the more modern reflexivity and criticism express themselves, the weaker the institutions become. And if the process continues—so went the argument—it will reach a point at which these institutions will simply dwindle into extinction.

However, this is where we find a surprise. These weak institutions can survive and will, as Berger has shown,[22] not as a matter of course but out of a resilient and renewed commitment from those who are part of them. It was the dissolution of the taken-for-granted certainties and the "weakening" of modern institutions, particularly the churches, that led social scientists to the impression that modern pluralism would inevitably lead to the decline of religion. Pluralism, as the "coexistence and social interaction of people with different beliefs, values and lifestyles,"[23] does not necessarily lead to an increasing secularism, not even to secularization, though this has occurred in northern Europe, for example (which thus became the paradigm for predictions about the rest of the world).

We are bewildered in the face of an issue that we have falsely diagnosed, and often, in order to avoid recognizing it, we evade it. What needs to be recognized is that pluralism, which accompanied incredulity and doubt in the systems of belief and values, does not eliminate beliefs and values; it only makes them more diverse with very different levels of commitment depending on where one is situated in the spectrum of the pendulum movement between fundamentalism and nihilism.

---

21. "The reflexivity of modernity has to be distinguished from the reflexive monitoring of action intrinsic to all human activity. Modernity's reflexivity refers to the susceptibility of most aspects of social activity, and material relations with nature, to chronic revision in the light of new information or knowledge. Such information or knowledge is not incidental to modern institutions, but constitutive of them—a complicated phenomenon, because many possibilities of reflection about reflexivity exist in modern social conditions." Anthony Giddens, *Modernity and Self-Identity: Self and Society in Late Modern Age* (Stanford, Calif.: Stanford University Press, 1991), 20.

22. Berger, "Protestantism," 794. Berger here relies on the work of Helmut Schelsky.

23. Ibid., 782. Berger concludes this essay with this comment: "The church, while it announces the coming triumph (indeed, that is the core of its message), still bears the marks of Jesus' kenosis. Where is one to look for the presence of this kenotic Jesus? Probably not in the self-assured, triumphalist institutions that merit the appellation of 'strong churches.' I would think that he is more likely to be found in those 'weak' places—where people are unsure of themselves, groping for a few glimpses of truth to hold onto, even where it seems that the roof is about to fall in" (796).

In summary, amid the corroding former certainties, modernity launched the search for new ones, or else surrendered to nihilism. And, ironically, among the new certainties—the sciences, political economy, psychoanalysis, self-help techniques, and so forth—was inserted another one: that secularization and the decline of religion would inevitably be yoked together. The renaming of the present (as in "postmodernity") is often an evasion of a problem caused by the misreading of the symptoms of modernity itself. In other words, the failure to diagnose a preexisting condition led to the renaming of the illness as if it were a new condition.

Since the Enlightenment the Christian church has been painfully aware of the challenge to its claim to truth. But in places where the Enlightenment has not been so decisive a factor as in the North Atlantic axis, the church is confronted by equally profound alternative religious convictions. Its vitality leads to new certainties regarding what grounds the church and its claims and gives it an identity. What is it that makes the church thrive in such contexts while its élan falters in its most traditional fortresses, as in the old continent?

PROFILES OF CHURCH AND MINISTRY

The answer to the question of what makes the church thrive may be found precisely in the contexts where the Enlightenment had its harsher impact and where the scientific worldview became dominant, sidelining other forms of knowledge.[24] In Europe and North America spirited responses to this crisis have come through the emergence of varied profiles of church and ministry, which in turn sheds some light on the process of understanding the Christian churches around the world.

Avery Cardinal Dulles, in his influential *Models of the Church*,[25] uses "models" to perform two functions. One is called the "explanatory" function. This is when a model describes a given ecclesial formation, offering the outline of its most prominent features. In this sense, models are similar to what Max Weber called "ideal types,"[26] which his colleague and friend Ernst Troeltsch applied to his ecclesiological studies. They do not correspond to any actually existing reality (this is why they are called "ideal"), but lift up dominant characteristics

---

24. See Michel Foucault, *Power/Knowledge: Selected Interviews and Other Writings 1972–1977* (ed. Colin Gordon; New York: Pantheon, 1980), 81–82.

25. Avery Dulles, *Models of the Church* (New York: Doubleday, 1987).

26. "[A]n ideal type is formed by the one-sided accentuation of one or more points of view" according to which "concrete individual phenomena . . . are arranged into a unified analytical construct" (*Gedankenbild*); in its purely fictional nature, it is a methodological "utopia [that] cannot be found empirically anywhere in reality." Max Weber, "Objectivity in Social Science and Social Policy," in *The Methodology of the Social Sciences* (ed. and trans. E. A. Shils and H. A. Finch; New York: Free Press, 1949), 90.

that help the observer to recognize and categorize the characteristics of a given social formation. The second function of models is "exploratory." Models, for Dulles, are exploratory when they play a prescriptive role, as in the model of a car that is built to envision and test its possible actual construction.[27]

Different from models and types are "profiles." Profiles, similar to ideal types, can be descriptive, but they are not ideal in the sense that they detect an actual reality that they aim at representing. They might be similar also to the exploratory function of models, but not as a goal or perfection to be achieved. Instead, a profile exposes characteristics that are real but that may not be so obvious for the casual observer. Profiles detect and expose. Akin to case studies, however, they offer glimpses into patterns that far exceed the characters and communities they describe. In their detecting and exposing function, profiles register a search for certainty in an era shaken by uncertainties.

A refreshingly ingenious source for describing these robust profiles that express the church's search for certainty can be found in literature that presents sketches of the church and its ministry. Fictional works of literature like novels work with profiles, detecting and exposing actual realities. Novels that deal with the church and its ministries do precisely that, and they are legion. Three novels will suffice to present some of the different profiles of the church that have become normative, revealing their promises and exposing their quandaries. They all come from a particular period in the history of the West, the period between the two world wars.

The choice I have made among an array of novels that can help in drawing profiles of ministry is somewhat arbitrary, though in this case not entirely. These novels are from a particular period in places that were experiencing turmoil, excitement, and dreadful prospects, thus heightening uncertainties. Two are from the United States and a third from Spain; all reflect a state of affairs in which the world was reconfiguring itself. Fascism was reaching out its tentacles to grip several European countries, while the United States was emerging as the new hegemonic center. Consequently, sociologists and theologians were attentive to the social, political, and economic formation of religious life. Near the end of the nineteenth century and the beginning of the twentieth, Max Weber,[28] Emile Durkheim,[29] Ernst Troeltsch,[30] and H. Richard Niebuhr,[31] to mention the most celebrated, all attempted to classify and examine the social

---

27. Ibid., 16–18.

28. Max Weber, *The Protestant Ethic and the "Spirit" of Capitalism and Other Writings* (ed. and trans. Peter Baehr and Gordon C. Wells; New York: Penguin, 2002).

29. Emile Durkheim, *The Elementary Forms of the Religious Life* (trans. Joseph Ward Swain; New York: Free Press, 1965).

30. Ernst Troeltsch, *The Social Teaching of the Christian Churches* (trans. Olive Wyon; Chicago: University of Chicago Press, 1976).

31. H. Richard Niebuhr, *The Social Sources of Denominationalism* (New York: Holt, 1929).

structure of emerging forms of religious consciousness, communities, and ecclesial formations.

Immediately after these towering figures in sociology and theology made public their work, Bonhoeffer published his dissertation *Sanctorum Communio* (1930), which carries the revealing subtitle, "A Theological Study of the Sociology of the Church."[32] In his work, Bonhoeffer, while affirming the phenomenological approach to the social formations or types of ecclesial communities, draws theological implications that sociological observations might provide, without being restricted to them or using them as a limiting matrix for ecclesiology. He raises the question of what it means to make a theological (*dogmatische* is Bonhoeffer's term) study of social phenomena. Certainly he meant nothing less than to witness or discern God's presence in the very fabric of the social matrix. Bonhoeffer was in search of a theological approach to reading the data collected under the auspices of a methodological atheism in which the "God-hypothesis" plays no role, or in his now-famous expression, *etsi deus non daretur* (as if God did not exist).[33]

Works of fiction instead of sociological analysis or an intra-textual study of ecclesiological dogmas proffer the possibility of finding a third option. Novels are not sociological studies or theological treatises. A work of fiction does not do that. It is not theology, and if it pretends to be, it is bad theology; and it is not sociology either, but it does often combine the description of socio-cultural realities and the delineation of religious convictions even when it exposes a deep, pervasive anti-religious stance.

A novel, any novel, in the words of Georg Lukács, is "the epic of a world that has been abandoned by God."[34] As defined by Lukács, it always has a theology encoded as if in the negative of a film, *sub contraria specie*, to borrow an expression of Luther's theology of the cross. And it relies also on social observation and keen perception of sociological phenomena. It provides evidence of a perceived abandonment, yet the same abandonment is already a profound theological statement. The social sciences remain at the phenomenological level of social formations and interactions. Novels do not share their scientific precision but detect the spiritual void of their times, the frantic search of the ever-elusive meaning of the "vanishing present," in the apt expression

32. Dietrich Bonhoeffer, *Sanctorum Communio: A Theological Study of the Sociology of the Church* (DBWE; trans. Richard Krauss and Nancy Lukens; Minneapolis: Fortress Press, 1998); German edition: *Sanctorum Communio: Eine dogmatische Untersuchung zur Soziologie der Kirche* (Munich: Chr. Kaiser, 1986).

33. Bonhoeffer, *Letters and Papers from Prison* (ed. E. Bethge; New York: Macmillan, 1968), 158, 168–69.

34. Georg Lukács, *The Theory of the Novel: A Historico-Philosophical Essay on the Forms of Great Epic Literature* (trans. Anna Bostock; Cambridge, Mass.: MIT Press, 1971), 88.

of Gayatri Spivak.[35] This is the reason why, unlike the sciences, the novel is ruled not by analogy but by irony, the use of words to convey a negation by affirmation, or concealing something to reveal it. As Lukács says again, "For the novel, irony consists in this freedom of the writer in his relationship to God. . . . Irony, with intuitive double vision, can see where God is to be found in a world abandoned by God."[36] By detecting an absence in the appearance of a presence, or vice versa, a presence in the appearance of an absence, novels are capable of crafting visages and detecting profiles that are more nuanced than sociological taxonomies yet more generalizable than the hair-splitting exercises that theological or dogmatic scholarship often ventures into.

The first profile that detects a condition and describes an option in search of certainty in a world that no longer takes for granted its grounding in the reality of God is *Elmer Gantry*, by the Nobel Prize–winning author Sinclair Lewis. The novel was published in 1927, just a couple of years after the "Scopes Trial" in Dayton, Tennessee. The trial received mass media treatment and marked the public triumph of evangelical creationism. Lewis makes reference to the trial,[37] but his main concern was portraying a fictional preacher for whom the novel was titled. The Reverand Gantry was not the type of fundamentalist whom the prosecution in the Dayton trial vindicated. He was the embodiment of what Max Weber had described some years earlier as a charismatic leader,[38] surrounded by followers filling his bank account to the brim and moving with ease through a variety of "evangelical" denominations and nondenominational churches as well. While "charismatic leader" is a type, "Elmer Gantry" is a profile. The novel is celebrated as one of the most acute analyses of hypocrisy in recent times. Nevertheless, its greater merit is to diagnose in its latency the emergence of a profile of ministry that would become a worldwide phenomenon some decades later. What marked this form of leadership and the sense of certainty it provided to the flock that followed was not dependent on dogma, church structure and polity, inerrancy of scriptures, and, most importantly, not even his persona as such; he offered himself as a depository of longings, failures,

---

35. Gayatri Chakravorty Spivak, *A Critique of Postcolonial Reason: Toward a History of the Vanishing Present* (Cambridge, Mass.: Harvard University Press, 1990).

36. Lukács, *Theory of the Novel*, 92.

37. Sinclair Lewis, *Elmer Gantry* (New York: Penguin, 1967), 374.

38. "As Weber treats charisma in the context of authority, its bearer is always an individual 'leader.' His charismatic quality has to be 'proved' by being recognized as genuine by his followers. This is not, however, as Weber is careful to point out, the ordinary case of leadership by 'consent' of the led, in the usual democratic meaning. The authority of the leader does not express the 'will' of the followers, but rather their duty or obligation. Furthermore, in the event of conflict there can in principle be only one correct solution." Talcott Parsons, "Introduction," in Max Weber, *The Theory of Social and Economic Organization* (trans. A. M. Henderson and Talcott Parsons; New York: Oxford University Press, 1947), 65.

and desires. His leadership was to be a catalyst, eloquently giving the people the assurance of their self-righteousness. So Lewis describes Elmer Gantry's call to be a player on "Christ's team":

> He had but little to do with what he said. The willing was not his but the mob's; the phrases were not his but those of the emotional preachers and hysterical worshipers who he had heard since boyhood. . . . He was certain . . . of being the center of interest in the crowd.[39]

Lewis presents the profile of an emergent form of evangelicalism in which what sustains the church is not the deposited faith it holds, the binding doctrines of Protestant orthodoxy (*fides quae creditur*), or the teaching office of the church, as in Roman Catholicism (*magisterium episcoporum*). However, it is also not the pietistic inner certainty of faith (*fides qua creditur*), nor the holiness movement of the puritan awakenings. It was rather the collective experience of spontaneous and structurally flexible doctrine and morals catalyzed by a charismatic leader intuitively aware of the mechanisms of mass psychology.

While the bilateral agreements have been a beacon of hope for those of ecumenical persuasion, the emergent phenomenon that Lewis describes completely bypasses them and is oblivious to their relevance or irrelevance. His description of this profile combines inspirational sentimentalism with biblical literalism surrounded by an aura of hypocrisy.

At the same time, a different option presents itself in the form of power and splendor. In the same year that *Elmer Gantry* was published (1927), another monumental name in North American literature, Willa Cather, offered to the public *Death Comes for the Archbishop*. While Lewis presents the rootlessness of a church in a society in the effervescent process of urbanization and its gravitation toward charismatic leaders, Cather reverts to an earlier context and its ensuing results. She locates her narration of events in the second half of the nineteenth century while the Roman Catholic Church was going through a vigorous moment of ecclesial renewal while trying to establish its ground on that bastion of world Protestantism, the United States.[40] The work covers the vocational trajectory of a French Jesuit priest, Father Latour ("the tower"), who is sent to New Mexico, a territory that has recently been part of Mexico and incorporated into the U.S., to establish the church among many indigenous

---

39. Lewis, *Elmer Gantry*, 53.

40. It is worth noticing that this period coincides with the conversion of Cardinal Newman from the Church of England to Roman Catholicism (1848) and of the Oxford Movement trying to bring the Church of England back to Rome. It is also the time of Vatican Council I (1869–1870), in which papal infallibility was declared, and just after the doctrine of the immaculate conception of Mary was promulgated (1854).

people (Hopi and Navajo) who had been evangelized by earlier Spanish and Mexican Catholic missionaries, but whose parishes, now in U.S. territory, were outside of any episcopal jurisdiction. As the consecrated bishop of Mexico, Father Latour starts to implement the Romanization of the local parishes, often clashing with the indigenous clergy and their autochthonous piety. An elderly indigenous priest thus describes his church to the bishop in defiance of the new imposing ecclesial policies zealously implemented by the bishop:

> We have a living church here, not a dead arm of the European church. Our religion grew out of the soil, and has its own roots. We pay a filial respect to the person of the Holy Father, but Rome has no authority here. . . . Our people are the most devout left in the world. If you blast their faith by European formalities, they will become infidels and profligates.[41]

Cather represents the Hopi and Navajo people with sympathy, but for all their indigenous inculturation, they were missing the most important lesson: the virtue of church discipline, church structure, and obedience to Rome and the ordination vows attached with it. And that was what the bishop was bringing to them. The "European formalities" were "catholic," meaning of universal validity. Certainty is guaranteed by this universal foundation that preserves truth from its inculturation in values that are regional and indigenous, therefore relative. While Lewis exposes and denounces the search for certainty in the volatile cult of charism, Cather presents with certain irony the self-assured importance of institutional "formalities" of power (in her description), and even as she reveals fascination with aesthetic-ritual institutionalism.

A third literary profile again has a distinctly different emphasis: praxis. The practical and pragmatic results of a model of the church have been championed in early modern time by pietism. Its remarkable herald, Jacob Spener, put it in the most succinct formula when he said that Christianity is not about doctrine, but about practice. "[I]t is by no means enough to have knowledge of the Christian faith, for Christianity consists rather of practice."[42] In the strange company of fellows to abide by this pietistic motto are liberation theologians as well as the promoters of the prosperity gospel. "You will know them by their fruits" (Matt. 7:16) is the biblical injunction that supports this stance. Certainty is assured by the results. Again, Max Weber, the sociologist, is helpful in diagnosing the impact of pietism on Protestant ethics.[43] In their popular interpretation

---

41. Willa Cather, *Death Comes for the Archbishop* (New York: Vintage, 1990), 146f.

42. Phillip Jakob Spener, "From the Pia Desideria: 1675," in *Pietists: Selected Writings* (ed. Peter C. Erb; trans. Theodore G. Tappert; New York: Paulist, 1983), 36.

43. Weber, *Protestant Ethic*, 87–98.

of the Calvinist doctrine of election, the Puritans emphasized the causal relation between election and prosperity. So if one is prosperous in life, that would be the litmus test of whether one belongs to the blessed elect. Election belongs to God alone and nothing we can do may change it, but if prosperity and a holy life are its fruits, Weber argues, then an implied argument of backward causation takes place: if one is industrious, disciplined, and successful in life, that evidence will in fact decide divine election. The results are valid as a criterion for certainty. Orthopraxis becomes the gauging tool for orthodoxy; epistemology precedes ontology.

Three years after Lewis and Cather published their works, yet another but distinct profile of the church was offered. Miguel de Unamuno, in 1930, wrote *San Manuel Bueno, Martyr*,[44] a short novel that narrates the story of a priest in a little Spanish village, Valverde de Lucerna. The story is narrated by a young parishioner, Angela Carballino, who, totally devoted to the priest, discovers that he has lost his faith in the course of his ministry. But with unreserved dedication he faithfully continues to serve his parishioners under the guise of "his pious fraud." Angela's brother, Lazarus, after returning from "America" as an atheist and believer in human social progress without religion, turns into Don Manuel's faithful disciple. He becomes an ardent follower of the priest, eventually knowing that Don Manuel is himself an atheist, yet convinced by his ministry and works of charity.

The great Spanish writer, in the tradition of giants like Cervantes or Calderón de la Barca, concludes his novella with a brief reflection regarding the manuscript by Angela that he presumably found and transcribed:

> I would like also, since Angela Carballino injected her own feeling into the narrative—I don't know how it could be otherwise—to comment on her statement to the effect that if Don Manuel and his disciple Lazarus had confessed to the people, they, the people, would not have understood. Nor, I should like to add, would they have believed the pair. They would have believed in the works and not their words. And works stand by themselves, and need no words to back them up. In a village like Valverde de Lucerna one makes one's confession by one's conduct.
>
> And as for faith, people scarce know what it is, and care less.[45]

Unamuno gives voice to a profile of church and ministry that provides another distinct foundation for certainty, in the midst of the most profound doubt, about what works and helps people here and now. Part and parcel of this help is not

---

44. The English edition can be found in Miguel de Unamuno, *Abel Sanchez and Other Stories* (Washington, D.C.: Regnery, 1996).
45. Ibid., 266.

only charity carried out by the priest and his disciple, but preservation of the parishioners' belief in the afterlife, which their actions are perceived to attest but their hearts and minds in secret deny. Sanctification becomes the guarantor of justification.

These three profiles, one charismatic-fundamentalist, another aesthetic-ritualistic, and the third cynical-pragmatist, represent the literary answers to the contemporary world and its search for certainties, whether we call it modern, late modern, or postmodern. The label does not matter. As Octavio Paz reminds us, "Humans have never known the name of the age they live in, and we are not an exception to this universal rule."[46] The description of its condition does matter, because it is a negative description: the *lack* of certainty that assails a culture and triggers the search for unassailable certainties. What characterizes these options is precisely a response in search of certainty in an inerrant writ, in the visible splendor of an institution, or in a pragmatic driven yearning for results.

IN DEFENSE OF A CHURCH PROTESTANT

Protestantism is a datable historical phenomenon. The word has its origin in the Second Imperial Diet of Speyer in 1529 in which the followers of the Reformation, being a minority in representation, were overruled in their appeal for religious freedom. They left the diet and returned with a "Letter of Protestation," defending their faithfulness to the scriptures and their freedom of conscience. Since then the word *Protestant* has been attributed to the followers of the Reformation cause. Three constitutive features, therefore, define the use of the word. Those who protested were a minority. Second, they claimed the scriptures as the principle for the judgment of doctrine (as opposed to Roman edicts, papal encyclicals, or the decisions of councils). Finally, they asserted freedom of conscience on matters pertaining to religion. Beginning in 1529, these three factors together shaped the definition of what "Protestant" means when applied to ecclesial formations. To phrase it negatively: as minorities, they did not have their share in the hegemony that controlled religious and political power; faithfulness to the Word of God meant that they did not submit unconditionally to human ordinances; freedom of conscience meant the rejection of an authority that rules against their minds and hearts.

Poignant in this historical description is that the definition of the word *Protestant* does not immediately entail any material content attached to it, as in a confessional document, a creed, or a catechism. It is strictly formal. Even the scriptures are not defined as to their content and limits. The canon, even if accepted prima facie, is not provided with a definition of what it entails. It

---

46. Octavio Paz, *La otra voz: Poesía y fin de siglo* (Barcelona: Seix Barral, 1990), 51.

remains open![47] This formal definition, however, describes more than a historically demarcated phenomenon. It describes an ethos proper to minorities who are open to the Word of God and who discern its implications in freedom. Where this is found, there is the church protestant.

The historical manifestation of such ethos is necessarily tenuous. Its existence is constantly at risk, because there is always the temptation to gravitate to a stable ground where certainty is ensured. The history of the historical mainstream Protestant churches is itself a documentary that attests to the betrayal of protestation, when it settles in the secure grounds of historical Protestant*ism*. The ecumenical movement, notwithstanding its noble efforts toward doctrinal appeasement of divisive factions and its social service, has never been exempt of conjuring totalitarian spectra.

Juan Luis Segundo suggests a connection between the present—articulated and globalized—economic system, on the one hand, and the evolution of the ecumenical movement, on the other. This connection presents the reverse side of the Reformation that split the Western church in the initial phase of the capitalist system ("financial capitalism"), when plurality was required to overcome the objective moral and doctrinal unity of the Middle Ages. Segundo writes:

> The so much championed "unity of the Christians," with its pastoral consequences, constitutes a clear ideological element. The ideal of the unity for liberation turned into the ideal of the unity to cover up conflicts, to minimize them in face of something more important and thus to serve, in an indirect way, to maintain the status quo . . . the ideology that places the [ideological] superstructure at the service of the existing order is, in most cases, not a conscious maneuver: it is an unconscious sliding of ideas through furrows that will prevent them from clashing with that order.[48]

Born from a historical event in 1529, the appellation "protestant" came to describe an *ethos* to be found where God-fearing faithful minorities exercise their freedom, often outside of what is currently defined by the proper noun *Protestantism*.[49] These minorities live in the almost unbearable tension between

---

47. In the extensive later confessional writings of the Lutheran Reformation, the canon as such is never defined as to what belongs to it or not. Luther (WA 2:325, 18–20) and Calvin (*Institutes* 4.9.14) explicitly rejects the church's need for a definition of the canon.

48. Juan Luis Segundo, "As Elites Latino-Americanas," in *Fé Cristã e Transformação Social na América Latina* (ed. Instituto Fe y Secularidad; Petropolis: Vozes, 1977), 186. See also Vítor Westhelle, "Ecumenics and Economics: Economic Justice and the Unity of the Church," in *El silbo ecuménico del Espíritu: Homenaje a José Míguez Bonino en sus 80 años* (ed. Guillermo Hansen; Buenos Aires: ISEDET, 2004), 157–76.

49. I will use "protestant" with lower case to designate this ethos as opposed to the proper noun "Protestant" that denotes a historical phenomenon.

the uncontrollable manifestations of the Spirit's charisma and institutional embodiment of the church.[50] They are found within and outside every denomination. To discern and detect their occurrence, when their visibility is so faint, is the task of an ecclesiology protestant.

Dutch Roman Catholic theologian Edward Schillebeeckx, in one of his last works, *Church: The Human Story of God*, expresses this protestant ethos in what could be taken as a testament to his witness:

> The church never exists for its own sake, although it has often forgotten this (as have many religions). For that very reason, in this "ecclesiological" book I shall not be saying too much directly about the church. We need a bit of *negative ecclesiology*, church theology in a minor key, in order to do away with centuries-long ecclesiocentrism of the empirical phenomenon of "Christian religion": for the sake of God, for the sake of Jesus the Christ and for the sake of humanity.[51]

Schillebeeckx's plea for a "negative ecclesiology" should not be understood as implying the tradition of negative or apophatic theology, which asserts that the majesty of God is such that it can be approached only by denying any human assertion about God. The reason for a "bit of negative ecclesiology" is that descriptions of its "majestic grandeur" have so often obliterated where and when it happens. The church protestant happens; it is always an event that points and testifies to its own end, both as goal and as consummation or extinction. This can be expressed only by a paradoxical statement: The "nature" of the church is eschatological.

---

50. Leonardo Boff, *Church, Charism and Power: Liberation Theology and the Institutional Church* (New York: Crossroad, 1985).

51. Edward Schillebeeckx, *Church: The Human Story of God* (New York: Crossroad, 1994), xix.

THE REPRESENTATIVE
AN UNEXAMINED QUESTION

2

> *Insofar as the Reformation was not simply a purification and reaction*
> *from abuses which had crept in, but was the origination of a distinctive form*
> *of the Christian communion, the antithesis between Protestantism and Catholicism*
> *may provisionally be conceived thus: the former makes the individual's relation*
> *to the Church dependent on his relation to Christ, while the latter contrariwise*
> *makes the individual's relation to Christ dependent on his relation to the Church.*
>
> Friedrich Schleiermacher[1]

Schleiermacher in the epigraph above clearly presents the distinction between Protestantism and Catholicism in *The Christian Faith*, the book that marked the beginning of modern Protestant theology.

The distinction, provisional as it might be, is sustained throughout Schleiermacher's ecclesiology even if further substantiated and nuanced. The merit of his statement lies in his defining of Protestantism as "a distinctive form of the Christian communion." But the ensuing antithetical formula does not convey this distinctiveness, for, as the author himself agrees, "Christian piety never arises independent and of itself in an individual, but only out of the communion and in the communion." Hence the antithesis by itself does not uphold the alleged distinctiveness. The distinctiveness seems to be predicated not on the relationship between Christ and the church but on the nature and function of the communion or the church insofar as it relates to any of its doctrinal loci: Christ, sin, creation, Trinity, and so forth. What does communion entail? Is it something shared or something given? How can the church make present that which otherwise, without *representation*, is only an absence? This crucial question has by and large remained unexamined. How is the "absent" represented? Is the church itself the "representative," or is it that which displaces a form of re-*presencing*?

---

1. Friedrich Schleiermacher, *The Christian Faith* (Edinburgh: T&T Clark, 1989), 103.

These two senses of representation are often conflated, and they are indeed contiguous, but the difference between them needs to be underscored lest we miss the ground on which ecclesial allegiances are founded. My argument is that most often the maze in which ecclesiological debates find themselves and get entangled results from the inability to distinguish these two senses. How do different ecclesial formations implicitly understand the relationship between the signifying and the signified? How does the church present itself and what it claims to be re-presenting? What is the role that the representational sign performs in communicating meaning? Does the church present itself as an "image," an icon that conveys by itself the divine (e.g., as in art, liturgy, music, architecture, etc.), or as a "proxy," a stand-in (e.g., as in politics or jurisprudence)? Much of the ecclesiological confusion issues from the fact that it is not clear whether the ministry and the identity of the church stand for something (Jesus, the scriptures, the confessions, the people, etc.) or whether the church's identity is the very re-presencing of the mystery (as in its sacraments, iconography, episcopacy, priesthood, etc.).

Philosopher and literary critic Gayatri Spivak, in her studies on postcolonial thought, brings back to the table this old distinction, which is of decisive importance for the study of ecclesiology.[2] Spivak, in the tradition of Hegel and Marx, presents the two senses of representation that are conflated and "run together: representation as 'speaking for,' as in politics, and representation as 're-presentation,' as in art or philosophy . . . between representation or rhetoric as tropology and as persuasion."[3]

This distinction can be traced back to the foundation of Western thinking when Aristotle distinguished between two basic human faculties, namely *poiesis* (production or labor, the foundation of the household and of the economy, in its etymological sense), on one hand, and *praxis* (action as intersubjective exchange, the foundation of politics, the city, and commerce), on the other.[4] For Aristotle the distinctiveness of *poiesis* and the verb *poieo* in contrast to *praxis* is that they designate an activity that results in the production of something,

---

2. Gayatri Chakravorthy Spivak, "Can the Subaltern Speak?" in *Marxism and the Interpretation of Culture* (ed. Cary Nelson and L. Grossberg; Chicago: Illinois University Press, 1988), 271–313; the same argument is repeated in her book *A Critique of Postcolonial Reason: Toward a History of the Vanishing Present* (Cambridge, Mass.: Harvard University Press, 1999), 256–65.

3. Spivak, *Critique of Postcolonial Reason*, 256f. The distinction is rendered in German as *Vertretung* (in the political sense of being a proxy) and *Darstellung* (in the sense of "presenting" something). But both are normally rendered by the same English noun, *representation*.

4. Aristotle, *Metaphysics* (bilingual ed.; trans. Hugh Tredennick; Cambridge, Mass.: Harvard University Press, 1933), 292–95 (6.1.1–6). Further in Vítor Westhelle, "Labor: A Suggestion for Rethinking the Way of the Christian," *WW* 4, no. 2 (1986): 194–206.

entailing an objective result, while *praxis* conveys a deed done that has an intersubjective effect but does not result in a positive and material outcome. It was only when Latin replaced Greek as the lingua franca in the Western world that these two senses collapsed into one word—*actio* (action).

The analogy to the Greek theater is fitting here. *Poiesis* describes the labor of those who built the theater, set the stage, and also wrote the play. *Praxis*, in turn, describes the activity of the actors performing the play. The verb *poieo* is used in the Septuagint to translate God's creative activity, including the Hebrew *barah* of which God is the exclusive subject. From there this term made it into the Nicene Creed, which confesses belief in God, *poieten ouranou kai gēs*, the "poet" of heaven and earth. In the New Testament the verb is used to describe Jesus' healings. The unique acceptation of *poiesis*, as opposed to *praxis*, was still held sharply by Basil in his *Hexameron*; while delivering his lessons to an audience of artisans, he employed it analogically to connect human labor and divine creation, even as he recognized the limits of the analogy.[5]

However, Aristotle's accepted distinction between *praxis* and *poiesis* in the Greek-speaking world of antiquity underwent a convoluted history after its reception in the Latin world. These two faculties, through the Middle Ages and well into modernity, were subsumed under the notion of action (*actio*) or practice (*praxis*, since Duns Scotus). The distinction between *praxis* and *poiesis* would return explicitly to the philosophical and theological vocabulary only with Hegel's *Phenomenology* in the section regarding the master and bondsman relation.[6] Work or labor (*Arbeit* in the sense of *poiesis*) is presented by Hegel as the self-actualization of the human in transforming the material world in distinction to the interpersonal relation between the two exemplary figures.[7]

The uniqueness of this conception of production as self-production was further developed by Marx's definition of "work" (*Arbeit*) as a metabolism (*Stoffwechsel*) between the worker and nature.[8] This metabolic relationship (forces of production) was set apart from the sociopolitical sphere (intersubjective relations of production), to which the term *praxis* was normally applied. *Praxis* in its narrow sense, with its intersubjective structure, constitutes itself discursively as explanatory narrative and public communication. It is the medium of human communicative action, moral deliberation and juridical legislation, and all that

---

5. Basil of Caesarea, *The Hexameron*, in *Nicene and Post-Nicene Fathers*, 2nd ser., vol. 8 (ed. Philip Schaff and Henry Wace; trans. Blomfield Jackson; repr., Peabody, Mass.: Hendrickson, 1995), 51–107. For the limit in the analogy he relies upon, see particularly pages 59f. (Homily 2.2).

6. G. W. F. Hegel, *Phenomenology of Spirit* (trans. A. V. Miller; London: Oxford University Press, 1977), 111–19.

7. Ibid. See my article "Theorie und Praxis III. Fundamentaltheologisch," in *Die Religion in Geschichte und Gegenwart* (4th ed.; Tübingen: J. C. B. Mohr [Paul Sibeck] 2005), vol. 8.

8. Karl Marx, *Das Kapital: Kritik der politischen Ökonomie* (Berlin: Dietz, 1962), 1:192.

is required for procedural actions in the polis; it pertains to the life in the polis and the actions necessary to administer it: in short, politics. *Poiesis*, on the other hand, describes all the activity that aims at providing the objective means for the sustenance of life (including intellectual nourishment, hence the etymological root of the word *poetry*) as well as its preservation in the form of human biological reproduction: in short, economy.

Oeconomia in medieval society entailed basically domestic relations, relations of production and reproduction at a time when the household and the economy, in the modern sense of the term, shared the same social space.[9] It was in this institutional reality with its distinctiveness that the Aristotelian *poietic* faculty, as opposed to the political faculty, was preserved. And it is from this background that it should be read and understood.

A similar thing happens with the English word *representation*, which translates in this case two German words, *Vertretung* and *Darstellung*. Following Spivak's choice of spelling to distinguish the two uses of the term, the first is rendered by "representation," while the latter is conveyed by the hyphenated "re-presentation";[10] or one could underscore the distinction by naming the first representation and the second re-*presencing*.

If this distinction is applied to ecclesiological analysis, some of the intricacies of ecclesiological debates can be elucidated. Finnish theologian Risto Saarinen uses an analogous distinction when commenting on two different etymological meanings of the word *communication*, which also has an ambivalent meaning signifying two different processes altogether and closely related to the two senses of representation.[11] These two meanings derive from alternative Latin roots: *co-unio* and *co-munus*. In Saarinen's words:

> The one [*co-unio*] dealing with communion or *koinonia* (Greek) should be obvious to all theologians. . . . The other root meaning deals with the Latin word *munus*, which can mean a gift, a task, or both. A communicating person has or knows the *munus*, the gift and task.[12]

---

9. Bonhoeffer, recognizing the difficulty with the modern separation of the household from the means of production, divides Luther's use of the medieval *oeconomia* to describe one of the mandates established by God (along with the civil government [*politia*] and the church [*ekklēsia*]) into two mandates: marriage (including family) and labor. Dietrich Bonhoeffer, *Ethics* (ed. Eberhard Bethge; trans. Neville Horton Smith; New York: Macmillan, 1965), 207–13 et passim. [DBWE 6:388–408]

10. Spivak, *Critique of Postcolonial Reason*, 256f.

11. Vítor Westhelle, "Margins Exposed: Representation, Hybridity and Transfiguration," in *Still at the Margins: Biblical Scholarship Fifteen Years after the Voices from the Margin* (ed. R. S. Sugirtharajah; London: T&T Clark, 2008), 70–72.

12. Risto Saarinen, "Communicating the Grace of God in a Pluralist Society," in *The Gift of Grace: The Future of Lutheran Theology* (ed. Niels Henrik Gregersen, Bo Holm, Ted Peters, and Peter Widman; Minneapolis: Fortress Press, 2005), 67.

The two senses, conveying different notions, are implicated in each other. The imparting of a gift or favor (*co-munus*) certainly has implications for interpersonal relations (*co-unio*). But the two ought to be distinguished according to which is given primacy in a given ecclesial formation. An example of the importance of this distinction is the debate over the Latin expression *communio sanctorum,* in which *sanctorum* (the plural genitive of *sanctus*) can be either holy things or holy people gathered. But the ambiguity in the translation is further determined also by the ambivalence of *communio.* Hence the translation can be either "the impartation of holy things" or "the assembly of the saints."

When primacy is given to one of these meanings, the authenticity and authority of the church and its teaching are ultimately grounded there. Two of the examples given in the previous chapter, Sinclair Lewis's *Elmer Gantry* and Willa Cather's *Death Comes for the Archbishop*, illustrate the emphasis in the communion as *co-munus*. Something was imparted that did not depend on interpersonal relations: the charismatic personality and the biblical inerrancy in one case, and the institution with its splendid liturgy in the other. Bishop Latour was not the representative of his church, in the sense of *Vertretung*, the political sense of "standing in" (as, for example, a presiding cleric in a Protestant denomination), but he embodied it in an objective and even ontological sense. Cyprian's maxim "Where is the bishop, there is the church" (*Ubi episcopus, ibi ecclesia*) summarizes this stance. In the case of *Elmer Gantry*, it is not the bishop but the charismatic authority that is the re-presencing of the church. In both novels, the mechanism of representation works in the same sense of imparting something that belongs to what the essence of the church is claimed to be.

In the third example, Unamuno's *San Manuel Bueno, Martyr*, there is nothing to impart. In their unbelief, the priest of Valverde de Lucerna and his disciple Lazarus could only offer themselves in the interaction with the people, representing the people's dreams and hopes not unlike the way in which a politician or a lawyer would, regardless of their beliefs or personal disbelief. Their authenticity was validated even though they did not personally believe in anything that they represented. But their acting out was self-validating.

This case of disbelief in Unamuno's novella brings up a controversy in the early church that lasted for a good part of the fourth and fifth centuries, the Donatist (after the north African bishop Donatus) outcry against priests who during the persecution by Roman Emperor Diocletian (303–305) committed apostasy. This controversy, however, does not bear upon the unbelief of the priest in the novel. On the contrary, the apostasy the Donatists decried was the betrayal of the trust of the people by handing over to the imperial authority sacred documents to be burned, and also some of the faithful into the hands of persecutors. The Catholic orthodoxy won the dispute with the argument that the holy possessions of the church, the sacraments, were valid independent of the personal disposition of the one who dispenses them. The dispute therefore pitted the interpersonal relations among the believers (the position held by the Donatists) against the ontological value of the sacred things in and of themselves. Unamuno's work carries the Donatist argument to its extreme by affirming that what matters is the faithfulness of the priest in carrying out his duties toward the congregation that gathers around him. His faithful actions and interactions with the people, not the intrinsic value of the church and the sacraments apart from him, authenticate his ministry.[13]

Keeping in mind the distinction of the two senses of representation, and also of communication, how do we adjudicate the truthfulness of the church? If the principles upon which each of the basic profiles of the church are erected follow Aristotle's distinction of human faculties, then neither can be deemed wrong. Nevertheless, one still cannot be reduced to the other, and this seems to be the dilemma of the ecumenical movement. What is in dispute is not, primarily, conflicting doctrines or diversity in biblical interpretation. Neither is it the variety of charismatic manifestations or the authority of the teaching office of the church. The irreducible quandary lies in the ambivalent understanding of what the church is representing. Or is the church ultimately not about representation at all, in either sense of the word? But if not, why is either form of representation so intrinsic to the church's identity?

THE CHURCH BETWEEN ECONOMICS AND POLITICS

In classical antiquity Aristotle's distinction between the human faculties of *poiesis* and *praxis* was understood to be embodied in fundamental social institutions.[14] One comprised the realm of the household (*oikos* in Greek; *domus* in Latin). This included the entire realm of production for the sustenance of life and also its biological reproduction. From there we have the word *economy*, which, until the high Middle Ages and before modern capitalism developed, retained the same meaning and in a single social location combined labor and marriage. The other comprised the civic order, the courts, the military,

---

13. During the Reformation, the accusation of Donatism was made against the Reformation by John Eck in his *404 Articles*, ##227–33. See "John Eck's Four Hundred Four Articles for the Imperial Diet at Augsburg," in *Sources and Contexts of the Book of Concord* (trans. Timothy J. Wengert; ed. Robert Kolb and James A. Nestingen; Minneapolis: Fortress Press, 2001), 59–60. The Reformers made the same accusation against the Anabaptists. See Luther in LW 37:366; 40:250; and Melanchthon in the Augsburg Confession and Apology 8, in *The Book of Concord* (ed. Robert Kolb and Timothy J. Wengert; Minneapolis: Fortress Press, 2000).

14. See Ruth Mohl, *The Three Estates in Medieval and Renaissance Literature* (New York: Columbia University Press, 1933), 10f.

and government, all encompassed in the *polis* (Greek), and *politia* (Latin), the etymological forerunners of the word *politics*, which until the American and the French Revolutions was the entitlement of the nobility. Though diverse in its applicability, there is a fundamental core element that distinguishes each of these instituted mandates, an operational principle at the nucleus of each that still remains the same. In the case of the household or the economy it is human reproduction and labor, the production of the means for the sustenance of life and its reproduction. As far as government and civil society are concerned, the operational principle is human intercommunication for the sake of building a reasonable, equitable, and peaceful order in the earthly city in and through which people ought to be protected and evildoers coerced. These therefore become the two basic ways in which humans *represent* in the double sense of "representation." As Spivak acutely observed, there is a correlation between these institutional dimensions of life and the two senses of representation. "*Vertretung* [is] representation in the political context. Representation in the economic context is *Darstellung*."[15]

In the Middle Ages, to these two fundamental institutions—*oeconomia* and *politia*—was added a third, the clergy or *ecclesia*.[16] These three institutions working in organic harmony formed the *corpus christianum*, the body of Christendom that had the papacy at the head. This arrangement was sustained for centuries by the "Donation of Constantine," a document forged in the Middle Ages that says that Constantine had given the papacy primacy over government and secular affairs of the empire. The document was proven a forgery in the middle of the fifteenth century by the Italian humanist Lorenzo Valla. Luther read a new edition of Valla's refutation early in 1520, at the dawn of the Reformation, and impressed on other reformers the conviction that the "Donation" was the forgery of the Antichrist embodied by the one seated at the papal see.[17] Within this background it is understandable that the Reformers' main concern was to dismantle the idea of the *corpus christianum*,[18] the organic unity under the papal head, and to stress the separation between secular and spiritual regimes. Luther's intention was the same when he put forth his famous distinction of the two regimes, or as it was called in the twentieth century, the "two kingdoms doctrine."[19] Melanchthon in the Augsburg Confession and Apology 16 relies

---

15. Spivak, *Critique of Postcolonial Reason*, 262–63.

16. This class was already hinted at by Aristotle when he listed "priests" as a distinct class in his *Politics*. Mohl, *Three Estates*, 10.

17. Heiko Oberman, *Luther: Man between God and the Devil* (New York: Image, 1992), 42.

18. Jürgen Küppers, "Luthers Dreihierarchienlehre als Kritik an der mittelalterlichen Gesellschafts auffassung," *ET* 8 (1959): 370f.

19. The most comprehensive study of this distinction can be found in Ulrich Duchrow, *Christenheit und Weltverantwortung: Traditionsgeschichte und systematische Struktur der*

on the same distinction, and so does Calvin.[20] This was the main concern of the Reformers; after all, they were contextual theologians responding to the occasion and its challenges.

However, in the late 1520s, Luther, while not rejecting the distinction between the spiritual and the secular, started to emphasize and focus on the discernment between the different institutions and their grounding as God's mandates. For this he furthered his reflections on the already familiar distinction of the three estates, *oeconomia, politia,* and *ecclesia,* the household, the public realm, and the church. Luther simply adopted the distinction of each estate from its common usage, but instead of framing it with the notion of the *corpus christianum,* the Christian body, he deconstructed it, stressing the uniqueness and peculiarity of each of these institutions. Furthermore, he did not equate the *ecclesia,* the church, with the spiritual regime. For him the church was an earthly reality as much as the economy and civil government. But his most important contribution was to emphasize the unique character of each, particularly of the economy (the domain of the household) and of politics or civil government, and how they are distinct from the church.

Under Luther's pen this model of the three orders or estates, while heuristically appropriate for his ends, underwent some changes worth noticing. For example, he does not see the clergy as a distinct class or caste (thus his criticism of monastic life)[21] but includes all of the human race insofar as all descend from Adam (the preachers, but the listeners, *auditores,* as well). Luther saw the church, as an institution, as one of the orders mandated by God since creation and distinct from the other two—household and civil government. It was the first one given to humans, with the establishment of the Shabbat.[22] The institution of the household (the creation of Eve and the tending of the garden) came next, followed by the civil government (normally regarded as a remedy for the Fall). As he writes in his *Lectures on Genesis* of 1535–1536: "Here we have the establishment of the church [*ecclesia*] before there was any government of the home [*oeconomia*] and of the state [*politia*]."[23] The church is an instrument to allow the Word of God to be announced to the whole creation and for the human response to be expressed. Henceforth was the household or economy instituted

---

Zweireichelehre (Stuttgart: Klett, 1970), 503f. See also Vítor Westhelle, "The Word and the Mask: Revisiting the Two-Kingdoms Doctrine," in *Gift of Grace,* 167–78.

20. John Calvin, *Institutes of Christian Religion* (Louisville: Westminster John Knox, 1960), 4, chap. 20.

21. However qualified this criticism was, monastic life was more an impediment than anything else to one's reception of justification. See the instructive collection of essays *Luther und das monastische Erbe* (ed. Christopher Bultmann, Volker Leppin, and Andreas Lindner; Tübingen: Mohr Siebeck, 2007).

22. This argument is laid out in detail in the introduction.

23. *LW* 1:103; WA 42:79.

to provide for sustenance or nourishment, while civil government was mandated for the sake of social order, defense, and protection. Luther called these institutions *larvae*, masks through and by which God works as if through instruments. In his words: "Three institutions [*Stände*] were ordained by God in which we live with God and good conscience. The first is the household; the other the political and worldly regime; the third the church or priestly order—all according to the three Persons of the Trinity."[24] For Luther they did not form classes, strata, or castes discretely separate from each other but were functions of human society in which all participate in one form or another, both passively and actively. As he regarded the church as made not only of the priestly class but of all who worship, so is the case with the household and the civil government.

What is important in Luther's adoption of the medieval three-estates typology are the functional or instrumental changes he brought about, concerning in particular the distinction between the household or economy and the political order. Aristotle, millennia ago, in the *Politics*, had already made clear the distinction between the citizens and the oligarchy, on the one hand, and, on the other, husbandmen, craftsmen, and laborers of all kind who "will of necessity be slaves or barbarians"; the latter fairly corresponding to what we would now call immigrants.[25]

Now the church is this reality that stands squarely in the in-between spaces—spaces where life is produced and reproduced—and the spaces of political life, of human communication, policy-framing and mores-forming activities. In the case of the church, what describes its nucleus is not primarily a given human activity. In the church, unlike the other institutions in which labor and action work as operational principles, the Word of God is first addressed to humans, out of which ensues the human response.

This "third space," to borrow an expression of Homi Bhabha,[26] the space between spaces, distinguishes itself from the other two not as a demarcated territory but as something that could be called anti-territorial. In economy and politics I know myself and I construct my identity to the extent that I participate in these two activities that define the two distinct forms of self-representation, one by production and procreation, the other by interaction in the sociopolitical sphere. In the first, identity is "produced"; in the second, it is "recognized." But in the case of the "third space" called church, something different happens. Here there is no human self-representation (and every time there is, it is called idolatry or demonry, as we will see later); the human is not the subject that pro-

---

24. WA TR 6:266 (#6913). Such use of the *vestigia trinitatis*, common from Augustine through Scholastic theology, is unusual in Luther. See Bayer, "Nature and Institution: Luther's Doctrine of the Three Orders," *LQ* 12, no. 2 (Summer 1998): 125–59.

25. Mohl, *Three Estates*, 11.

26. Homi Bhabha, *The Location of Culture* (New York: Routledge, 1994), 36–39.

duces or recognizes her- or himself. In this "third space" the human is exposed ("I was naked," Gen. 3:10) but also sheltered ("and God made garments of skin . . . and clothed them," Gen. 3:21). The creature is addressed by God, and only responds in shame, praise, lament, prayer, or revolt. This is what is behind the Jewish zeal that the name of God not be pronounced. We don't address God; it is always the other way around. This tenet is the same behind the Protestant article by which the church stands or falls: justification by grace through faith. This implies that justification is not by works, when we represent ourselves as in the household, nor by the laws that regiment our political and civil existence. Certainly *works* and *civil law* need to assist the church, for in it there are liturgy and by-laws, architecture and committees, music and bookkeeping, sermons and social services, new generations of members and instruction on how to proceed in everyday life. But this is not what makes the church distinct.

This is the reason why, strictly speaking, we cannot define the church as such. It is not of our doing. We can only refer to it as this elusive "third space" determined by God's enunciation of the Word and the promise to be present materially in the elements of the sacrament. What we "do" is not our action, but only our *re-action*. The church happens as God speaks; Luther called it the *creatura envangelii*, the creature not of our doing and making, but of God's good word of promise. In this sense, even if Luther never used the expression "creature of the word" (*creatura verbi dei*), it was indeed clear that "the church is established by the word of God."[27] Church happens!

While taking for granted the creedal marks of the church (*notae ecclesiae*: one, holy, catholic, and apostolic), the Reformers refer to the church in nonessentialist but functional features, namely, the gathering of the saints (*congregatio sanctorum*) under the two forms in which the Word of God expresses itself: the audible proclamation and the visible sacramental elements. All the rest— processions, hymnody, flowers, and candles—are not binding for the church to be one or to have an identity. What is essential for the church to happen is the gathering of the people and the Word delivered in its two forms, preached and administered in the sacraments! This lowers the bar for a minimalist ecclesiology. In fact, in his address to the Evian Assembly of the Lutheran World Federation in 1970, Swedish theologian Gustaf Wingren polemically proposed a reading of Article 7 of the Augsburg Confession that suggests an understanding of the church as encompassing a freedom for "more than merely 'unity of [Christian] churches.'"[28] In fact, he was suggesting what Luther himself did

---

27. *LW* 1:104.

28. The reference is to be found in an adversarial account given by David P. Scaer, *The Lutheran World Federation Today* (St. Louis and London: Concordia, 1971), 27.

when he said that the church was created for Adam, which means for the whole of humanity and in fact encompasses the whole of humanity.[29]

However minimalist, lean, and elegant this ecclesiology may be, hailed by the famous *satis est*, "it is enough," of AC 7, it is really not enough as long as it is not recognized that these functions do not happen in a vacuum but are intertwined with the two other mandates. They pertain to the neighboring realms adjacent to the church and are in a tense relationship with them. A biblical illustration might be helpful. In Revelation 22 we find the description of the tree of life producing its twelve kinds of fruits, one for every month, and its leaves healing the nations. There is no temple in the new Jerusalem; instead there is this tree of life. As in paradise, this tree is the church for all the nations, all the children of Adam. As in paradise, this tree produces the fruits that nourish and the leaves that heal, which are gifts of the tree that correspond to the tasks assigned to the two other spheres adjacent to the church: the household that produces sustenance and the civil order that must defend and protect (Luther used a play on words in old German to describe the tasks mandated to the *oeconomia* and the *politia*: *nehre und wehre*, "nourishment and protection"). These correspond to the two shapes by which the Word functions: enunciation and embodiment.

THE CHURCH'S TEMPTING VICINITIES

I will later dwell on the question of adjacency that pertains to the relationship of the church to its neighboring realms, the household and politics, but now I need to bring home the argument. The temptation of the church is always to find or allow itself to be entangled by one type of its self-representation in order to acquire a stable identity. Some churches move into presenting themselves chiefly as a household, others as a public open forum.[30] But these two are still

---

29. Joseph Sittler made a similar claim in his controversial "Call to Unity" address to the World Council of Churches assembly held in New Delhi in 1961. In a similar vein and verve see also Guillermo Hansen, "On Boundaries and Bridges: Lutheran *Communio* and Catholicity," in *Between Vision and Reality: Lutheran Churches in Transition* (Geneva: LWF/DTS, 2001), 408: "A catholic practice means the concrete embodiment of plurality, for it bridges the apparent incommensurability of local identities with the universal plot of the gospel. . . . [T]he catholic nota is the event whereby our communities seek to communicate and link their destiny to those beyond the immediate border." See along the same lines Nancy Bedford and Guillermo Hansen, *Nuestra Fe: Introducción a la teología cristiana* (Buenos Aires: EDUCAB/ISEDET, 2008), 72f.

30. Even as attempts have been made to correct the abuses of the church falling into the captivity of the household model with its patriarchal hierarchy (see Letty Russel, *Church in the Round: Feminist Interpretation of the Church* [Louisville: Westminster John Knox, 1993], 42) or in favor of a "community of argument" against political suppression of difference (see Kathryn Tanner, *Theories of Culture: New Agenda for Theology* [Minneapolis: Fortress Press,

manners by which the church represents itself, entailing either an "economic" or a "political" ideal. While both have been successful in the history of Christendom, they have equally surrendered either to the household paradigm or to the political one. The following are the two types of churches that have established their identity on one or another of those paradigms. Certainly the two are often intertwined, making their discernment more difficult. But they are both indeed distinct in themselves by the fact that both have their sense of identity conceived as a construal and not an event in which the word and not the text or an office is what constitutes church.[31]

THE *POIETIC* TYPE[32]

In the Western world since antiquity, there have been two human faculties through which identity is construed, as I have already observed. The one defined by Aristotle as *poiesis* is what pertains to human production or labor. *Poiesis* becomes the operational principle that lies at the core of the construal of human identity through the means that provide for the sustenance of life and its biological reproduction. This is what we came to call "economy" in the original and encompassing sense of the word. Identity in this realm is a *given*; it is something laid out there (*dargestellt*) and can be passed on as a gift or alienated when unduly appropriated by others.

This *poietic* type has been normative for some ecclesial formations in defining themselves. Churches that follow this type understand themselves as the very means through which their ministries deliver the message they have amassed, administered, and kept. The church in this case has a sacramental character; it relies on its own resources and is defined in essentialist terms. The church does what it ontologically already is. The church is already one, holy, and catholic—pure even if in need of being always purified, but it is so out of its own assets.[33] It is not a public over against other publics, but a public on its own.[34]

Representation in this type of ecclesial formation is understood as re-presencing, the act of presenting itself for that which it already is. As a systemic and self-enclosed domain, whatever it takes in from the outside does not change

1997], 123f.), still the imagery used remains within the territorial confines of either household or politics.

31. On the distinction between text and event, see Jean-Luc Marion, *God without Being: Hors-Texte* (trans. Thomas A. Carlson; Chicago: University of Chicago Press, 1991), 144–49.

32. "Type" is here used in the sense developed by Weber and Troeltsch. It is descriptive of an "ideal" formation that lifts up dominant traces of a "real" social configuration that is similar to what a caricature does in portraying a real person.

33. Thus the warning of Vatican Council II: *Ecclesia semper purificanda.*

34. Reinhard Hütter, *Suffering Divine Things* (Grand Rapids: Eerdmans, 2000), 28–29.

or challenge its inner constitution. It becomes an *autopoietic* system.[35] It has a task to perform, a work to be done in delivering and disseminating that which essentially it is.

This church type emphasizes its systemic structure as an organism, as a body whose members are in the function of the whole, and in this entirety each part finds its nourishment. No one is its representative in the political or juridical sense of the term. The one who speaks does not speak *for* it; the one who speaks, speaks as church, as the *pater familias* in old Roman law, the head of the household (*domus*). To paraphrase Napoleon's mot regarding the state, the "representative" of this type would say *je suis l'Église*, "I am the church." Such churches are not exclusive to any denomination, confession, or movement, but their salient characteristics are readily detectable. The episcopacy models the church and can be empirically found in the large spectrum of Christianity with different degrees of intensity, from Eastern Orthodoxy to the Roman Catholic Church to Pentecostalism, as well as in mainline Protestant churches.

The ontological dimension this form of representation assumes provides for a strong sense of identity and a seemingly unassailable ground of reliability, particularly appealing in times of prevailing uncertainty. The lack of democratic participation in its internal constitution is compensated by a sense of belonging in the organic unit of its household. But it is also a type that is entangled by the "economic" paradigm in which the church is the result of its own striving to produce and reproduce its own identity.

THE *PRAXIC* TYPE

Identity in the *praxic* type is won through human interaction, *praxis*, the basis of politics and civility. What one produces or brings forth is not decisive; what counts is human intersubjective activity. Representation is obtained by recognition in and through which one acts out a role. This is the domain covered by the notion of politics in its broad sense. While in the economic paradigm authority is grounded in power, in the political paradigm authority is founded on legitimacy. Representation has the sense of being a presence instead of an absence (*vertreten*). Identity in this type is not construed or produced but is acquired and acted out in the acknowledgment of the legitimacy of the roles being played.

The *praxic* type has been dominant and appears in ecclesial formations that stress the communication of the message as a communal event that shapes their

---

35. Influenced by the biologists Humberto R. Maturana and Francisco J. Varela, Niklas Luhmann, "Closure and Openness: On Reality in the World of Law," in *In Autopoietic Law: A New Approach to Law and Society* (ed. Gunther Teubner; Berlin: de Gruyter, 1987), 335–48, defines *autopoiesis* as an ontologically self-enclosed social system.

inner constitutional form. The words of the character Shug in Alice Walker's novel *The Color Purple* are exemplary: "They came to church to share God, not find God."[36] Contrary to the "economic" paradigm, here the church is what it does; its identity is not a given but must be acted out. Those who speak, speak *for* the church but not *as* church. It posits itself as a reality among others, which it understands itself to be related to and determined by. The church is not an organic self-enclosed system but is open to the vicissitudes of communicative action and is shaped by them.[37]

The church in this type presents itself as a transient reality without a nature or an essence of its own. It stands for something other than itself. This is the reason why the apostolic mark of the church is important here. As much as the apostles were eyewitnesses to the grounding events of the faith—the life, death, and resurrection of Jesus Christ—so is the church in giving continuity to that witness to every generation. Church functions; and its function, not its intrinsic nature, determines its reality. The lack of a sacramental re-presencing is compensated by a sense of communal and democratic participation. Leadership is defined accordingly by proxy, by a stand-in who is given custody by the community of its own well-being. But no ontological value is attributed to this act of surrogacy; it is always contingent on the rules by which policy is established and changes made in function of the challenges.

As in the former (*poietic*) type, this too can be found in the life of churches that lay emphasis on their congregational matrix. When Melanchthon in AC 7 called the church a *congregatio* and not a *communio sanctorum*, he evaded the ambiguity of *communio* and thus defined it as a gathering of the people of God, giving voice to this type of ecclesial formation. This "formation" is therefore contingent on the circumstances surrounding a gathering. Hence it is always being formed and re-formed, as the Protestant motto well describes: *Ecclesia reformata semper reformanda est.* The reformed church is always a reforming church. The church is in motion; it is *ecclesia viatorum*, the church on the way.

As in the case of the economic paradigm, one can detect the presence of the political archetype across the ecumenical spectrum, though the churches of the Reformation are the first to come to mind. Base Christian communities in the Roman Catholic Church and prayer, healing, and exorcism gatherings in Pentecostal and free evangelical churches are expressions of the broader appeal of the *praxic* type. The healthy alternative it promotes against the economic paradigm can also leave it entangled in the political paradigm. While it does

---

36. Alice Walker, *The Color Purple* (New York: Pocket Books, 1982), 201.

37. As much as Luhmann's system theory of *autopoiesis* provides the sociological grounding for the *poietic* type, Jürgen Habermas is the one who has articulated the sociological and philosophical arguments for the *praxic* type. See his *The Theory of Communicative Action* (trans. Thomas McCarthy; Boston: Beacon, 1984).

not "produce" its identity by its work, it acquires it by its actions, and by its actions it stands or falls. Success and the enjoyment of legitimacy sanction its validity, and these become also its captivity.

Yet, as has been already suggested, what does it mean to say that the church's integrity—its image, figure, and character—constitutes a divine endowment neither worked out from its own resources nor acquired through its actions? And how is it related to the adjacent economic and political realms that are always and unavoidably immersed in it? How is it to be church without capitulating to the temptation to construe identity by either form of representation? How can the church exist in this enticing vicinity of economics and politics that offer it tempting ways to construe an identity and to represent itself? These are questions that the following chapters will address.

MEANINGS OF TRADITION   3
GIVE AND TAKE

The contemporary's report is the occasion for the one who comes later. . . .
There is no follower at second hand.
Søren Kierkegaard[1]

Someone must have traduced Joseph K.
Franz Kafka[2]

WHOSE TRADITION? WHOSE TREASON?

The two basic meanings of representation, one following an "economic" and the other a "political" paradigm, have found their respective support in two irreducible meanings of tradition. Each one of them works with principles so diverse that the possibility for negotiating a compromise is very tenuous, if it exists at all. For example, when the declaration *Dominus Iesus* was issued in 2000, it argued that the Protestant communions could not be called churches because they lacked apostolic succession and the valid Eucharist.[3] The argument resides in a particular understanding of tradition. And when Matthias

---

1. Søren Kierkegaard, *Philosophical Fragments: Johannes Climacus* (trans. Howard Hong and Edna Hong; Princeton, N.J.: Princeton University Press, 1985), 104.

2. Franz Kafka, *The Trial* (trans. Willa and Edwin Muir; New York: Knopf, 1992), 1.

3. For the quote see chap. 1, n. 8. The same argument was made again by the Sacred Congregation for the Doctrine of Faith in the 2007 document "Responses to Some Questions regarding Certain Aspects of the Doctrine of the Church." The following question was clearly presented: "Why do the texts of the Council and those of the Magisterium since the Council not use the title of 'Church' with regard to those Christian Communities born out of the Reformation of the sixteenth century?" And the response is unequivocal: "According to Catholic doctrine, these Communities do not enjoy apostolic succession in the sacrament of Orders, and are, therefore, deprived of a constitutive element of the Church. These ecclesial Communities which, specifically because of the absence of the sacramental priesthood, have not preserved the genuine and integral substance of the Eucharistic Mystery cannot, according to Catholic doctrine, be called 'Churches' in the proper sense."

Flacius Illyricus and associates undertook the writing of what is known as the *Centuria of Magdeburg* (1560–1574), a different understanding of tradition was operative. The *Centuria* (centuries) was a compilation of church history aiming at showing that the Reformation was the true continuity of the church catholic through the centuries since its primitive origins.

Tradition means handing over something or someone, passing down a possession or a body of information, surrendering something. Its meaning is obtained from the Latin verb *tradere*, from which the word *treason* is also derived. The Donatist controversy in the early church provides a classic example of what constitutes the two disputed meanings of tradition. For the Donatists, the handing over to the Roman Empire of the sacred texts to be burned and people to be imprisoned, tortured, and killed during the time of Christian persecution was treason. For them what was to be passed on was the integrity of the actions. Tradition was the handing over of a given practice. The Roman church, then already with the support of the Roman Empire after Constantine, argued that the treacherous actions of priests or bishops did not compromise at all what they delivered in performing the sacraments. The sacraments worked *ex opere operato*, by their own intrinsic merits apart from the character of the one who presided over them. No matter who delivered the gift, it was the gift that counted, independent of the hands that handled it.

These two different meanings of what is handed over—whether it is a practice or a "product"—are to be discerned; they sponsor two conflicting views of what tradition means. One is tied to the notion of representation as a stand-in for something or someone who is absent or is not acting *motu proprio*, by his or her own self. The person is acting out a role or a call, and it is only as such, and insofar as the person is called and as such acknowledged, that the representation is operative. This acting out is what is passed on. To use the example of the Lord's Supper, in the words of institution, as reported by Paul in 1 Corinthians 11:23-26, the emphasis is placed on "*Do* this in remembrance of me," and not on "This *is* my body, which is given for you" (Luke 22:19). It is the event that is passed on. In the other sense of representation, as re-presencing, the opposite is the case: the emphasis lies on the gift that is passed on. Tradition entails the handing down of an objective reality, something that has merit in itself.

From the time of the early church, these two streams of the understanding of tradition can be detected, and they became explicit in the dispute over the formation and reception of the canon of the scriptures.[4] Is it the church that engenders the canon, or is the canon simply received and acknowledged by the church? The letters of Paul, by the end of the first century, were already

---

4. See Bruce Metzger, *The Canon of the New Testament: Its Origins, Development, and Significance* (Oxford: Clarendon, 1987).

circulating as a collection. In the middle of the second century, Irenaeus regarded the four Gospels (the *Tetramorph*) we have today in the New Testament as the "pillar and ground of the Church."[5] At the beginning of the third century, Origen was working with a collection of books that might have been the same as we have today in the New Testament. The canon as we know it won universal reception in the church toward the end of the fourth century. But no formal justification of it was presented. The church fathers "were ratifying what had already become the mind of the Church."[6]

THE OPEN CANON AND THE ENCLOSED SILENCE

The question of the authority by which the church makes this ratification of its mind still remains. If the authority lies in the reception itself, there is no objective content that is given a perennial value. It depends on a given community's interface with a given content that will be always shifting. Schleiermacher expresses this sense of unease with closure, drawing the implication that tradition is made by the process of active reception. In *The Christian Faith* he writes:

> Hence even though the Canon is fixed in many Confessions of the Church, this ought not to prevent further unrestricted investigation of the matter; critical enquiry must ever anew test the individual writings of Scripture with a view to decide whether they rightly keep their place in the sacred collection.[7]

And he goes even further to suggest that "the peculiar inspiration of the Apostles is not something that belongs exclusively to the books of the New Testament."[8] Apostolic inspiration is, therefore, something affirmed by the reader in whom this inspiration is also at work, for the "authority of Holy Scripture cannot be the foundation of faith in Christ; rather must the latter be presupposed before a peculiar authority can be granted to Holy Scripture."[9] Schleiermacher is defending a non-objectivist position on the interpretation of the scriptures. Its authority is not intrinsic to it but dependent on the faith of the reader. To phrase it even more radically, Søren Kierkegaard, a few decades

---

5. Irenaeus, *Against Heresies* 3.11.8., in *Ante-Nicene Fathers*, vol. 1 (ed. Alexander Roberts and James Donaldson; Peabody, Mass.: Hendrickson, 1994), 428.

6. Everett Ferguson, "Factors Leading to the Selection and Closure of the New Testament Canon," in *The Canon Debate* (ed. L. M. McDonald and J. A. Sanders; Hendrickson, 2002), 320; cf. also Bruce Metzger, *Canon of the New Testament*, 237–38.

7. Friedrich Schleiermacher, *The Christian Faith* (Edinburgh: T&T Clark, 1989), 603.

8. Ibid., 599.

9. Ibid., 591.

later, regarded the scriptural report as the "occasion" that serves as a register of the reader or hearer who believes it. And he concluded, "There is no follower at second hand. The first and the last generation are essentially alike, except that the latter generation has taken the occasion in the report of the contemporary generation."[10]

The objective content is just an "occasion"; it does not convey anything by itself. What is decisive is to act it out. On the other hand, this definition is determinedly different in the other stream of interpretation of tradition, where what is passed down is not contingent upon the act of reception. It has an ontological quality, something that is passed on independent of the receptivity or affection of the receiver. But what is passed on cannot be the apostolic witness of the scriptures as such, for in this case Kierkegaard's argument would hold. If the scriptures are available to all in every generation, they will be the occasion, but not more than the occasion, for the believer. For this other understanding of tradition, there must be something else that enshrines the *gift* that is conveyed and is not contingent upon affection and reception.

This gift needs to be an extrascriptural norm that exercises authority over the scriptural witness and its reception, which ensures that the gift is being delivered regardless of its reception. This understanding of tradition has a long history in the church, and one that presents us with a very clear alternative to the meaning of tradition based on scriptural reception. The earliest version of understanding tradition as the impartation of the gift reaches far back in the history of the church, but not as far as the very early church. It dates back to the early Constantinian era.

The argument for this gift that the church holds and can dispense at its will was developed in orthodox Christianity by Basil of Caesarea late in the fourth century, in *On the Spirit* of 374.[11] He purported to explain the institution of some practices that he regarded as normative, as, for example, crossing oneself or turning to the geographical east in prayer. "What writing has taught us to turn to the East at the prayer?"[12] Basil's own question is answered with another rhetorical question: "Does not this come from that unpublished secret teaching which our fathers guarded in a silence out of the reach of curious meddling and inquisitive investigation?" And he continues: "This is the reason for our tradition of unwritten precepts and practices, that the knowledge of our dogmas may not be neglected and condemned by the multitude through familiarity."[13]

---

10. Søren Kierkegaard, *Philosophical Fragments*, 104f.

11. Basil, *On the Spirit* 27.66, in *Nicene and Post-Nicene Fathers*, 2nd ser., vol. 8 (ed. Philip Schaff and Henry Wace; trans. Blomfield Jackson; repr., Peabody, Mass.: Hendrickson, 1995), 40–43.

12. Ibid. 27.66.(41.)

13. Ibid. 27.66.(42.)

In other words, the scriptures and their reception are not enough; they must be supplemented by this unpublished secret additional information. Basil then goes on to give a further reason for the keeping of this secret knowledge that has been handed down outside of the scriptures: "One form of this silence is the obscurity employed in the Scriptures, which makes the meaning of 'dogmas' difficult to be understood for the very advantage of the reader: Thus we all look to the East at our prayers."[14]

This passage of Basil would find its way, throughout the Middle Ages, into textbooks of canon law that argue for an extrascriptural source for Christian dogmas in order to supplement and clarify the scriptures.[15] What is the source of this special endowment, where is it kept, and how is it transmitted? It comes from the presumed teachings and deeds of the glorified Christ's forty days on earth after his resurrection. Precious little is recorded in the New Testament about those days between Easter Sunday and Ascension. This silence is rather significant because that was the time Jesus was fully revealed and his mission finally understood by the disciples.

The ending of John's Gospel (21:25) offered a clue: "[T]here are also many other things that Jesus did; if every one of them were written down, I suppose that the world itself could not contain the books that would be written." A legend thus emerged. The glorified Jesus revealed to the apostles secrets that were not registered in writing. Hence such revelation was and is not available to scrutiny and thus cannot become the occasion for the faith of the believer who scrutinizes it. However, the apostles, so goes the legend, who were the eyewitnesses of his resurrection and hearers of these supposedly secret teachings, presumably kept them and decided not to render them in writing. And these teachings would then be transmitted from these original apostles to their successors, the bishops in their historic succession.[16]

The presumption of this secret knowledge is thus the necessary and exclusive condition to justify the historic episcopate, the uninterrupted historical

---

14. Ibid.

15. Heiko Oberman, "Quo Vadis? Tradition from Irenaeus to *Humani Generis*," *SJT* 16 (1963): 234.

16. Heiko Oberman, *Forerunners of the Reformation: The Shape of Late Medieval Thought* (Philadelphia: Fortress Press, 1966), 54–55. For a reading in support of the secret teachings in the English Reformation, see Sir Thomas More, *The Dialogue concerning Tyndale* (ed. W. E. Campbell; London: Eyre and Spottiswoode, 1927), 98. More claims, "[W]e should well know that his word and ordinance needeth none other authority but himself, but is to be believed and obeyed, be it written or unwritten." But his argument, to use the old English saying, went to the pot when Tyndale repudiated More's claim by saying, "[W]hile Christ may well have preached many unwritten sermons, the 'pith and substance' of all that the church needs to know is entirely present in the written text of the Bible." See William Tyndale, *An Answere Vnto Sir Thomas Mores Dialoge* (ed. Anne M. O'Donnell and Jared Wicks; Washington, D.C.: Catholic University of America Press, 2000), 24.

succession of bishops since the time of the apostles. And in the West it also justifies the pope as the first among equals as the direct successor of the apostle Peter, to whom primacy among his peers was given according to the Roman Catholic reading of Matthew 16:18: "[Y]ou are Peter [*Petros*], and on this rock [*petras*] I will build my church."

It is not irrelevant, however, that the notion of a historic succession of bishops commencing with the apostles is actually older than Basil. It comes from Irenaeus in the second century of our era. However, Irenaeus used it for precisely the opposite reasons from the ones claimed by Basil and the medieval canon lawyers. He was appealing to the apostolic tradition in order to establish the clarity and the wholeness of the scriptures against those who asserted that the scriptures "are ambiguous and that the truth cannot be extracted from them."[17]

IRENAEUS AND APOSTOLIC SUCCESSION

Irenaeus, unlike Basil, was writing in a time in which the canon of the scriptures had not yet been fully acknowledged and received by the church. Many of its writings were rejected or accepted in the name of this secret knowledge kept by those who "maintain that the Savior privately taught these same things not to all but to certain only of his disciples." Aware of the legend about the secret knowledge imparted to the apostles during Jesus' forty days on earth after the resurrection, Irenaeus claims that "the entire Scriptures, the prophets, and the Gospels, can be clearly, unambiguously, and harmoniously understood by all, although all do not believe them."[18] And he goes on to say that we

> have learned from none others the plan of our salvation, than from those through whom the gospel has come down to us, which they did at one time proclaim in public, and, at a later period, by the will of God, handed down to us in the Scriptures, to be the ground and pillar of our faith.[19]

For Irenaeus, the church does not establish or engender the canon; it receives it, and this reception is an act of humility in accepting it as ground and pillar of the faith of the church.[20] His argument is for tradition to be grounded on the act of reception. Once this canon has been received, it is the whole church

---

17. *Against Heresies* 3.2.1., in *Ante-Nicene Fathers*, 1:415. The declaration *Dominus Iesus* uses this passage of Irenaeus in support of the apostolic succession of bishops. This argument cannot be sustained by any close reading of the text.

18. Ibid. 2.27.2. (p. 398)

19. Ibid. 3.1.1. (p. 414)

20. See Oscar Cullmann, "La tradition," *CT* 33 (1953): 41–52.

that keeps it and is sustained by it, for it is clear to all. For Irenaeus, and, we might add, for the Reformers as well, this makes any further claim for a historic succession or any other possession of secret knowledge at best obsolete or redundant. Is it not ironic that it is in the fourth century, exactly around the time when the canon had been accepted and received, that the argument of a secretly kept oral tradition was raised? And this argument was raised in order to set apart a particular office of the church as possessing this gift that exceeds and supplements the scriptural records, presuming their insufficiency.

The merit of Basil was to recognize in his time that there was no reason whatsoever to maintain the historic succession as a sign of unity once the canonical scriptures had been received, unless there were a divine secret knowledge to be preserved outside of the scriptures. He clearly affirmed the secret teachings and thus inaugurated a new way to understand tradition to which many, even during medieval times, and above all the Reformers, took exception.[21] The Reformers said no to this proposal and kept the faith of the ancient church as it has been preserved in the scriptures. At least this is what the Apology of the Augsburg Confession 7 and 8 clearly states: "The opponents say that universal traditions ought to be observed because they are thought to have been handed down from the apostles. Such religious people! . . . Therefore the intention and counsel of the apostles ought to be sought from their writings."[22]

THE REACTION OF THE REFORMERS

Does this sound familiar—the argument for a special knowledge that is kept secret from most baptized Christians, a knowledge not shared by all members of the priesthood of all believers? It should, for anyone familiar with Luther's *Bondage of the Will* (1525). Luther was arguing against Erasmus, the humanist Catholic (albeit reluctant) who was unable to join the Reformation because he was not able to give up the conviction that some secret knowledge must be lodged somewhere in the church, since it is impossible for the average Christian to unveil the secrets hidden in the obscurity of the scriptures. Luther's case against Erasmus is not that the scriptures are self-evident. Nothing could be less characteristic of Luther than this fundamentalist claim.[23] His argument is rather that the scriptures are clear (*claritas scripturae*), and that their perceived

---

21. Oberman, "Quo Vadis?" 235.

22. *The Book of Concord* (ed. Robert Kolb and Timothy J. Wengert; Minneapolis: Fortress Press, 2000), 181.

23. See the study by Miikka Ruokanen, *Doctrina Divinitus Inspirata: Martin Luther's Position in the Ecumenical Problem of Biblical Inspiration* (Helsinki: Vammala, 1985), 146: "Luther's principle of *theologia crucis* legitimates the critical approach to the Bible avoiding all divinization of the letter. . . . But . . . applying an external criterion to the theological evaluation of the Bible would mean applying ideological criticism alien to the essence of the Christian faith."

obscurity is the result of human resistance to accepting the guidance of the Spirit's work in the whole church. The obscurity of the scriptures for Luther necessitates prayer, meditation, and temptation so that the Spirit might reveal its meaning for us. It does not call for a secret knowledge. He explicitly rejects that idea. "It is true that for many people much remains abstruse; but this is not due to the obscurity of scripture, but the blindness or indolence of those who will not take the trouble to look at the very clearest truth."[24] Therefore, says Luther, "on this account I have attacked the pope, in whose kingdom nothing is more commonly stated or more generally accepted than the idea that the Scriptures are obscure and ambiguous, so that the spirit to interpret them must be sought from the Apostolic See of Rome."[25] "The Scriptures are perfectly clear."[26]

GIVE AND TAKE

For several centuries after Basil the distinction between the two senses of tradition was not clearly demarcated—for a simple reason: in addition to their role as ministerial leaders, bishops were also for the most part the great theologians of the church, versed in the exposition of the scriptures. Edward Schillebeeckx summarizes the issue succinctly:

> In the first millennium we see that the teaching authority of the ministry and theology usually overlap. Although many laity and monks were theologians, the episcopate was in fact the *ordo doctorum*: the bishops proclaimed the faith both as ministers of the church and professional theologians.[27]

In the high Middle Ages, however, with noble rank as a qualification for the bishopric and with the practice of simony, the buying of church offices, bishops were no longer the main theologians of the church, as in the earlier centuries. The two streams in the understanding of tradition become sharply divided. One argument sustaining that tradition was made by those who were expositors of the scriptures (*expositores sacrae paginae*), whereas the other relied on an intrinsic (and ontological) endowment given to the office to be dispensed at will. Schillebeeckx presents the argument:

---

24. *LW* 33:27.
25. *LW* 33:90.
26. *LW* 33:99.
27. Edward Schillebeeckx, *Church: The Human Story of God* (New York: Crossroad, 1994), 225.

After the cathedral schools came into being, . . . later to be followed by scholarly-academic theology in the first European universities, a new status of doctors or magisters in theology developed: the guild of master theologians. And because in feudal times the bishops came predominantly from the nobility, often with hardly enough theological training, a marked difference arose between the *magisterium episcoporum* and the *magisterium theologorum*, a field of tension which has led to much crossing of boundaries on both sides.[28]

By the time of the Reformation this difference became unbridgeable. A decision had to be made on what constitutes tradition. Is it the passing down of a practice, the practice of biblical exposition for every generation, or is it the handing down of a received endowment deposited in the church? The former follows the "political" paradigm; the latter the "economic" paradigm of the two senses of representation (chapter 2, above). Protestantism by and large has privileged the first, while Catholicism has emphasized the second. The difference, therefore, is not the common assumption that Protestants have one source of authority, the Bible, whereas Catholics have two, the scriptures and the tradition. In fact, both rely on tradition, but they have different ways of understanding what it entails. As Cardinal Ratzinger (later to become Pope Benedict XVI) explained it:

> The real antithesis in the concept of the church between Catholics and Protestants is not between Scripture and tradition but between Scripture and office. Protestants interpret the Scripture without the Petrine Office, and therefore they are not *given* Scripture, but *take* it.[29]

The distinction between "given" and "take" in Cardinal Ratzinger's text points indeed to the distinction between that which comes in and of itself as a "gift," with an objective quality attached to it, and that which is "taken" or, better said, received. While one relies on what a given office is endowed with, the other lays emphasis on the biblical and theological exposition and its effective communication and reception. In one case the scripture is given for what the "office" says it entails, regardless of the reception, whereas in the other the elucidation is made for the sake of its reception, hence the need to make it understandable for a given public.

---

28. Ibid.

29. Joseph Ratzinger, "Ein Versuch zur Frage des Traditionsbegriffs," in *Offenbarung und Überlieferung* (ed. K. Rahner and J. Ratzinger; Freiburg: Herder, 1965), 28. Cited by Steven Paulson, "Lutheran Assertions regarding Scripture," *LQ* 17, no. 4 (Winter 2003): 379.

FUNCTIONS THAT DIVIDE THE CHURCH

It would be a mistake, however, to equate Catholics and Protestants in every respect with the alternatives of "give" and "take." In Protestantism, its orthodox faction claims that faith is the assent to an objective content given in the scriptures and the confessions of the church (*fides quae creditur*–the faith in that which is believed), laying emphasis on the giving. Protestants of pietistic persuasion stress the receiving side of faith (*fide qua creditur*–the faith that believes). In this case, what grounds the church is not the content of the faith that it holds, but the subjective act of trust of the believers. On the Roman Catholic side, Leonardo Boff, while still a Franciscan monk, worked with an analogous distinction. He claims that there "are two functions, not divisions, in the Church."[30] One is the learning and receiving function (*ecclesia discens*), while the other is the teaching and giving function (*ecclesia docens*). In the Roman Catholic context his comments were a criticism of the pre–Vatican II "pathological" one-sidedness of his church as *ecclesia docens*, the church that teaches and delivers.[31]

The New Testament and early church scholar Robert Wilken, who grew up a Protestant and was trained as a Protestant theologian but later converted to the Roman Catholic Church, explains the difference between "giving" and "receiving." He tells the story of a pastor who, in confirmation class, would have the students memorize Luther's Small Catechism a year before he would explain what it means. Wilken adds:

> I first learned of this pastor when I was a young man, and like others my age I guffawed. How ridiculous! The whole point of catechism instruction is to help young people understand the meaning of the Lord's Prayer, the Ten Commandments, the Creed. What is the value of having youngsters memorize the words of the Catechism without telling them what they mean? Now years later I realize that this pastor was much wiser than I.[32]

Explaining the meaning is a performative act that is vested in the effective reception of what is communicated or shared. However, stresses Wilken, "meaning is ephemeral, and the meanings one learns at twelve years of age are not the fullness of the words one memorizes."[33] Learning something by heart even without knowing its meaning is something given; it comes with an

30. Leonardo Boff, *Church: Charism and Power; Liberation Theology and the Institutional Church* (trans. John W. Diercksmeier; New York: Crossroad, 1992), 139.
31. Ibid., 141f.
32. Robert L. Wilken, *Remembering the Christian Past* (Grand Rapids: Eerdmans, 1995), vii.
33. Ibid.

endowment whose value might not be fully appreciated, but one must trust the giver and treasure it for a value that cannot even be estimated.

The Reformation, largely in opposition to the "economic" paradigm, made a different claim leaning toward the "political" paradigm. There was no secret endowment. The appraisal of scripture was in its use and function. In other words, the scripture was worth its use, and in its use the scripture found its value. Yet this is the option . . . in case we remain attached to this binary opposition. Each is internally coherent and makes sense once one accepts the presupposition by which the argument inherent to it works. Sacred cows abound in church circles too. This is what I need to examine next.

ON THE AUTHORITY OF THE SCRIPTURES

4

MORE THAN ENOUGH

> *So I opened my mouth, and he gave me the scroll to eat. He said to me,*
> *Mortal, eat this scroll that I give you and fill your stomach with it.*
> *Then I ate it; and in my mouth it was as sweet as honey.*
>
> Ezekiel 3:2-3

Salman Rushdie, the famous Indian writer/novelist, was giving a reading to university students in Delhi when a young woman put up her hand and said, "Mr. Rushdie, I read your novel *Midnight's Children.* It is a very long book, but never mind, I read it through. The question I want to ask is this: fundamentally, what is your point?" Before Rushdie could even attempt an answer, she spoke again, saying that she knew what he was going to say and that the point of the exercise was the whole effort—from cover to cover. When Rushdie tried to say that it was something like that, the young student snorted, "It won't do." "Please," he begged, "do I have to have just one point?" "Fundamentally," she said with firmness, "yes."[1] The young student's question can very well be applied to the "very long" sacred texts, scriptures. And unlike Rushdie's text, the scriptures fundamentally have one point: they point to Christ. Nevertheless, despite the fact that they have one point, texts regarded as sacred are subject to different treatments. Some are to be emulated and are themselves a locus of devotion. Others are submitted to interminable interpretations in the attempt to find their meaning. While the first option demands that the text be accepted, the second expresses deep longings that are evoked by the text about a past long gone or a future yet to come. Either option has an impact in the community called church; it shapes it and frames it.

---

1. This incident has been taken from Salman Rushdie, *Step across This Line: Collected Nonfiction 1992–2002* (New York: Modern Library, 2003), 146.

The dispute that the Reformation stirred under the principle of *sola scriptura,* the scripture alone, has been easily rendered as an allowance voucher either to fundamentalist and magisterial claims or to the foundationalist freedom of a Humpty Dumpty claim that "it means what I choose it to mean." But these options, which are trenches in the present ecumenical warfare, are not what the Reformers meant by *sola scriptura.* What is at the core of the argument is something quite different. For the church the question posited is a relatively new one, unforeseen by the Reformers. The question is: Does the church authorize the proper use of scripture, or does it enable that which it announces?

Between the Reformation's understanding of *sola scriptura* and the understanding of this Reformation mantra in the present day stand the traumatic events unleashed by the European Enlightenment of the eighteenth century, events that changed our views of science, of politics, and of religion. As far as Protestant theology is concerned, *sola scriptura,* or the scriptural principle, as it is known, seems to have been the first casualty. When Luther and the Confessions describe the scriptures as entailing law and promises, the scriptures present these through prophets and apostles. Prophecy is what points to the gospel, the fulfillment of which is testified by the apostles as witnesses of the life, deeds, death, and resurrection of Jesus Christ as attested in the scriptures. This understanding was grounded in two fundamental assumptions that remained unchallenged throughout Christendom until the time of the Enlightenment. The first was that Jesus Christ is the fulfillment of the Old Testament prophecies. The second was that the miracle accounts, particularly the resurrection of Jesus, were factual events and should be regarded as such today.

The philological work of Hermann Samuel Reimarus (1694–1768) put these assumptions into question.[2] Gotthold Ephraim Lessing (1729–1781) furthered and radicalized his predecessor's work, rendering the truth claim of the miracle stories and the resurrection as nondemonstrable by reason. This left two options for those who felt the impact and wanted to remain faithful to the Christian message. One was to surrender reason, a *sacrificium intellectus,* and cling to the literal sense of the scriptures, no matter what reason might argue. This gave birth to what is known as *fundamentalism.* The other was to ground Christian faith on some foundation other than the scriptures, such as a moral postulate, a feeling of absolute dependence, a ground of being, authentic existence, universal history as revelation, and so forth, of which the scriptures would be a dated and circumstantial expression. This has been called *foundationalism.* Both fundamentalism and foundationalism are products of the Enlightenment. One kept the *sola scriptura* but subjected it to an anachronistic misreading; the

---

2. *Fragments from Reimarus* (London: Williams & Norgate, 1879), particularly the chapter "On Miracles and Prophecies," 69–83.

other simply evaded it. Much of the current debate over the authority of the scriptures, particularly in the United States of America, is a debate over these two options, with the participants not realizing that the responses offered still leave the basic question unchallenged. Both foundationalism *and* fundamentalism are, in fact, celebrations of the Enlightenment's biblical criticism. Both are a concession to Lessing's thesis that "accidental truths of history can never become the proof of necessary truths of reason."[3] Fundamentalism opted for the truths of history without the aid of reason, whereas foundationalism sought the truths of reason without historical claims of the Bible. It was an affirmation of Lessing's thesis though validated through the different truths Lessing proposed as exclusive and exclusionary options.

The problem that plagues both answers, prompting the modern alternative of either having reason (along with will and feelings) alone as arbiter or requiring blind assent to the letter lies in Lessing's thesis itself, insofar as it is assumed that it addresses the *sola scriptura* principle.

The scriptural principle for the Reformers addressed an entirely different problem from the one that prompted Lessing's quest for truth against or apart from biblical-historical claims. The Reformers' question was not one that concerned primarily reason, logic, or even historicity. It was a question of *power*, namely, who controls evangelical rhetoric, the art of proclaiming the gospel? Once this is understood, the answers that foundationalism and fundamentalism gave to the Enlightenment become the fallacies of a misplaced question. The irony in all of this controversy is that the *sola scriptura* principle as it was used by the Reformers was an attempt to prevent precisely the fallacy produced by both fundamentalism and foundationalism, that is, to ground the teachings and practice of Christianity anywhere else but in grace, in faith, in Christ as attested by the apostolic witness and registered in the scriptures. *Sola scriptura* is "alone" only insofar as alone is faith, alone is grace, alone is Christ, *sola fide, sola gratia, solus Christus.* This is the reason why, since August Twesten (1789–1876) in the early nineteenth century coined the expressions,[4] we speak of *sola scriptura* as the "formal principle" of evangelical Protestantism, while justification, entailed by the expressions *sola fide, sola gratia,* and *solus Christus,* is called the material

---

3. Gotthold Ephraim Lessing, *Lessing's Theological Writings* (ed. Henry Chadwick; London: Adam & Charles Black, 1956), 53.

4. August Twesten, *Vorlesungen über die Dogmatik der evangelisch-lutherischen Kirche, nach dem Kompedium des Herrn Dr. W. M. L. de Wette* (2nd ed.; Hamburg: Friedrich Perthes, 1929), 280–82, where he distinguishes an "objective material principle" (*objective materiale Princip*) as the doctrine of justification and a "formal principle" (*formale Princip*) as the scriptures. He then (p. 284) identifies a third "subjective or generative principle" (*subjective, erzeugende Princip*), which he describes as the "alertness of conscience" (*Regsamkeit des Gewissens*). See the informative essay by Erik M. Heen, "The Distinction 'Material/Formal Principles' and Its Use in American Lutheran Theology," *LQ* 17, no. 3 (Autumn 2003): 329–54.

principle. In other words, the scriptural principle is the apostolic principle, that is, what was attested by the apostles as inculcating Christ and him crucified and resurrected. For the Reformers the "successors" of the apostles include anyone who brings the prophetic and apostolic witness to be heard and read by his or her contemporaries.

SOLA SCRIPTURA: THE NEGATIVE PRINCIPLE

The *sola scriptura* principle is not an invention of the Reformation. It was inherited, as were many other theologumena, from late medieval theologians, preachers, and philosophers. It was used with different emphases and nuances by Roger Bacon, John Wycliffe, John Hus, Marsilius of Padua, William Occam, Jean Gerson, Wessel Gansfort, and others. All of them, like Luther, used it primarily as a negative principle to oppose the claims of a special and independent authority as argued by the Roman Curia, which I have already discussed in the previous chapter.

The first time this argument was explicitly stated was when Basil of Caesarea in his treatise *On the Spirit* (of 374) explained the institution of practices like crossing oneself or turning to the east in prayer that he regarded as normative and divinely ordained. Here Basil is relying on a fundamental distinction between "dogma" and "kerygma" where the former is a silent reverential observance and the latter a proclamation to the entire world.[5] The reason for the distinction, which has been preserved in most of Orthodox and Roman Catholic theology, is to permit dogma to interpret and supplement scripture. Modern Protestant theology has also invoked it, as in the nineteenth-century proposal by Karl Friedrich Kahnis to introduce an "ecclesial principle" alongside the formal and material principles.[6] More recently, Carl Braaten suggested that between the Reformation's clear and exclusive distinction between *ius divinum* and *ius humanum*, a third concept of law should be introduced, which he called *ius ecclesiasticum*.[7]

Luther objected forcefully to this argument for a "silent" or "secret" (Basil's words) tradition entailing the assumption of divinely sanctioned rites. He made his objection very clear in his *Bondage of the Will*, as I have shown in the previous chapter.

---

5. Basil, *On the Spirit* 27.66, in *Nicene and Post-Nicene Fathers*, 2nd ser., vol. 8 (ed. Philip Schaff and Henry Wace; trans. Blomfield Jackson; repr., Peabody, Mass.: Hendrickson, 1995), 41–42.

6. See "Schriftprinzip," *Die Religion in Geschichte und Gegenwart* (3rd ed.; Tübingen: Mohr, 1961), 5:1540–1543.

7. Carl Braaten, *Mother Church: Ecclesiology and Ecumenism* (Minneapolis: Fortress Press, 1998), 97.

The clarity and sufficiency of the scriptures are old themes in Christian theology, first emerging in the struggle against Gnosticism. Much before Luther, in the late second century, Irenaeus had already refuted these secretive private lessons and asserted that there was nothing obscure in the scriptures and that they were understandable by all though not believed by all. For Irenaeus the apostolic witness left in print, the scriptures, was more than enough to anchor the faith of the church.

SCRIPTURE AS INTERPRETER ITSELF: THE POSITIVE PRINCIPLE

Luther's often-quoted thesis that the "scripture interprets itself" (*scriptura sui ipsius interpres*) is well known.[8] Gerhard Forde,[9] Oswald Bayer,[10] and Steven Paulson[11] have independently phrased this notion well when they say that we do not interpret the scripture, but the scripture interprets us. But how is this brought about? The common English translation is not precise and suggests that one should be using the scriptures against the scriptures in order to find the correct meaning. This is in fact a post-Enlightenment translation, which, although not completely wrong, misses the sharpness of the literal translation. It should literally be translated as "the scripture is in itself the interpreter." The word *interpres* in Latin is a noun, designating that which stands between two values or "prices" (*inter-pres*). The etymology of the word points to the exchange of merchandise in markets of antiquity. It was often the case that because of differences in the languages or dialects spoken by the merchants bargaining for the value of their goods, an interpreter was needed to convey the value or the price asked by a merchant of another in the process of negotiating an exchange. Analogously, the thesis that the scripture interprets itself has the precise meaning that it is not interpreted but is the interpreter itself. The scripture stands between two "values" and allows for the exchange to happen.

What are those values? Luther's concise definition of what theology is about says it all: *homo peccator et Deus salvator,* or simply Jesus Christ and us. The scripture interprets this exchange, Christ in our stead and we in the stead

---

8. WA 7, 97, 20–22 is the locus classicus for the expression.

9. Gerhard O. Forde, *A More Radical Gospel: Essays on Eschatology, Authority, Atonement, and Ecumenism* (Grand Rapids: Eerdmans, 2004), 71.

10. Oswald Bayer, *Gott als Autor: Zu einer poietologischen Theologie* (Tübingen: Mohr Siebeck, 1999), 298.

11. Steven D. Paulson, "Lutheran Assertions regarding Scripture," *LQ* 17, no. 4 (Winter 2003): 381.

of Christ. That is why Luther could call it a happy or marvelous exchange.[12] As our interpreter, the scripture makes intelligible to us a language that for us is foolishness (*moria*, 1 Corinthians 1). We come to the "market" with the notion that we can barter with the valuables we think we have, and the interpreter tells us that they are worth nothing. Yet the other party is giving even himself to us. What is this if not a foolish and scandalous exchange? Nothing for all, all for nothing! If we try to do something, even that little we suppose we retain (*facere quod in se*) in this exchange, we destroy the gift, and the happy exchange turns into a miserable deal. A gift can only be given if it is free and without any reciprocity; otherwise it is no longer a gift. Its sheer reception is called faith. Hence *sola scriptura* stands between two other *solae*, *solus Christus* and *sola fide*, the gift and the reception conveyed by grace alone, *sola gratia*.

The problem with foundationalism in all its liberal colors is that it took the scripture to be negotiated by the theologian or philosopher who stands between the scripture and its reader and gives the hermeneutic key to know its worth, that is, the worth of the scriptures, not the worth of Christ. The fundamentalist with all shades of biblical legalism does the same thing as the negotiator, asserting its immense purchase value, but in the exchange loses Christ. Between the two, foundationalism and fundamentalism, it is only the price tag that each puts on the scriptures that is different, but the scripture still is merchandise in the market of ideas and morals. For each, the scripture is a value in and of itself and no longer the interpreter. In contrast, to say that the scripture is itself the interpreter does not put a price tag on the scripture. Therefore, the scripture, like the interpreter in the marketplace, does not have a value in itself. Its importance is to make possible the exchange, a very foolish yet happy exchange at that. Hence it is not valueless, but value free.

Worth noticing is that this process in which the means of exchange become the end of a bargain is a modern phenomenon typical of capitalist economies. It is not surprising that this problem of the scriptures turning into a commodity is a phenomenon that coincides with the triumph of capitalism. In pre-capitalist economies the "interpreter," that is, money, is a means and not an end in itself; it exists only to make possible the exchange of goods. In capitalism a reversal occurs. As Marx put it in his classical description of this transition to capitalism, we move from the formula C-M-C (commodity-money-commodity) to M-C-M, by which money is transformed into capital. Accumulation thus becomes an end in itself.[13] Fundamentalism and foundationalism are approaches to scrip-

---

12. *Mirabilis mutatio.* WA 31/2, 435, 11; *LW* 17:225.

13. See Karl Marx, *Das Kapital: Kritik der politischen Ökonomie* (Berlin: Dietz, 1962), 1:161–91 (chap. 4, "Die Verwandlung von Geld in Kapital"). His early insights into this phenomenon can be found in Karl Marx, *Grundrisse: Foundations of the Critique of Political Economy* (New York: Vintage, 1973), 201–18, 667–68.

ture ruled by a similar capitalist ethos. While the Reformers conceived of the reader under the law facing scripture to be the reader under the gospel (R-S-R), foundationalism and fundamentalism see scripture under examination by the reader to be transformed into the scripture interpreted (S-R-S).

MORE THAN ENOUGH: RHETORIC AND DIALECTICS

Is *sola scriptura* sufficient? Is alone enough? Simply put, no! It is not enough because it is more than enough! If I were just to say that it is not enough, lurking behind that statement would be the suspicion of a suggestion that we need a further Gnostic knowledge to complement what is lacking or not clearly exposed in it. This is a position that Irenaeus and a number of theologians leading to the Reformers so often criticized, and that foundationalists are reintroducing. But if I were to say that it is simply enough, lying in wait would be the suspicion that the scripture is no longer the interpreter but a value, or the value in itself, as fundamentalist merchants of the scripture advertise.

However, grammatically speaking, the expression "more than enough" can have two meanings. In a *rhetorical* sense, we can use the expression to denote something that exceeds expectations. A gift that comes with no strings attached (only in this way is it a gift) and that enriches our lives beyond what we had envisioned can be described as "more than enough" in this rhetorical sense; it is something that comes by sheer grace. But "more than enough" can also be interpreted in a *logical* sense as that which exceeds a condition set or a requirement made, and the excess is superfluous or overcharged.

What would be the right choice between these two senses of "more than enough"? Cannot both be true? In fact, the scripture is more than enough, as it is the interpreter that presents the story of a gift that is self-surpassing, a gift that we call gospel and all that points to it and inculcates Christ (*was Christum treibet*). It is the story of God who becomes flesh and dies the death of a sinner, of the greatest sinner (*maximus peccator*), so as to meet us on our terms, we who have nothing to bargain, we who stand condemned by the law, we to whom all is given, even God's own self. This is the rhetorical sense of "more than enough."

But the logical sense to "more than enough" is also true. There is plenty in the scriptures that exceeds what for us is necessary and sufficient, even as it is salutary for times and places in which it was promulgated and will serve us as examples if correctly understood, that is, according to its "grammatical, historical meaning," as Luther insists.[14] This is what Luther says clearly in "How Christians Should Regard Moses" (1525):

---

14. *LW* 39:181.

One must deal cleanly with the Scriptures. From the very beginning the word has come to us in various ways. It is not enough simply to look and see whether this is God's word, whether God has spoken it; rather we must look and see to whom it has been spoken, whether it fits us. That makes all the difference between night and day. . . . The word in Scripture is of two kinds: the first does not pertain or apply to me, the other kind does. . . . The false prophets pitch in and say, "Dear people, this is the word of God." This is true, we cannot deny it. But we are not the people.[15]

THE UNIVERSAL WORD SPEAKS DIALECT

The question is, to whom are the words addressed? If the words are spoken to the one who is totally sinner (*totus peccator*) and entail the promise of Christ who makes us wholly righteous (*totus iustus*), this is the word for all of us that the scripture interprets. Now if the word addresses a particular individual or groups of people and is bound to that particular situation and context, it is a different and distinct kind of word; it is equally the Word of God, but we might not be the people to whom it is addressed. If it is not the universal Word that brings us to Christ in the midst of our *totus peccator* condition, if it is a particular word that addresses a political, economic, social, familial, gender, race, or sexual situation, then this word needs translation (*trans-latio*, bringing over from a given context to another context), because the universal Word also speaks dialect.[16] This is the distinction between what is apostolic and what is not, even if spoken by an apostle. In one of his many criticisms of the book of James, Luther said:

And this is the true test by which to judge all books, when we see whether or not they inculcate Christ. For all the scriptures show us Christ, Romans 3 [21]; and St. Paul will know nothing but Christ, I Corinthians 2 [2]. Whatever does not teach Christ is not [yet] apostolic, even though St. Peter or St. Paul does the teaching. Again, whatever preaches Christ would be apostolic, even if Judas, Annas, Pilate or Herod were doing it.[17]

---

15. *LW* 35:170.

16. The expression is from Pedro Casaldáliga, *Creio na Justiça e na Esperança* (Rio de Janeiro: Civilização Brasileira, 1978), 211.

17. *LW* 35:396. This is also the reason that Luther in criticizing the spiritual (allegorical, tropological, and anagogical) exegesis argues that "literal meaning," which was the medieval alternative, "is not a good term" and prefers "grammatical, historical meaning" (*LW* 39:181).

Even Christ's own command when he bids the ten healed lepers to "go to the priest and make sacrifice does not pertain to me," says Luther, and he adds: "The example of their faith, however, does pertain to me; I should believe Christ, as did they."[18]

Is Luther contradicting himself? Has he not earlier made the case that the scriptures are themselves the interpreter? And does he now also claim that they need to be translated? Legalists and liberals alike would charge Luther with trying to have it both ways. And so he does, because, for him, interpretation is not translation. And it is important to stress the meaning of each. The scriptures are both the interpreter and that which needs translation, depending on the use implied. The scriptures are our immediate interpreter insofar as their words are for us, both as the universal Word that condemns us and leads us to the promise, and as the civic mandate that pertains to worldly affairs. And these two coincide when we are brought by them to Christ. However, the scriptures need to be translated whenever the dialect employed does not speak to us. And this distinction remains through the eschaton: *duplex est forum, theologicum et politicum;*[19] there are two distinct contexts, one theological and the other political. In today's dialect we would say: Theology and ideology are different orders of discourse. One pertains to the ultimate, the other to penultimate realities. One is the Word that alone speaks, promises, and delivers; the other is a dialect that the Word speaks for circumstances demarcated by time and space. One does what it says (*sacramentum*); the other exemplifies what the doing implies for a given context (*exemplum*).[20] By making this distinction, Luther steers away from the strictly "political" paradigm, often associated with Protestantism, but he still does not proceed completely into the "economic" paradigm.

Yes, the Word speaks dialect, a specific mode of carrying a conversation confined to a given context and addressing particular issues that pertain to and are demarcated by that context. From the same root *dialect* we have the word *dialectics*, which, before Hegel gave it an ontological meaning, was one of the ancient basic human arts in what was called the *trivium*, in which it was complemented by grammar and rhetoric. Dialectics was the art of mastering the logic or rationality of a given dialect, a conversation within a given context. For example, varied are the dialects of the courtroom, a marketplace, a street gang gathering, church liturgies, a church convention, and so forth. Each entails its own rules and logic, which are bound to the very context of the dialect employed.

Luther used the distinction between the Word as law and gospel that pertains to all, on the one hand, and other narratives that address only some

---

18. *LW* 35:174.
19. WA 39/1, 320, 2–3.
20. For a typical description of the distinction, see WA 5, 639, 13–16.

persons and under certain circumstances, on the other. Thus he describes them as two different linguistic arts: rhetoric and dialectics. Dialectics for Luther was what we would call the logic of an argument, by which a postulate, proposition, or mandate is put forward, sets and begs its counterpart, and demands a fitting response. In a commandment a proposition is made and a response is expected. It presupposes an exchange, an interaction that might not be a happy one. Dialectics was regarded as the art of reasoning within the rules of conversation in the context of a given "dialect." It is the craft Luther employed in the disputations. It implies an understanding and discernment of the rules and the context in which a debate takes place. The context in which it happens must be specified by reading it grammatically and historically.[21] Luther's criticism of the spiritual meaning in biblical exegesis as a tool of interpretation was precise and incisive because "spiritual" exegesis (entailing allegorical, tropological, or anagogical meaning) sought a universal meaning in a particular dialect and did not "deal cleanly with scripture." Rhetoric, on the other hand, is just telling the story, proclaiming it. Such is the gospel, which Luther again and again defined simply as a discourse or story about Christ that grasps us as the overwhelming gift of God. It does not make a proposition to be argued, nor is it about a conversation among different parties. It is pure deliverance in both senses of the term: it dispenses and releases in the same act; it is law and gospel.

THE RULE OF GRAMMAR

How do we discern these two genres? It is vital to know if the text is "for me." But could I not be in denial? For Luther this discernment is made possible by the primary liberal art and the most important of the *trivium* for theology as theology: grammar. "Among the human sciences devised, the most useful for the theological propagation is grammar."[22] Why grammar? Because it is grammar that reveals what genre is being employed by scripture, whether it is dialectics or rhetoric, whether it is the external form or the inner energy. The latter releases the force in the word-event that it becomes. *Ergon* and *energeia* are the terms often used to describe these two aspects of language that grammar discerns.[23] The universal Word as *energeia* is that which effects my conviction as sinner and announces the unconditional gospel. It does what it says and says what it does. Different from this universal Word are the circumstantial expressions that survive for our edification in the letter of the scriptures. This

---

21. *LW* 39:181.

22. WA 6, 29, 7–8.

23. See Richard M. Morse, *New World Soundings: Culture and Ideology in the Americas* (Baltimore: John Hopkins University Press, 1989), 11–15. Cf. Vítor Westhelle, "Communication and the Transgression of Language in Martin Luther," *LQ* 17, no. 1 (Spring 2003): 1–27.

distinction corresponds to the one Luther uses between Christ as a sacrament and as an example. The sacrament enfolds us for what it is; it is the means of grace itself. The example, on the other hand, indeed needs a translator. Foundationalists, with their liberal strategies, evade the distinction and invent a new grammar alongside of scripture. They create an "Esperanto" that is as salutary as the actual Esperanto is in the world today: worthless. Fundamentalists, with their legalistic strategies, conflate the distinction and idolize dialectics, legislating it as the only lingua franca.[24]

For Luther, the question left for theological discernment was about the distinction. Thus he writes from Coburg to Justus Jonas in June 1530: "We start with this distinction: the Decalogue is the dialectic of the gospel and the gospel the rhetoric of the Decalogue, and thus we have all of Moses in Christ, but not all of Christ in Moses."[25] In other words, Moses is enough, yet we never make it—we don't meet the standards; Christ is more than enough, and we don't need to make it.

In his commentary on the Ten Commandments in the Small Catechism, Luther provided the example of how to translate a dialect, even one that Luther could praise as much as the Decalogue, while proclaiming himself to be a new disciple of it.[26] He turned negative statements into positive ones, making very clear what is positively for us ("*Wir sollen . . .*") out of what was negatively formulated for the people of Israel ("*Du sollt nicht . . .*"). Even if you are not under the civil charge of murdering someone, the Fifth Commandment applies to you, because you must "help and support [the neighbors] in all of life's need." He does this exemplarily in his commentary on the Third Commandment in the Large Catechism. There he distinguishes the outward sense that concerned only the people of the First Testament from the Christian meaning. For the latter it means having not only the duty but also the right and privilege to have time both for hearing the Word of God and for leisure (also for the common folk, who were not socially protected, he insists). Or he could go even further than that, as he did in the "Theses concerning Faith and Law":

---

24. One might be reminded, as an illustration, that the commandments of God, dictated by God, that came down to the people were written by Moses and carried his handwriting, his dialect, his peculiar calligraphy, as it were. According to Exodus, the original tablets written by God (see Ex. 31:18; 32:15-16) were broken when Moses saw the idolatry of the people. The message could not be more suggestive: for an idolatrous people even a text written in God's own handwriting would become an idol and, as idols do, would arrest the gaze from the One to whom the gaze should be directed. Again this would put a price tag on the scriptures, turning it from the interpreter into a value in itself.

25. . . . et coepi iudicare, decalogum esse dialecticam euangelii et euangelium rhetoricam decalogi, habereque Christum omnia Mosi, sed Mosen non omnia Christi. WA Br 5, 409, 28–30.

26. . . . ego hic factus sum novus discipulus decalogi. WA Br 5, 409, 26.

> 49. [I]f the adversaries press the Scriptures against Christ, we urge Christ
> against the Scriptures. . . . 52. For if we have Christ, we can easily estab-
> lish laws and we shall judge all things rightly. 53. Indeed, we would
> make new decalogues. . . . 54. And these decalogues are clearer than the
> Decalogue of Moses.[27]

Indeed, *tempus mutat mores et leges*, time changes customs and laws.

However, with the antinomian controversy raging (1535), Luther makes it
clear that not anything goes, and he continues:

> 58. Nevertheless, since in the meantime we are inconstant in spirit, and
> the flesh wars with the spirit, it is necessary, also on account of inconstant
> souls, to adhere to certain commands and writings of the apostles, lest the
> church be torn to pieces.[28]

Certain commands demand an affirmative response, and not just anything.
But which ones are they? The response can only be one that follows from
Luther's and the Reformers' apostolic or scriptural principle: those that do not
divert us from but lead us to hearing the story of God in the flesh, crucified and
resurrected. Luther adds, if the question is "Christ or the law, the law would
have to be let go, not Christ." In other words, any law that pretends to have
universal validity except the one that declares every one of us equally totally
sinner, *totus peccatori*, thus leading us to Christ, is a grammatical confusion of
dialectics and rhetoric. For example, any law that would prescribe works and
conditions for belonging in the priesthood of all believers, for being listeners
and proclaimers of the Word, must be let go, for nothing can keep us from the
love of God.

THE PROPER USES OF THE LAW

Therefore, Luther distinguished between two senses or kinds of law and justice,
what the later confessors phrased as the first and the second uses of the law.
The first use is the civil or political use of the law, the "logical" or dialectical
use. The second is the theological use, the one that the rhetorical "more than
enough" addresses. The civil use belongs to the dialect that addresses particular
contexts and situations and that can and will change according to civil arrange-
ments and political contracts. Why is the civil the first use and the theological
use the second? Because the civil use concerns the relation to the neighbor in

---

27. *LW* 34:112–113.
28. *LW* 34:113.

ever-changing circumstances. Because we are all creatures, human beings in God's continuing creation, before we are believers.

The first use of the law applies to all, Christian and non-Christians alike; and it is to be found in the scriptures and also elsewhere, because it refers to local expressions of the orders of creation. It is the set of laws framed by Moses for the Jewish people and written in the heart, finding expression in Roman law, in the civil code of Luther's Saxony (*Sachsenspiegel*),[29] in the Constitution of the United States, or in Koranic legislations of Islamic countries. These laws apply to all, but not all phrase it in the same way. Luther, for example, found the justification for polygamy given in Deut. 25:5-6 a "very good" rule that protected a widow and kept the name and lineage of a deceased father.[30] For that context it was a good law and its example should teach us that we should enforce legislation toward those same ends. These civil uses of the law, wherever they are found, need translation, for they are dialect-bound. Not only *tempus* but also *situs mutat mores et leges* (time and location change customs and laws). When the Word speaks dialect, when the first use of the law is concerned, it is for Luther still the law of God spoken to a given community or individuals; but its meaning for us needs to be translated, carried over from one place to another, from one time to another. And the means of its translation is communicative or dialogical reason, "the head of all [temporal] things . . . the all-best, yes, something divine."[31] This communicative reason is what can be exercised across human communities regardless of religious allegiances. And the end of reason is to prevent chaos, produce equity (*Billigkeit*), and bring about civil justice and peace for the proclamation and the hearing of the Word. This is the *telos*, the goal and the end of all laws.

These laws are the expression of something deeper, which for Luther, following Paul and the later natural law tradition, can be found in every human heart. The Decalogue and all the other biblical prescriptions are but an expression of natural law codified in given dialects. Thus, says Luther, "I keep the commandments which Moses has given, not because Moses gave commandments, but because they have been implanted in me by nature, and Moses agrees"[32]—or even, as we have seen, insofar as Moses agrees. Luther keeps the commandments of Moses insofar as Moses agrees with natural law. "Moses" is a dialect, which even gives us language to help us in our conversation toward finding our own voice to achieve equity. And this is an ideological task, a civic and political exercise that theologians alone will not accomplish, for their

---

29. *LW* 35:167.

30. Ibid.

31. Et sane verum est, quod ratio omnium rerum res et caput at prae caeteris rebus huius vitae optimum et divinum quiddam sit. WA 39, 175, 9–10.

32. *LW* 35:168.

proper forum is the Word proclaimed. But as members of a civil community, they are called upon to testify as to the way the people of the Bible carried out such conversations and such dialectics, the contextual results they have achieved, and the example this provides us.

But is Luther sponsoring a double theory of truth by which revelation stands beside a natural and perennial truth, that is, a metaphysics? Definitely not! His point is only that natural law sustains us like crutches in the provisional affairs of this world. This is what natural law discloses and what is universal about it. The fact that there is so much coincidence in legislations from all over the world and through all times as to what conveys our civil and social obligations attests to this common sense of what is right and wrong. But this is also why in different societies with their different dialects there are varied amazing ways in which this natural law might be expressed and which are always subject to change. But is there one code that is immutable? No, there is none. (From all we know, the only one there ever was was broken, and what we are left with are dialects trying to convey it; Exod. 32:19). All that we have are our hearts that are also broken and fail in every attempt to express that image of God implanted in them.

Here is a simple example. We all share the sense that in our hearts there is something written along the lines of the Fifth Commandment, "Don't kill." However, this general law is concretely rendered with many variations through time and space. Some societies think this pertains to all living creatures. Many think that it is right to kill that which threatens our human lives, including some bacteria or those labeled as terrorists. Some think that it pertains to all *human* beings, including the arch-murderer Cain (Gen. 4:15). Some include the unborn; others also those who are brain-dead. Still others think that it applies to all humans except those condemned in a court of law to be executed. According to the option chosen by a local dialect, does anything go? Certainly not, because our broken hearts reflect their brokenness in communities severed from one another precisely over these "translations." Yet it is the same longing of the hearts to find expression of the law written in them that also forms communities. And these communities long for broader fellowship of all the human race and all creatures as much as they assert their differences that are at once expressions of sin, of the injustices we create and perpetrate, and symptoms of our yearning to live out the law written in the heart and give to it a timely and contextual expression.

We all in our stations of life need these crutches to get along, no matter what shape or form they are cast in. For Luther, they took three shapes: the household (*oeconomia*), the state (*politia*), and the church (*ecclesia*). Yes, even the church as a visible, institutional, or empirical reality is nothing but a crutch to help us in our infirmity as much as the state and the household are.

ANTINOMIANISM?

Natural law is only the shorthand for the universal human search to live together under the condition of utter sinfulness, which we normally call original sin. This does not imply metaphysics, a universal truth that raises our nature to an immutable status beyond nature's vicissitudes. It implies, however, reasoning through our ever-changing infirmities to find institutions that address them. And these institutions always change because God is not only the creator, but the one who continuously creates; and we are not only sinful, but indeed sinners; we keep finding new ways to dodge our condition and go against it. "Antinomianism" is the name we give to this attitude of living without these institutions as if the crutches that carry us were only addictions from which we have been set free. This would be like believing that throwing away the crutches would by itself heal us.

The work or function of the law in its two uses or senses is finally only one, to bring us to Christ, to be the pedagogue of Christ. Theologically, it brings us to Christ because it finally accuses us, leaving us with nothing but a promise received in faith, that is, nothing but everything. Politically, it institutes systems and structures fit to times and places in which the Word as law and gospel can be proclaimed. This is why justice is such a precious and overwhelming topic in the scriptures. It is the pedagogue of justification. It teaches us what we can never accomplish: the imputation of a righteousness we can only receive as a gift. Injustice is so detrimental not only because it creates a "noise" in God's communication to us, but also because in denying the love of the neighbor, we simultaneously change the love of God into the love of an idol that suits ourselves. The laws of Moses and all the other dialects that try to render the law written in our hearts warn us of this detrimental transformation.

The two senses of the law come together only in the *eschaton*, which happens in every moment of judgment, in all *eschata* (plural). These are the moments that the Augsburg Confession calls the "terrors that strike the conscience when sin is recognized."[33] These are the very moments in which the law in both its uses comes to its end and fulfills its task and the rule of God reigns. This is why Luther insisted so much that the law in its civil sense must address us, must be a dialect that speaks to us so as to bring terror into our conscience. (If terror does not strike us first, what we get is terrorism.) Only then can it also be theologically useful. But it must always strike us before them, me before you, for only then can I love you before myself; only then can we love others before ourselves; only then can we love the Other before ourselves—otherwise

---

33. Augsburg Confession 12, "Concerning Repentance," §§3–4, in *The Book of Concord* (ed. Robert Kolb and Timothy J. Wengert; Minneapolis: Fortress Press, 2000), 45.

it simply would not be love. For Luther the end of all laws is love.[34] And we reach this end only if the law fulfills its task in us in the first place. This is why the Formula of Concord (Solid Declaration) 6 defines antinomianism as prescribing the law to others, but not to ourselves insofar as we regard ourselves the true Christians.[35] Antinomianism is as much living without the law as it is applying to others what we do not apply to ourselves. In this sense, ironically, it reverses Luther's maxim in affirming that the end of all love is the law.

Is scripture alone enough to be the ground and pillar of the church? It is more than enough. More than enough in a double sense. First, it exceeds anything we can bargain for, and in fact leaves our bargaining as worthless and detrimental insofar as it inculcates Christ in us, being for us the interpreter of the absolutely unequal exchange between what we bring (brokenness) and what Christ brings (wholeness). And, second, it also exceeds in providing us with a plethora of examples, some indeed superfluous, that pertain to different circumstances showing how this works out in our everyday life with its challenges, limits, circumstances, and possibilities.

The church neither authorizes the correct meaning of the scriptures, nor enables floating meanings chosen at whim. The church is the custodian of the events it attests to and the chronicler of the events that keep on happening and are the verve of the church. "Therefore every scribe who has been trained for the kingdom of heaven is like the master of a household who brings out of his treasure what is new and what is old" (Matt. 13:52).

---

34. Si enim lex contra charita temest, non est lex. Se charitas est domina et magistra legis. WA 42, 505, 11–12.

35. "[W]e reject and condemn as a harmful error . . . the teaching that the law is not to be urged . . . upon Christians and those who believe in Christ but only upon unbelievers, non-Christians, and the impenitent." Formula of Concord, Solid Declaration, art. 6, "Third Use of the Law" §25, in *Book of Concord*, 591.

CHURCH AND TRINITY

THE PROMISE AND LIMITS
OF AN ANALOGICAL REASONING

5

God has no unity,
How am I to have it?
Fernando Pessoa[1]

The dominant images of the church have been historically associated analogically with the Trinity: the people of God, the body of Christ, and the temple of the Holy Spirit. These are images that suggest complementary relations, but the emphases in one or the other of them correspond also to theological postures and are connected to different church traditions and confessions. It should not be surprising to find in Roman Catholicism, with its highly sacramental and incarnational Christology, a prevalence of the body of Christ image. In the Protestant tradition, with its stress on the Word of God addressed to humans, the image of the people of God is underscored. In the Radical Reformation of the sixteenth century as well as in the contemporary Pentecostal movement, the temple of the Holy Spirit best expresses the self-understanding of the church. These three images, as well as the many others found in the Bible,[2] can be seen in their diversity as the justification for the plurality of churches.

Ernst Käsemann advanced this argument against the idea that the New Testament canon grounds the unity of the church. This is a summary of his response:

---

1. "Deus não tem unidade, / Como a terei eu?" Fernando Pessoa, *Poesias Inéditas* (1919–1930) (Lisbon: Ática, n.d.), 166.
2. Paul Minear, *Images of the Church in the New Testament* (Philadelphia: Westminster, 1960), lists no less than ninety-six images of the church.

The New Testament canon does not, as such, constitute the foundation of the unity of the church. On the contrary, as such (that is, in its accessibility to the historian) it provides the basis for the multiplicity of the confessions. The variability of the kerygma in the New Testament is an expression of the fact that in primitive Christianity a wealth of different confessions were already in existence. . . . If the canon as such is binding in its totality, the various confessions may, with differing degrees of historical justification, claim as their own larger or smaller tracts of it, better or less known New Testament writers.[3]

While the canon suggests pluralistic imagery, the use of the trinitarian motif suggests unity in diversity.[4] The discussions surrounding the Trinity, however, have themselves been a source of basic disagreements. A basic difference can already be found in the language of the Eastern Greek churches in comparison with the Western Latin churches to designate the persons of the Trinity. As Orthodox theologian John Zizioulas argues, in the East the word for "person" (*prosōpon,* which in the Latin West was translated by *persona*) was in the early church given an ontological weight through "*the identification of the 'hypostasis'* [a self-subsisting entity] *with the 'person.'*"[5] In the Latin West, *persona* had a theatrical association with the mask the actor wears in performing a thespian role and is not descriptive of the *being* of the person who is performing the act. Zizioulas argues that the Greek Orthodox church fathers introduced a new ontology unknown to the great Greek philosophers and actually against their metaphysical assumptions. Instead of starting with a unitary essence and substance in defining being, and only then moving into the multiplicity of existing entities, that is, from the one

---

3. Ernst Käsemann, "The New Testament Canon and the Unity of the Church," in idem, *Essays on New Testament Themes* (London: SCM, 1971), 103f.

4. This argument has been advanced in a study of Latin American Protestantism by Argentinian theologian José Míguez Bonino in *Faces of Protestantism in Latin America.* The author finds in liberal denominations an emphasis on the first person of the Trinity, while the second person is dominant in "evangelicalism," and Pentecostalism stresses the third person. José Míguez Bonino, *Faces of Protestantism in Latin America: 1993 Carnahan Lectures* (Grand Rapids: Eerdmans, 1997), 107–29. Later he adds: "*However, neither did the church err in emphasizing, along with the unity of that work, the distinction of its dimensions:* 'the father is not the Son nor the Spirit, the Son is not the Father nor the Spirit, the Spirit is not the Father nor the Son.' Such formulas are not just plays on words. What have been called 'properties' or 'appropriations' refer specifically to that necessary distinction. God is Father, Son, and Holy Spirit when creating and preserving the world, when inviting to faith in Jesus Christ and in building the church, when fertilizing and directing history. *God is so, however, in a different way and thus incorporates human beings in God's work—'commissions' them—in a different manner.* To honor the unity of that work and respond to the diversity of those distinctions is at once the task of the thought and practice of the church" (142).

5. John D. Zizioulas, *Being as Communion: Studies in Personhood and the Church* (Crestwood, N.Y.: St. Vladimir, 2002), 36.

to the many, the Greek fathers started with the persons in order to define *being* as a communion of persons. This ontology arises out of their exploration of the mystery of the Trinity, in which being itself is the result of the communion of persons. This is of importance for the grounding of the church, as the body of Christ, in the Trinity itself, with which it is in perichoretical union,[6] being at the same time, as it is the body of Christ, the people of God, the principle (*archē*) of the Trinity, and the temple of the Spirit. "Christ *in-stitutes* and the Spirit *con-stitutes.* The difference between these two prepositions: *in*—and *con*—can be enormous."[7] The difference between *instituting* and *constituting* is parallel to the two senses of representation presented earlier. "The 'institution' is something presented to us as a fact . . . 'con-stitution' is something that involves us in its very being . . . because we take part in its very emergence."[8]

The ecclesiological implications of Zizioulas's proposal are indeed significant. But the great merit of his interpretation of the Trinity is that he tries to balance the ontological reality that is *given,* "a *fait-accomplit* . . . presented to us as a fact,"[9] with the human freedom of participating in this communion. And he is probably right when he says that the Eastern Orthodox churches have the capacity of balancing this enormous difference of that which is given without the freedom of our choosing and that which is constituted by our free participation. This then accounts for the "fact that Orthodoxy has not experienced situations similar to those of the Western churches, such as the problem of clericalism, anti-institutionalism, Pentecostalism, etc."[10] In other words, Zizioulas suggests that Orthodoxy has achieved a tenuous balance between the two senses of representation: representation as re-*presencing* and representation as stand-in. One relies on the "economic" paradigm, the other on the "political" one.

But in spite of trying to keep the balance, Zizioulas falls back into a univocal definition of the church by finding its truth in the Eucharistic celebration, which belongs to the category of the "given," that is, under the "economic" paradigm. In the Eucharistic assembly, he writes,

---

6. *Perichoresis* is a term used originally in Greek Orthodoxy to describe the relation of the persons of the Trinity. It can be defined as co-indwelling, co-inhering, and mutual interpenetration. It allows for the individuality of the persons to be maintained while asserting their community.

7. Zizioulas, *Being as Communion,* 140. Indeed, this distinction is very important for Zizioulas. Cf. Miroslav Volf, *After Our Likeness: The Church as the Image of the Trinity* (Grand Rapids: Eerdmans, 1998), who offers an excellent commentary on the Greek theologian from a Protestant perspective, although he does miss this distinction; see, e.g., p. 215.

8. Zizioulas, *Being as Communion,* 140.

9. Ibid.

10. Ibid.

God's Word reaches man and creation not from outside, as in the Old Testament, but as "flesh"–from inside our existence, as part of creation. . . . Christ Himself becomes revealed as truth not *in* a community, but *as* a community. So truth is not just something "expressed" or "heard," a propositional or logical truth; but something which *is*, i.e. an ontological truth: the community itself becoming the truth.[11]

The bracketing of the trinitarian relations by focusing only on its Christological aspect, even if that needs to be defined relationally, leads to a definition of the church composed of only one aspect of the trinitarian relations insofar as its relation to the world is concerned, that is, the economic Trinity. And this is the incarnation of the *logos*. In this sense, reference to the Old Testament is revealing, where we find a God *with*, *among*, and even *in*[12] its people, but never *as* the people. In this manner, the truth of the incarnation or the incarnation as truth conceals the importance of the external Word, as precious for the Protestant tradition as it has also been for the Hebrew faith. A good number of the Protestant churches go by the rule that where the Word is, there the church is (*ubi verbum, ibi ecclesia*). But for Zizioulas, and he would claim this for Orthodox churches in general, where there is the Eucharist, there the church is.[13] That is, the truth instituted by Christ in the Eucharist and constituted by the Spirit in the communion is salvation. This leads Zizioulas to an "overrealized eschatology."[14] To put it bluntly, institutional re-*presencing* overrides event.

Nevertheless, it has also been clear that the emphasis on the Word and its proclamation places Protestantism too easily in the camp of the "political" paradigm. The Christ proclaimed is not at the same time the incarnate Christ according to his human nature, but being absent he is proclaimed by proxy, revealing a certain Modalist or even docetic tone in the argument.[15] In addressing this problem, the Trinitarian grounding of ecclesiology in Eastern

---

11. Ibid., 115.

12. The reference is to the Hebrew sense of Shekinah, the indwelling of God among the people.

13. Both in the declaration *Dominus Iesus* and in the document "Responses to Some Questions regarding Certain Aspects of the Doctrine of the Church," the Sacred Congregation for the Doctrine of Faith of the Vatican makes a similar claim referring to the "valid Eucharist," along with the Sacrament of Orders (apostolic succession), as a true mark of the church.

14. Volf, *After Our Likeness*, 101.

15. Zizioulas finds this a problem of the Western theology in general "*because the term 'person' lacked an ontological content* and led towards Sabellianism (the manifestation of God in three 'roles')." The suspicion of Modalism or Sabellianism has been often raised in particular to the Protestant neo-orthodoxy movement of the twentieth century. Some see in it even some more radical forms of docetism and Gnosticism. See Paul Tillich, *A History of Christian Thought from Its Judaic and Hellenistic Origins to Existentialism* (ed. Carl E. Braaten; New York:

Orthodoxy, as presented by Zizioulas, offers a needed correction, albeit a one-sided correction.

A WESTERN READING

In an original argument, S. Mark Heim[16] makes a proposal similar to that of Zizioulas in rethinking trinitarian language, with one fundamental difference from the one worked out by Zizioulas. He does not start with the different persons of the Trinity to identify the work of the economic Trinity—the Father as the principle (*archē*), the Son as the "instituter," and the Holy Spirit as the "constituter" of the church—as Zizioulas does with zest. Instead, he appeals to the Western tradition of not separating the work of the Trinity according to the persons of the Trinity.[17] Heim's distinction is not among the persons but among three different forms of relations, or what he calls "dimensions" of the Trinity. One is an "impersonal" relation that he describes as both an indwelling of one in another[18] and a radical sense of emptiness that has roots in the Jewish-Christian tradition. He exemplifies this relation with the experiences of God's presence "described in natural or impersonal categories: wind, fire, a consuming presence in which mortal creatures threaten to disintegrate."[19] The second relation he calls the "iconic dimension," in which there is a personal relationship with the divine in the form of its living manifestation among humans. In the Christian tradition it would be Jesus Christ. The third is the "communion dimension," in which

> [t]he triune persons do not only share the one and the same divine life (the constant process of impersonal exchange). They do not only meet each other as distinctive others, honoring and enacting their identities toward each other. They also enter into communion with each other *as different persons*.[20]

Touchstone, 1967), 34. Ernst Bloch, *Atheismus im Christentum: Zur Religion des Exodus und des Reichs* (Frankfurt: Suhrkamp, 1968), 75f.

16. See his *Salvations: Truth and Difference in Religion* (Maryknoll, N.Y.: Orbis, 1995). A summary argument is also found in "The Depth of Riches: Trinity and Religious Ends," in *Theology and the Religions: A Dialogue* (ed. Viggo Mortensen; Grand Rapids: Eerdmans, 2003), 387–402.

17. The classical formulation is Augustine's: *opera ad extra sunt indivisa*, the external work of the Trinity cannot be divided.

18. The example he uses is a blood transfusion. See Heim, "Salvation as Communion: Partakers of the Divine Nature," *TT*, 61, no. 3 (October 2004): 322–33.

19. Heim, "Depth of Riches," 392.

20. Ibid., 397.

Heim's typology of the trinitarian dimensions exemplifies that distinction between the economic paradigm of representation and the political one in an enlightening way. The economic paradigm is similar, though not identical, to the impersonal dimension in that a relation is established through an object, the "gift" that is passed on, without implying the direct intersubjective relationship of the iconic dimension. The latter is better described by the political paradigm. By using different categories, by not conflating the impersonal and the iconic dimensions, and by showing what different kinds of relations they are, Heim is touching on the same problem that I already examined earlier when two different forms of representation are conflated. His third dimension, communion, is what I shall address and examine further.

TRINITY: A CONTEXTUAL SECOND-ORDER DISCOURSE

I have argued elsewhere[21] that the doctrine of the Trinity is a second-order discourse to make sense of a fundamental dilemma that emerged from the passion narrative of Jesus Christ. How are we to speak of a God who becomes human and suffers the consequence of assuming the most deprived state of humiliation and sinfulness? Although the conception of the Trinity is not, strictly speaking, biblical,[22] it provided semantics for framing the Christian story of the life, passion, death, and resurrection of Jesus and furnished the church with an explanation for its existence as the people of God, the body of Christ, and the eschatological anticipation of the spiritual presence. A concept of God emerged that connects the church to the past and creation, to the presence of Jesus, and to the foretaste of a future to come by the outpouring of the Spirit. This idea was already present in the early Orthodox Church when Maximus the Confessor expressed it: "The things of the Old Testament are shadow (*skia*); those of the New Testament are image (*eikōn*); and those of the future are truth (*alētheia*)."[23]

---

21. Vítor Westhelle, *The Scandalous God: The Use and Abuse of the Cross* (Minneapolis: Fortress Press, 2006), 30–34.

22. Schleiermacher was eager to remind us of this and "to make the point that the main pivots of the ecclesiastical doctrine–the being of God in Christ and in the Christian Church– are independent of the doctrine of the Trinity." Friedrich Schleiermacher, *The Christian Faith* (Edinburgh: T&T Clark, 1989), 741.

23. Cited by Zizioulas, *Being as Communion*, 99. Hegel makes a similar move in his overall conception of the self-realization of the Spirit that is first perceived by "intuition" (*Anschauung*), then by "imagery" (*Vorstellung*), to finally reach its truth in the "concept" (*Begriff*). A similar argument is developed by Juan Luis Segundo, who defines God as "the One before us, the One with us, and the One ahead of us." *Our Idea of God* (Maryknoll, N.Y.: Orbis, 1974), 21–31.

Although the doctrine of the Trinity is still a benchmark for most of the Christian churches, its reinterpretations to address present challenges are rather faithful to its conceptual inception. The doctrine emerged as a contextualized attempt to explain the faith of the church and the biblical legacy in the face of the challenges the first Christians met.

Three contextual factors were of decisive importance for the formulation of the doctrine. First, the Christian community emerges from the very heart of Judaism. The apostles and the first adherents to the faith were Jews who would gather in synagogues and who were interpreted by Jews and Gentiles as a dissident and marginal group but still within Judaism. The group's dissident character or even apostasy was due to the fact that they identified Jesus of Nazareth not only as the waited messiah but as the son of God who even dared to say, "Whoever has seen me has seen the Father" (John 14:9). The utterly transcendent God of inaccessible glory, whose face not even Moses was allowed to see, was now a God with his people in the flesh. And more, this messiah was the one executed as a criminal on the mount of the empty skull (Golgotha), the place abandoned by God. The attempt of the church was to maintain the radical affirmation that Jesus was the Christ, the only son of God, without, however, abandoning the radical transcendence of God, a notion that those early Jewish-Christians could not part with. This was the first challenge to which the concept of the Trinity tried to respond—to be true to the apostolic witness of the New Testament as well as to respect the core of the Jewish faith. Additionally, this had to be accomplished while keeping the accepted canon of the Hebrew Bible in its integrity in the emerging new Christian canon, notwithstanding significant opposition among followers of Gnostic persuasion. Hence the first challenge was to forge the reality of diversity into the very concept of the divine unity. With this gesture the church could be conceived as being "one" even when it held opinions that seem contradictory, as in the joining of the transcendent and the immanent without surrendering either or blending the two. The church could claim the communion that the Father in his utter transcendence and the Son in human flesh enjoyed through the Holy Spirit.

Second, as soon as the Christian faith made its incursion into the Greco-Roman cultural and philosophical milieu, it faced another challenge, the philo-sophical conception of the impassibility of the divine being. If change in a substance conveys its finitude, then something that existed before is no longer there in the altered state. Hence God cannot be the cause of Godself (for in such a case what God is now, is not what God previously was). God cannot be eternal (for if God has changed, then God is no longer the same, for something that was divine is no longer). However, for God to be God necessitates that God be both immutable and eternal, which carries the logical conclusion that God must be impassible, or apathetic, for *pathos* means to be moved and suffer change. The trinitarian discussions were an attempt to dispute this argument by creating a new definition of what the divine being is. The contribution of Zizioulas pertains precisely to this point. His argument is that the early orthodox patristic theologians did not start from the unitary essence of being and then deduce individualities. Instead, they began from the diversity of persons as *hypostases* (subsisting entities) in order to define *being* as the community of these persons. The second challenge was to express in the midst of finitude and death the very presence of the divine and life. The poignant words of Rubem Alves say it well: "God died; long live God."[24]

The third circumstantial factor was that by the year 60 C.E. it was relatively clear that the mission toward the Jews was becoming a failure.[25] New leaders of Christian communities (like Paul and his collaborators) who themselves came from Judaism began the missionary work among the Gentiles in the Greco-Roman cultural and religious world. In this context the challenge was no longer to convey the message of Jesus Christ to people who had an utterly transcendent notion of God. It was also not the strict philosophical context of the Greek academies with their concept of God's impassibility or apathy. The work of these missionaries was to make inroads particularly in the popular classes. Popular religiosity offered a plethora of divinities to be worshipped, each with its qualities, virtues, and vices, offering different and appealing goods in the retail market of religious options. The account of Paul's experience in Athens (Acts 17) that led to his famous address at the Areopagus gives a vivid image of the religious context in which the mission toward the Gentiles was carried out. Additionally, in the political realm the emperor was endowed with divine attributes and called *kyrios*, lord, or even *deus*, god. And in this politico-religious system order was maintained by the anecdotal *panem et circenses* (bread and circus), or by massacre and repression. And not rarely, as the many Christians martyred in the arenas attest, the two strategies would be combined. However, among the poor and oppressed, among whom were many of the early Christians, we find a strong eschatological expectation with apocalyptic overtones. Ernst Käsemann, who claimed that apocalyptic is "the mother of all Christian theology," defined Christian apocalyptic as the imminent expectation of the *parousia*, the presence or coming of Christ, in which God would radically change the destiny of this old eon, drastically reversing its perverse course.[26] In this sense apocalyptic is

---

24. Rubem Alves, "Deus Morreu; Viva Deus!" *Liberdade e Fé* (Rio de Janeiro: Tempo e Presença, 1972), 19. The Portuguese *viva* is not only an interjection of acclamation as in English but also the imperative of the verb "to live": calling God back to life.

25. See Vítor Westhelle, "Paul's Reconstruction of Theology: Romans 9–14 in Context," *WW* 4, no. 3 (1984): 308.

26. Ernst Käsemann, "Die Anfänge christlicher Theologie," in idem, *Exegetische Versuche und Besinnungen* (Göttingen: Vandenhoeck & Ruprecht, 1964), 2:100.

not something that deals exclusively with a 180-degree turn in the historical axis expected at the time of the second coming. *Parousia* has also a social dimension, for the eschatological moment that brings it is socially located; it begins with the little ones at the margins (*ta eschata*). And it has also a geographical sense, for it would reach the ends of the earth (*eschatou tēs gēs* Acts 1:8; 13:47). This event is not only the expression of the relation between Father and Son, as in the incarnation, but extends itself to the last things, both in time and in space, as the work of the Spirit who anoints to bring good news to the poor, release the captives, restore sight to the blind, and liberate the oppressed (Luke 4:18). And this was the third challenge that helped to shape the trinitarian doctrine: there was an eschatological vision by which the Holy Spirit was bringing a reversal of the doomed ways of the world. This paradigmatic reversal that the last will be first was already announced and anticipated in a condemned criminal who is executed and is resurrected to life in the power of the Spirit. And while this was born out of the Spirit, it was also carried out in defiance of the imperial power. The one executed is called *kyrios*, or Emmanuel, God among us.

This is the importance of the trinitarian principle in framing an ecclesiology in which its communion, to use the analogy proposed by Maximus, "shadows" the utterly transcendent God, the *extra nos*, "images" God's presence among God's people, *in nobis*; and anticipates the final revelation of the "truth,"[27] *pro nobis*.

These elements of the trinitarian principle born of the church's own struggle with its context form the basis for the formal criterion of ecclesiology. They are the foundation for the three signs or marks that the Protestant Reformers used to define the church: the proclamation of the Word, the celebration of the sacraments in which Christ is experienced as present, and the gathering of the eschatological people, people who know themselves to be at the *eschaton*, or at the margins, where the Spirit breathes life when life is hanging at the edge. Martin Luther already used these constitutive elements of the church as early as 1519.[28] John Calvin mentions them a number of times in the *Institutes*.[29] But the classical definition was made popular by Melanchthon in the Augsburg Confession 7, which states: "The church is the assembly of saints in which the gospel is taught purely and the sacraments are administered rightly. And it is enough for the true unity of the church to agree concerning the teaching of the gospel and the administration of the sacraments."

---

27. In Greek, *alētheia* (truth) might have its etymology in *alēthē*, the overcoming of oblivion. Cf. Zizioulas, *Being as Communion*, 45.

28. *LW* 35:67.

29. John Calvin, *Institutes of the Christian Religion* (Louisville: Westminster John Knox, 1960), 4.1.3, 7, 9, 10, 11, and 12.

What was being attempted with this definition was to provide the church with the identifying marks that made it visible and gave it a form. But it is in this context that Melanchthon brings up the Donatist controversy (AC 8), and so does Calvin.[30] These corruptions that the Donatists fought, however, do not cancel the validity and effectiveness of the church's witness even if its truth lies hidden from our eyes and can be seen only by God. The observable criteria expounded for the definition of the church are only formal, that is, things that can be observed by anyone without presupposing theological content. The classical Protestant definition of the church as the congregation of believers among whom the Word is proclaimed and the sacraments rightly administered still begs the question about its theological or material criterion.

The distinction between formal and material criteria can be illustrated by an example from the academic field. What are the formal and material criteria for writing the final paper for a graduate course? The formal criterion is the level of adherence by the student to the style manual adopted by the school, the length of the manuscript as specified by the program or the course, the number of sources employed for the research, and the correct use of grammar, syntax, orthography, and so forth. But even within these parameters, this hypothetical paper can be either a very mediocre piece or one of outstanding brilliance. To make the latter judgment as to its quality is to apply the material criterion, which will depend on the assembly of data, the consistency of the argument, the knowledge of the field covered, the originality of the argument, and the like. These traits defy objective measurements and quantification. To identify the material criterion for the definition of the church, we must make a similar move and look to the content behind the formal features that are enough to recognize the church, but not enough to determine its "quality," that is, its faithfulness.

LUTHER AND THE MATERIAL CRITERION

In 1539 Martin Luther published one of the most significant texts of the later period of his life, *On the Councils and the Church*.[31] Like Melanchthon and Calvin, he did not go on to discuss the essentialist definitions of the marks of church (*notae ecclesiae*) as we find them in the Nicene-Constantinopolitan Creed: one, holy, catholic, and apostolic. The Reformers defined the church by its ministerial function: the gathering of the people, the proclamation of the gospel, and the administration of the sacraments as instituted by Christ. And that, as Melanchthon had proclaimed, is enough (*satis est*). Yet even if Luther had earlier agreed with this definition, in *On the Councils and the Church* he apparently departs from

---

30. Ibid., 4.1.13. Both Melanchthon and Calvin find in the Anabaptists the contemporaneous version of the Donatist movement.

31. The references are to part 3 of the treatise found in *LW* 41:143–78.

that parsimonious definition and lists seven marks or "possessions" by which the church is "recognized."[32] But he is not, at least for the first six marks, introducing anything really new; he is just qualitatively unfolding those formal signs of the church. These six are as follows: The first is the Word of God that is proclaimed. He then lists separately the sacrament of baptism and that of the altar, Holy Communion. The fourth mark is the office of the keys, the confession of sins (both privately and publicly) and absolution or announcement of forgiveness, which at that time for the Reformers was no longer a sacrament as such but a rite of returning to baptism. Then in the fifth and sixth place come ministry and public worship, which unfolds what happens when the Christian people gather as the congregation of the saints; someone is assigned and is acknowledged as the minister to lead the congregation while it worships in public. To this point, Luther maintains the minimalist definition of the church according to the formal criteria discussed above. But is this enough (*satis est*)?

The next mark, the seventh, does not unfold directly from the traditional definition of the church and its unity like the previous six Luther listed. He writes: "Seventh, the holy Christian people are externally recognized by the holy possession of the sacred cross."[33] But "cross" here and most often in Luther functions as metonymy; it designates something with which it is associated, namely, suffering. He often used the words *cross* and *suffering* interchangeably.[34] This is how he describes it: The Christian people as church

> must endure every misfortune and persecution, all kinds of trials and evil
> from the devil, the world, and the flesh (as the Lord's Prayer indicates)
> by inward sadness, timidity, fear, outward poverty, contempt, illness, and
> weakness, in order to become like their head, Christ.[35]

For the Reformer, human suffering not only was a reality in life but necessarily designated the place in which the church becomes identical with Christ in our midst. Conformity to Christ is and must be a recognizable mark of the church as it embraces the reality of evil in any of its manifestations, such as suffering, illness, persecution, oppression, marginalization, trial, or any other form by which sin torments human existence.

Among the seven external marks of the church, this last one has more than a formal characteristic, a quality, a gravitas to it; it is a scar or even an open

---

32. *LW* 41:148. See also *Christian Assembly* (Mpls.: Fortress Press, 2004).

33. *LW* 41:164.

34. Regin Prenter, *Luther's Theology of the Cross* (Philadelphia: Fortress Press, 1971), 3, goes so far as to assert that the cross of Christ is for Luther essentially "identical . . . with the cross we are called upon to bear."

35. *LW* 41:164.

wound. The visibility of this mark, different from the others, upsets the apple cart, so to speak. It lacerates the well-arranged traditional marks of the church either in the creed, in the Reformation, or in any other ecclesiastical definition of the church. But if this mark, this wound, is of people gathered in the midst of the passion of the world to hear the promise of the gospel and feel the solace shared as a balm in the elements of the sacraments, there and that is the true church. This is why this last mark is the decisive *material criterion* of the church. Amid the suffering of the world, the church is there waiting for the Word to be proclaimed and the sacraments to be administered; it is already there hidden or latent, as Luther said, waiting to be manifest in the gathering of the people around the Word and the sacraments. According to him, already "Christ is living in the poor and despised."[36]

This is the point made by Dietrich Bonhoeffer when in his ecclesiology he claims that "the church is Christ existing as church-community."[37] This is a theological statement on a sociological reality that indeed is already in the world; it is real, not a model to be implemented, built, or developed. To use an expression by Luther again, "The people of Christ are the poor, the insignificant, the faint-hearted, the harassed, the lowly, the fearful."[38] Bonhoeffer is reacting against the notion that the church is an ideal to be sought after, or that it will never be fully attainable in this world. He adds:

> Neither of these views does justice to the genuinely historical nature of the empirical church. The first is mistaken because Christ entered history; the church is therefore his presence in history. *The history of the church is the hidden center of world history*, and not the history of one educational institution among others. . . . it is not Ought that effects Is, but Is that effects Ought.[39]

The "is" is already the latent church in the Christ and him crucified in the midst of the empirical reality of this world, which "ought" to take shape in Christ preached and his gifts bestowed in the water of baptism that kills and brings to new life, and in the bread and the cup that are shared in communion. It is not about an institution in search of its ideal; it is already here where Christ is

---

36. *LW* 10:190.

37. "Kirche ist Christus als Gemeinde existierend." Dietrich Bonhoeffer, *Sanctorum Communio: A Theological Study of the Sociology of the Church* (DBWE; trans. Richard Krauss and Nancy Lukens; Minneapolis: Fortress Press, 1998), 211 et passim. He is paraphrasing an expression coined by philosopher G. W. F. Hegel: "God existing as community." Georg Wilhelm Friedrich Hegel, *Lectures on the Philosophy of Religion* (one-volume edition: The Lectures of 1827; ed. Peter Hodgson; Berkeley: University of California Press, 1988), 473.

38. *LW* 16:121.

39. Bonhoeffer, *Sanctorum Communio*, 211f. (emphasis in the original).

in the flesh and all its frailty. This is the reason that the Protestant motto *ecclesia reformata semper reformanda est* (the church reformed is always a reforming church) is misleading if understood to mean that it is still in search of being what it ought to be, or in the words of Bonhoeffer again, "It is not Ought that effects Is." The same can also be said of the definition of the church in Vatican II: *ecclesia sancta simul et semper purificanda* (the church holy and at once always being purified).

Although Luther never objected explicitly to the *satis est*, the "is enough" of the Augsburg Confession 7, it is plausible to assume that he did not do it because he was in agreement with those marks of the church insofar as they were the *formal* criteria to discern the church. However, what he adds to the "enough" belongs to a different order of criteria. Cross and suffering in the reality of this world make up a material criterion required to recognize the social location of the church as the historically existing God in Christ.

TYING ENDS TOGETHER

The discussion so far and the elucidation of the material criterion have enabled me to address the questions and queries regarding the church's integrity, including its image, figure, and character; its relation to the adjacent economic and political realms; how it is to be church without capitulating to either form of representation; and how the church exists in this enticing vicinity of economics and politics. The material criterion points to where the church *already* is. This prevents the church from falling prey to either the economic or the political paradigm, and from construing its identity through the sacraments or acting it out through its proclamation. Without it what we have is either a void of sacramental ritualism or else an empty rhetorical impersonation by which the congregation is but a free association of the like-minded.

KOINŌNIA

6

BETWEEN THE IDOL OF THE HOUSE
AND THE DEMONS OF THE STREET

Whoever wishes to know how much at home we are in entrails
must allow himself to be swept along in delirium through streets
whose darkness greatly resembles the lap of a whore.

Walter Benjamin[1]

THE HOUSE AND THE STREET

The two paradigms–the "economic" and the "political"–that ground two modes of representation are distinct modes for the construal of identity. In the economic paradigm, identity is an objective reality that is a given. There is no transaction; you take it or you leave it. It does not stand for something else; it is what it re-presents. In what is given is the gift embedded. In ecclesiology this identity takes many forms: the Eucharist, an ecclesiastical office, a liturgy, the Bible, confessional writings, a charismatic leader, a holy site, and so forth. In this case the church is seen as a household in which these "gifts" are produced, reproduced, and kept; stored in it is the very content of the faith (*depositum fidei*). The household of faith constitutes a family in which the members belong regardless of personal idiosyncrasies; in it one is family. A consummate example of this way of affirming a church identity is to say that in the "gift" received is the truth regardless of one's personal conviction. Since Augustine's affirmation that by himself he would not have come to faith if the church had not moved him to,[2] the church has developed the doctrine of implicit faith

---

1. Walter Benjamin, *The Arcades Project* (trans. Howard Euland and Kevin Mclaughlin; Cambridge, Mass.: Belknap Press of Harvard University Press, 1999), 519.

2. Augustine expressed this in his dispute with the Manicheans: "For my part, I should not believe the gospel except as moved by the authority of the Catholic Church. So when those on whose authority I have consented to believe in the gospel tell me not to believe in

(*fides implicita*), which says that people need not necessarily believe personally in some revealed truth provided that they belong in obedience to the church that holds these truths, as a household that bestows identity on its members and to which obedience and subservience are due. An image comes here to the fore: the house. The house functions as a model[3] of the church with all the images it evokes.

On the other extreme of the spectrum we have church formations that follow the political paradigm. In this the identity is construed by interpersonal relations. What counts is the interrelationship among people. Recognition comes through the role one plays in standing for that which is absent. The roles and rules of performance authenticate the truth that is being claimed. In ecclesiology, the church following this paradigm is identified by how, among different people, a common version of the truth can be shared. The church is an assembly of representatives in which what counts is the role one plays in representing the inaccessible truth. What is revealed or manifested is not the essence of the thing itself but how it is lived out in the lives of people who perform their role in *representing* that which is of the essence. The truth being represented is validated according to its intersubjective communicability. The point here, opposite to the house model, is not belonging but mutuality. The apostle Paul's long admonition to the Corinthians (1 Corinthians 14) that speaking in tongues can only be edifying if it is translatable so that the community can understand is an example of this view of community; it stands in sharp contrast to what is given even as pure mystery (*mysterium* is the word that in Latin was translated as *sacramentum*, hence the English *sacrament*). Translatability is accessibility to meaning. Authority is not granted to what is given as such, but to the authenticity conveyed in a meaningful exchange that happens in an encounter. Streets, roads, pathways are metaphors for accessibility. They in themselves are nothing except for the function they carry out. The words of the poem by António Machado aptly convey this idea: "Walker, there is no path; you do the path by walking."[4] This is the street model of the church. Any street, boulevard, avenue, or narrow pathway, regardless of the beauty of the surroundings, its flower-planted borders, or the smoothness of the pavement, is only a function of bringing people to meaningful encounters. But the point is not the road; it is rather that to which the road leads.

Manichæus, how can I but consent?" *The Nicene and Post-Nicene Fathers*, 2nd ser., vol. 11 (ed. Philip Schaff; repr., Peabody, Mass.: Hendrickson, 1995), 131.

3. "Model" is here being used in the sense that is applied in architecture or in industrial design, as discussed in chap. 1.

4. "Caminante, no hay camino; se hace camino al andar." Antonio Machado, "Proverbios y Cantares" 29, in *Obras Completas* (ed. Manuel; Biblioteca Austral; Madrid and Barcelona: Espasa Calpe, 1978), 239.

Certainly both models have been celebrated in the church, but they work in a tension-ridden relationship. Each of the two, as much as it manifests basic characteristics of the church, is also a form of its captivity. This way of phrasing the problem is not new. Anthropologist Roberto DaMatta has used the metaphors of "house" and "street" to characterize Brazilian culture as a constant movement between the outer space of the streets and the intimacy of the home.[5] Instead of the frozen separation between the public and the private,[6] DaMatta's metaphors allow for a fruitful way to address the overlapping features in the relation between civic spaces and those of intimacy, the first following the political paradigm and the latter the economic paradigm. Even while they remain distinct, there is a constant negotiation between these spaces. These metaphors describing a culture stand in clear contrast to the reality of globalization, in which a dramatic integration of worldwide relations is concomitant with a radical fragmentation of isolated territorial spaces, which are often not larger than a computer terminal from where one can navigate the World Wide Web. The streets have become spaces of displacement and the houses increasingly inaccessible from the streets, protected by walls, fences, and security systems. Those who cannot "web-in" become the excluded ones, the subaltern people of the world. And to these is also denied the possibility of maintaining the movement and exchange between the "house," or realms of intimacy, and the "street," or spaces where one exercises civic rights and duties. They are the homeless, the (illegal and also legal) immigrants, the landless peasants, the street children, the shut-ins, the imprisoned, the institutionalized, the children and women abused in their homes, among others. Globalization has meant for many the denial of the alternation of living contexts between civic spaces and realms of safety and shelter. And without such possibilities of contextualization, globalization becomes imperialism.[7]

If DaMatta's metaphors are inapt to describe this new situation, I take them to be very helpful in addressing in an analogous way the basic character of the church as an alternative space placed in (and as) this very transition between the civic spaces and the intimacy of the home, calling us out and gathering us in. The church, in its very catholicity, can be understood as a movement between "house" and "street" that bridges the cleft between globalization and fragmentation, between collectivism and individualism. Further, DaMatta's metaphors show more promise and biblical support as a way to describe the church as

5. Roberto DaMatta, *A Casa e a Rua: Espaço, Cidadania, Mulher e Morte no Brasil* (São Paulo: Rocco, 1985), 55–80.

6. For the classical distinction between the private and the public, see Immanuel Kant, "Beantwortung der Frage: Was ist Aufklärung," in *Ausgewählte kleine Schriften* (Hamburg: Felix Meiner, 1965), 1–9.

7. I owe this phrasing to my former colleague and now Bishop Antje Jackelén.

communio, a community that is both that which passes on the gift (*co-munus*) and the gathering of the people, or being one (*co-unus*).

Already in the Hebrew Scriptures the tent of the tabernacle provides an image for and prefigures the Christian church precisely by being this "house" on the way, occupying a middle position as neither the intimate space of the home nor the utter exposure of the street, yet both at the same time: the presence of the divine, yet in dynamic transition. To phrase it differently, what the *communio* ecclesiology does not do sufficiently is to convey the idea that the church is always a conjunctive reality—it is always the church *and,* the church *but,* the church *however.* . . . It is always something else, an elusive third, though not even a third *entity,* situated somewhere between the private and public.[8]

The evangelist Luke, in the book of Acts, often refers to the Christian community as those of the "Way" (*hodos:* road, way, street, path; cf. Acts 9:2; 19:23; 22:4; 24:22). But the same evangelist when referring to the gathering of the actual congregations describes them as the church that gathered in the house (Acts 2:46; 5:42), and so does Paul (Rom. 16:5).[9]

That the church might be described by these metaphors suggests, on the one hand, its gregarious character, the search for a space of healing, safety, and rest. Nevertheless, it is simultaneously called to break away from this very safety and move out of the familiar spaces and comfort zones. This calling is indeed already indicated by the very word *ekklēsia.* New Testament authors borrowed the word from the civil and political realm. *Ekklēsia* means an assembly of citizens called away from everyday routine, gathered to deliberate issues that pertain to civic and political life in order then to reenter it with a different attitude. *Ekklēsia* means a moment of discontinuity with the quotidian, but not as an end in itself; it suggests the possibility of a retreat in which deliberations are taken in order to return to the *polis.*

This dynamic simultaneity of risk-taking and safety is the reason why it is not wrong, but incomplete and thus misleading, to call the church a communion of salvation (*communio salutis*) or the place of salvation (*locus salutis*), when salvation is associated with being at rest. It is necessary to say also, in the same breath, that it is a community in transit (*communio viatorum*). As such, by being both a place and a way, the church proclaims a world that it itself does not know, but in which it believes, and for which it sacrifices itself in fulfilling its vocation of being the witness (*martyria*) to this other world and the

---

8. This is what denominationalism does at the cost of eschatology. See H. Richard Niebuhr, *The Social Sources of Denominationalism* (Hamden, Conn.: Shoe String, 1954), for a pointed denunciation of the treachery of the gospel and the evasion of the eschatological message of the kingdom in North American denominationalism.

9. See also Paul's (according to Luke) complementary use of *demosios* (public) and *oikos* (house) in Acts 20:20.

sacrament (*mysterium*) that anticipates it. Protestant ecclesiology expresses this incisively by presenting only two constitutive practices as sufficient (*satis est*) for the church's being (*esse*) and unity while gathered as a congregation. These are the announcement of another world or the World of the Other (done through the proclamation of the gospel), and the foretaste of its reality (the sacraments), even if further components might be necessary for the church's well-being and function (*bene esse*). But these are *adiaphora*, not of the essence, and they are changeable depending on context and circumstance. The minimalist ecclesiology that Protestantism inherited from the Reformation preserves in its core precisely these two functions of the church: the Word proclaimed that provokes and unsettles, and the sacraments that comfort and heal (baptism that *brings* us into communion and the Lord's Supper that *renews*, nourishes, and restores it). *Communio* ecclesiology gave expression to this vision of the church by grounding it in the doctrine of the Trinity, which simultaneously sustains the ideas that God is transcendent and also radically immanent. God is the Other, beyond and above us, who addresses us unconditionally, but who is also closer to us than we are to our own selves so that we can taste, savor, and feel the divine in the very stuff of this world. These two affirmations (utter transcendence and radical immanence) held paradoxically together are at the core of the doctrine of the Trinity, more than any and all trinitarian speculations.

If Cyprian defined the church as the requirement for salvation (*extra ecclesiam nulla salus*),[10] it might be so in at least two senses that the Greek word *sōtēria* and the Latin *salus* have. One is to heal, cure, preserve, and provide refuge. In this sense we are describing the house-function of the church. "Salvation" can also mean to deliver, to rescue, and to liberate. This sense would describe the street-function of the church. The idea of a salvation into another world (which would be a third sense of the term) is only a derivative and eschatological blending of the first two distinct semantic senses of the word *salvation*. Hence, if we follow the etymological meaning of the word, we can say that the church is the community of salvation insofar as, and only insofar as, it manifests itself in the places of perdition as a community that both heals and liberates.[11] Where this happens there is the church. Church happens! We *believe it*; we *do not* believe *in* it (*credo ecclesiam*, as the Nicene Creed formulates).[12] We believe it to be the

---

10. This expression is often quoted outside of its original context. Cyprian was opposing a papal disposition that accepted the baptism of those who belonged to heretical communities. In his opposition to the pope, Cyprian, ironically, played an anti-ecumenical role.

11. It is likely that the etymological root of the word *salvation* is the Latin *sal*, "salt." Salt was and is used to preserve or cure food. But it was often used as currency for the payment of wages earned; hence the connotation of something that affords one's freedom.

12. The Tappert edition of the *Book of Concord* has the correct translation, as opposed to the translation we have in both the *Lutheran Book of Worship* (Minneapolis: Augsburg Publishing House, and Philadelphia: Board of Publications, Lutheran Church in America, 1978) and

place of salvation, of healing and deliverance, when the evidences of our time point to the cross of our forsakenness. Where there is healing and deliverance, there is the church.

The time of the church in Protestant ecclesiology is symbolized by this void that extends itself from the moment of Jesus' death (God's *apousia*, absence) to his return and presence (*parousia*). It is not a time of dramatic events, great discourses, and certainties. It is the time of weakness and hope, the hope against all hope, as Paul describes Abraham's faith in Rom. 4:18, and as Brazilian bishop Dom Helder Câmara applied it to the church in calling it an "Abrahamic minority."

> They already exist; it is not necessary to create them. The Spirit of God raises them up deep within every race, in every religion, every nation, every human group. Who belongs to these abrahamic minorities? All those who, like Abraham, hope against hope and decide to work to the point of sacrifice for a more just and humane world.[13]

This is also what Luther meant in calling the church the community of the cross. It is the community that lives precisely in this time, in the Shabbat (which Luther in his Genesis lectures defined as the institution of the earthly church),[14] the distinctively Christian Shabbat that stands between Good Friday and Easter Sunday. Intriguingly, that was a time in the Gospels during which the apostles were silent!

CAPTIVITIES: THE IDOL AND THE DEMONS

The house and the street are complementary images that in tension suggest movement and at the same time a sense of homely calm and ease. Exposure and also a haven, risk and comfort, wanderlust and refuge are often the biblical notions attached to the church, which, as opposed as they are, also comple-

---

the Kolb and Wengert edition of the *Book of Concord* (Minneapolis: Fortress Press, 2000). For the Protestant argument against having the preposition "in," see John Calvin, *Institutes of Christian Religion* (Louisville: Westminster John Knox, 1960) 4.1.2 (vol. 2:1012f.).

13. Helder Câmara, "A Covenant That Deserves to Crown Your Journey," message to the Mani Tese [Outstretched Hands] youth movement at the climax of its 1972 march, Plaza Michelangelo, Florence, Italy, November 5, 1972. The Spanish version appears in Camara, *Proclamas a la Juventud* (ed. Benedicto Tapia de Renedo; Pedal. 64; Salamanca: Ediciones Sigueme, 1976), 187–92. The original Portuguese version appears in Câmara, "Justiça e paz: viagens 1972–1973," *Servicio de Apostillas* 36 (1973).

14. See *LW* 1:103, 106. Cf. Oswald Bayer, "Nature and Institution: Luther's Doctrine of the Three Orders," *LQ* 12, no. 2 (Summer 1998): 125–59.

ment each other. But interestingly, these two notions can also describe the two captivities of the church.

The two captivities of the church—one of working out its identity within the economic paradigm and the other of following the political one, of being identified either with the house or with the street—correspond to two well-known religious entrapments. The entrapment of the house is known as idolatry, while the one of the street is demonry, or the demonic.

In the beginning of the twentieth century, the young Hungarian philosopher Georg Lukács published *The Theory of the Novel*,[15] presenting a compelling analysis of modern society that is still valid a century later. The work starts with a comparative study of the forms of two literary genres of great Western literature, the classical epic and the modern novel, as exemplary expressions of the spiritual search and its perils. Although the distinction pertains also to very different historical periods, the importance of the study goes far beyond the historical restrictions and literary expressions that these genres represent. The study provides a sketch or a profile of two typical struggles against ailments that affect the human condition and to which the church is not immune. Of the two ailments, one knows "answers but no questions, only solutions (even if enigmatic ones) but no riddles, only forms but no chaos,"[16] while the other reflects "a world that has been abandoned by God."[17] If the second is well characterized by the experience of the demonic,[18] the first could be described by the tranquil arrest of the soul in the external image of its own projection and production: the idol.[19] The phenomena of these two shapes of the ailment of the soul are characteristic also of the captivities of the church. The idol pertains to the domain of the visible; the demon is an unseen and insinuating reality. In one the evil spirit takes an external commanding shape; in the other the spirit is like the inhaling of a contagious atmosphere that corrodes from within. But let us examine more closely these two symbols of the spiritual ailments of the soul[20] that have infested the church as well.

THE IDOL

The idol is the visible image that arrests the gaze and renders it incapable of seeing beyond the frame of the representation. As Lukács expressed it, the

---

15. Georg Lukács, *The Theory of the Novel* (trans. Anna Bostock; Cambridge, Mass.: MIT Press, 1971). (Original publication: Berlin: P. Cassirer, 1920.)

16. Ibid., 31.

17. Ibid., 88, 97, 103.

18. Ibid., 102–11.

19. See the extensive and insightful analysis of idolatry in Jean-Luc Marion, *God without Being: Hors-Texte* (trans. Thomas A. Carlson; Chicago: University of Chicago Press, 1991).

20. Although either idols or demons (unlike the devil) can be taken as neutral psychological categories, I use both of them insofar as they symbolize a psychological pathology, particularly when the nouns *idolatry* and *demonry* are employed.

answer is inscribed in the idol before the question emerges. The idol (as the story of golden calf in Exodus 32 well describes) is the visible assurance of a presence in the midst of a situation in which deliverance has not yet been fulfilled, and the one who stood for spiritual presence (Moses) is absent. The idol, through its visible presence, is a token of assurance that redemption is at hand. The phenomenon of the idol inherits all idealizations–from liturgical aestheticism to modern metaphysics–for the "essence" of the idol is deception wrapped in certainty; it is precisely to posit something for the sight (this is the meaning of the Greek verb *eidō*, from which we have *idol*), a visible assurance of what cannot be rendered in an image. Technically, this is the "theoretical" attitude as such, for *theōreō* also means "to behold," "to gaze at," "to contemplate," or, indeed, "to speculate."[21] The gazing at the idol's shape mirrors back as a spell.

However, the idol is more than that. It is not only having a glance of the representation and being by it absorbed–or absorbed by its "Being." In the words of Jean Luc Marion, it is freezing in a figure "that which vision aims at in a glance."[22] In other words, idolatry is the failure to realize that what is being gazed at is the very gaze of the one who stares at the image. Ultimately, the images that we idolize are images of the self.[23] The idol is something made up, an artifice, a fetish (from the Portuguese *feitiço* and the Latin *facticius*), which also could take the shape of a grandiose metaphysical system, a scientific demonstration, an ideological incantation, or an amorous infatuation.

One could argue that the whole analysis offered by the work of Feuerbach in his criticism of religion is precisely on target if it is read as a description of idolatry. His *Essence of Christianity* could be more properly named *The Phenomenology of the Idol.* In idolatry, Marx Wartofsky, commenting on Feuerbach, points out, "All the external objects of feeling become . . . self-directed feeling. They are objective aspects under which man adores his own nature. The idolatrous form of this self-realization is boundless individual egoism. . . . Feuerbach's sharpest attack is upon such idolatry."[24] But the end result of this idol production is not a simple projection of the individual self, as in narcissism (although this is also not excluded). For Feuerbach what makes the idol effective and visible while masking the fact that it is a projection is that we humans worship not the qualities of the individual devotee alone but the ideal ensemble of qualities

---

21. This is further elaborated in the chapter following the story of the golden calf in Exodus 33, when Yahweh denies Moses the sight of the divine face.

22. Marion, *God without Being*, 26.

23. See Michael Jinkins, *The Church Faces Death* (Oxford: Oxford University Press, 1999), 41–42.

24. Marx Wartofsky, *Feuerbach* (Cambridge: Cambridge University Press, 1977), 208–9.

of the species. And such qualities can be invested in other collectivities, such as a civilization, a nation, the state, a religion, an institution, a church. The idol emerges when faith sets sharp contours around every image that it adores, excluding all the rest. The idol is about framing![25]

Karl Barth is certainly the theologian in the last century who not only recognized the merit of Feuerbach's devastating criticism but grounded his early theology in this diagnosis: his age, the early twentieth century, was the age of the idol. However, the spirit of idolatry has been long recognized in the history of the Christian church in various ways. It is the form of sin that grows out of the individual and projects itself in the idol. It is the sin symbolically described by the narrative of the Fall in Genesis 3. It is also a recurrent motif in the New Testament references to the defilement that comes from the inside of the self and actually produces evil deeds. "*Hubris,*" "pride," and "sin of strength" have been used to describe this human behavior, the "spirit" that produces idolatry and falls prey to it: the drive to be like God. It endows the finite with attributes of the infinite while masking the mechanism through which this transmutation is accomplished.

The human proneness toward idolatry, even if recognized as not the only source of spiritual derangement, is indeed enough of a reality not to be dismissed. In it power is released for the sake of conquering and dominating others, which goes from personal relations (e.g., abuse) to the fetish-producing mechanisms of the global market. Our Western modernity with its trust in reason and quest for progress has seen and continues to see atrocities and terrors that make the Trojan War only a pale symbol of its condition. This is the spirit of an age that Dostoevsky was able to describe at its dawn with profound insightfulness:

> It is clear that evil is buried more deeply in humanity than the cure-all socialists think, that evil cannot be avoided in any organization of society, that a man's soul will remain the same, that it is from a man's soul alone that abnormality and sin arise, and that, finally, the laws that govern man's spirit are still so unknown, so uncertain and so mysterious that there are not and cannot be any physicians or even judges to give a definitive cure or decision, but that there is only He who says, Vengeance is mine, I will repay.[26]

---

25. Francis Bacon's famous distinction of different forms of idols is still helpful. They are the "idol of the tribe" (pertaining to the human race), the "idol of the cave" (pertaining to the individual), the "idol of the market" (pertaining to one's social group), and the "idol of the theater" (pertaining to schools of thought).

26. Fyodor M. Dostoevsky, *Dnevnik pisatelya* (1880), cited in "Dostoevsky," in *Encyclopedia Britannica* (1964).

Dostoevsky was recognizing in the utopian socialism of his time the human incapability to eradicate idolatry. Worse, even the best-intended efforts–and above all the best-intended efforts of a church–turn into idols when the depth of human sinfulness is forgotten. Dostoevsky died some months after this statement. Hence he did not get to know that idolatry took blunter and bloodier shapes than he ever could have imagined. His merit was to recognize that the idol insinuates itself not only in obviously evil minds but also even in the gentle-hearted efforts to provide for a caring community. Lukács, while acknowledging the utopianism of his youth, was even more aware of the fragility of his hopes, describing them as "those hopes which are a sign of a world to come, still so weak that it can easily be crushed by the sterile power of the merely existent."[27]

Juan Luis Segundo, reflecting on the criticism that Latin American theology's notion of structural sin has forgotten the power of the indwelling spirit of the idol, forgotten that sin is not only outside us, says: "[D]espite our protest of innocence, structural Sin also was 'dwelling' inside of us. Somehow we were part of it; we were its accomplices."[28] This is the recognition of one of the fundamental claims of the Judeo-Christian tradition–in spite of the rightful protest of Job–that somehow we are all responsible. And responsibility is this call to be accountable for the idols our heart creates and our arrested gaze perpetuates.

Idolatry in the church means its captivity to the house model. The idol sets in when something that might be good (*bene esse*) turns into that which is of the essence (*esse*): a liturgical formula that one will not let go of, an office that stands above any reproach, a charismatic leader whose persona is deemed infallible. I mentioned such an idolatrous tendency earlier when discussing novels by Willa Cather and Sinclair Lewis. The Reformers denounced it as the human proclivity to endow human ordinances (*ius humanum*) with divine right (*ius divinum*), turning a human production into the object of one's devotion.

THE DEMON

The manifestation of this "spirit" (*ruah* in Hebrew, *pneuma* in Greek), this breath that comes from inside and condenses itself (as if in a mirror), glazing the figure of the idol, has been greatly studied and analyzed. But it has also been criticized as being only one form of the ailment of the soul and not necessarily the only spirit to corrupt our existence. Since Valerie Saving-Goldstein's work

---

27. Lukács, *Theory of the Novel*, 153.
28. Juan Luis Segundo, *The Humanist Christology of Paul* (trans. John Drury; Maryknoll, N.Y.: Orbis, 1986), 174.

on women's experience,[29] much has been said about what one could call–after Lukács's suggestions about the form of the epic–the "Ulysses complex" of human behavior: the act of conquering and inflicting pain (Odysseus or Ulysses means "giver of pain").[30] What is this Ulysses complex? How can it be understood?

The answers to these questions lie at the opposite end of the spectrum of ailments that affect the community. It is the reverse side of idolatry and must be described as demonic. Different from the idol, the demon makes its appearance by an act of invasion, by possession. Instead of the self-assured positivity of the idol, the demon negates. Its psychology is not of the conqueror, who "sees" and so conquers (indeed: *veni, vidi, vice*); the demonic is the spirit of being homeless, of not belonging, of having been invaded, fragmented, and shaken. As a spiritual reality, the demon comes from the outside. Its realm is not the visible; it pertains rather to the human capability of having self-expression. In the New Testament many of the descriptions of demonic possession are, in fact, related to language. Demoniacs are unable to express themselves in an authentic way. The person possessed is dumb (e.g., Luke 11:14); the demon speaks instead of the person (e.g., Luke 4:31-37); or the person is no longer in control of his body language–the dumb spirit moves the possessed and throws him around (Mark 9:17-18). "Demons," said Roland Barthes, "above all those that are of language (and could there be any other?), need to be fought with language."[31] And this is how one is delivered: by getting back one's authentic language. A demon prevents one from speaking one's word, from naming one's world; demons are "divinities of impediment," as Hindu mythology would call them.

While the idol arrests the gaze that becomes fixed upon one's projected and idealized self, the demon is the anguish of a subject that cannot find its own self. In the words of Jan Patočka, "The demonic is demonic precisely in its ability to deepen . . . self-estrangement. Humans estrange themselves by becoming bound to life and its objects, losing themselves among them."[32] In vain is one's search for the self. In case of demonry there is no self-help. The possessed persons cannot recognize their own possession, while the spirit inside of the persons is indeed able to recognize the true spirit (and avoids it as much as possible). The possessed do not come, but are brought to Jesus. The demoniac needs others, needs a community to be delivered.

---

29. Valerie Saving-Goldstein, "The Human Situation: A Feminine View," *JR* 40 (April 1960): 100–112.

30. See the connection established between Odysseus and modern enlightened conceit in Max Horkheimer and Theodor Adorno, *Dialectic of Enlightenment* (trans. John Cumming; New York: Continuum, 1996), 46–80.

31. Roland Barthes, *Fragmentos de um Discurso Amoroso* (Rio: Francisco Alves, 1986), 71.

32. Jan Patočka, *Heretical Essays in the Philosophy of History* (trans. Erazim Kohák; Chicago: Open Court, 1996), 100–101.

While in the New Testament there are numerous instances of sin originating from within, as we saw in connection to the idol, also present is the opposite image of the enemy that comes as a robber to assail. The theological tradition has dealt with the realization of the demonic while trying to avoid adopting a dualistic framework in its theology. While demons are real, they should not be granted an ontic status, which is an attribute of a self-subsisting entity. This would end up in Manichaeanism, which Schleiermacher well described as one of the "natural" heresies of Christianity. This is the case because Manichean dualism would fundamentally change the basic Judeo-Christian *mythos* that affirms the goodness of all creation (even if not its perfection) and that all is from God (*creatio ex nihilo*).

Different attempts at accounting for the demonic, while remaining within the confines of the Judeo-Christian *mythos*, can be easily recognized. The most influential attempt goes back to Augustine and his etiological interpretation of original sin, which pervades the human character and leaves her helpless–though not changing (ontologically) her innately good nature. Augustine's explanation became the received view in Western Christianity even when it has prompted reactions, revisions, and dissent. Significant variations of this explanation have been offered and have become very influential, ranging from Schleiermacher's radical non-etiological rereading of the Augustinian heritage to Paul Tillich's "structures of destruction"[33] and, finally, reaching its most crisp expression in Latin American liberation theology's notion of structural evil.[34] In either of these variations–the etiological explanation of Augustine or the social causation of evil inaugurated by Schleiermacher–there is an external influence of sin, which renders the individual inept to work out her or his goodness.

The other option for interpreting the demonic casts, as it were, a shadow of malevolence in God. The metaphor of a *shadow* is decisive here, for if the demonic cannot be granted an ontological status of its own, it also cannot be something positive in God. The shadow is the negative image of the positive self, that which though lacking an existence of its own is indeed real. The shadow of God is God's concealed side, the *deus absconditus*. This argument in Judeo-Christian monotheism might be traced back at least to the book of Job. Later, the Kabala's notion of *zimzum*, the self-contraction of God in Godself, is suggested as an explanation for how the infinite allowed space for the finite

---

33. Paul Tillich, *Systematic Theology* (Chicago: University of Chicago Press, 1957), 2:60.

34. In modern theology, since Schleiermacher, we have the etiological interpretation substituted for a structural one. The difference is significant, but the logic of the argument is still the same, i.e., to avoid dualism and to exempt God from evil. See my article "Original Sin Revisited: Schleiermacher's Contribution to the Hefnerian Project," *CTM* 28, nos. 3–4 (June–August 2001): 385–93.

world by absenting itself. The demonic, as the result of this recoiling of God, is the condition of the possibility for finitude to have free room for its being.[35] A logical mode of reasoning akin to this has been also represented in the Christian tradition, for example, by the early Eastern Orthodoxy's notion of *stasis* (in the sense of "uproar," "dissension") in the relations of the Trinity,[36] by Maximus the Confessor's notion of the work of God being accomplished through opposites,[37] and by Martin Luther's theology of the cross. In Luther's terminology, demons do not belong to God and cannot be of divine essence, but are instruments (*Werkzeuge*) in God's own alien work (*opus alienum*). God's shadow is also the shadow of God; the genitive is both subjective and objective.

In contrast to the idol, either of the versions of the demonic reflects a possession of the will and renders one incapable of having a gathered self; it is the spiritual disorder of the one possessed, owned, enslaved. There is something active and aggressive in it. Demonry is not an omission; it is an active impediment, an injury that lames the self. (This is the reason why the popular notion of "sin of omission" is not sufficient to explain demonry.) Søren Kierkegaard raised this point well with the notion of the "sin of weakness" emerging in contrast to the idolatrous "sin of strength."[38] This notion is found in Paul Tillich and decisively in feminist theology.[39] Even as the Lutheran Confessions accounted for the "sin of strength," idolatry, in terms of being without fear of God (*sine metu Dei*), they have already described the spiritual state related to demonry as one of lacking trust in God (*sine fiducia erga Deum*). The recognition of this parallelism in the Confessions' understanding of sin and thus of the ailments of the soul is a point often missed in the traditional interpretations of the doctrine of sin.[40] The difficulty with some of this terminology, however, is that

---

35. Hans Jonas, *Der Gottesbegriff nach Auschwitz* (Frankfurt: Suhrkamp, 1987).

36. The classical text is in Gregory Nazianzen's "Third Theological Oration," in *Nicene and Post-Nicene Fathers*, 2nd ser., vol. 7 (ed. P. Schaff and H. Wace; repr., Peabody, Mass.: Hendrickson, 1995), 301.

37. Yves Congar, *I Believe in the Holy Spirit* (3 vols.; trans. David Smith; New York: Crossroad, 1997), 3:11–18.

38. See Paul Sponheim, "Sin and Evil," in *Christian Dogmatics* (2 vols.; ed. Carl Braaten and Robert Jenson; Philadelphia: Fortress Press, 1984), 1:370–75.

39. Note the critique of Tillich in Judith Plaskow, *Sex, Sin and Grace* (Washington, D.C.: University of America Press, 1980), although she admits that Tillich does recognize this form of sin (103). But her criticism still holds insofar as Tillich has failed to distinguish idolatry from demonry, which results in the ambiguity that Plaskow correctly points out (109). This point is well made by Jerome Stone, "Tillich and Schelling's Later Philosophy," in *Kairos and Logos: Studies in the Roots and Implications of Tillich's Theology* (ed. John J. Carey; Macon: Mercer University Press, 1984), 3–35. See also Eduardo Cruz, "The Demonic for the Twenty-first Century," *CTM* 28, nos. 3–4 (June–August 2001): 420–28.

40. Cf. AC 2. The Latin text further links the lack of trust with the notion of concupiscence, calling it a true sin (the German text mentions only the lack of fear in God–*Gottesfurcht*–and the lack of faith–*Glauben an Gott*). This marks a formidable disagreement

it tends to individualize the phenomenon. The notion of structural sin or the "hamartiosphere," although awkward and abstract, recognizes important collective aspects in the manifestation of the demonic. The spectrum of demonry, as in the case of the idol, is vast. It can go from colonialism and paternalism to personal drug addiction, passing through forms of ideological deception (as opposed to the idolatrous ideological incantation).

If Feuerbach was the one to define the religious profile of idolatry, it is Friedrich Nietzsche, with his criticism of the slave mentality of religion in general and Christianity in particular, who gave us the most elaborate description of the demonic: the privation of a gathered will. Long before the decried vainglory of the *Übermensch*, Nietzsche's "will to power" is an analysis and denouncement of the demonic power that cripples the spirit from the outside and renders it mute inside.[41] We might take as an example Kafka's *The Trial*, a prominent literary illustration of a dramatic description of this condition. Kafka's character shows well the demonic element of the entrapment in which the human, without intending to, finds himself a collaborator in his very alienation and does not find by himself the resources to be free.

The demonic in the church is its captivity to the street model, in which the church loses its proper voice, the voice that marks its difference from the world. In the name of being "relevant," the demon, as the lack of trust in God, adjusts the church to the ways of the world; the demon acculturates. In Miguel de Unamuno's novella discussed earlier, the lack of trust in God took the form of a piety that pronounced and performed only what the people in their deception wanted to hear and see; the demonic is the hypocritical spirit that illustrates what Jean Paul Sartre called "bad faith." The demon in the church mutes criticism, falls for what is trendy; it tells what one wants to hear; it is salt that has lost its flavor, yeast that has no leaven. It does not risk transformation but settles into the given. In his reflections on the church, Philip Hefner makes this point:

> Critical honesty recognizes that though the past is a trail of tears and broken dreams, it is also a vessel of God-given identity and possibility. Critical honesty together with faith recognizes that all facets of the past must be retrieved together, and, above all, that our retrieval of the past is governed by the challenge to act in obedience to the future that God can bring forth out of that past.[42]

---

between Lutherans and Roman Catholics until today: the Roman Catholic Church regards concupiscence not as a sin in itself, but as a disposition toward it. See the "Joint Declaration on the Doctrine of Justification," §§29–30.

41. Cf. Walter Kaufmann, *Nietzsche* (Darmstadt: Wissenschaftliche Buchgesellschaft, 1982), 379–80.

42. Philip Hefner, "The Church as a Community of God's Possibility," *CTM* 25, no. 4 (August 1998): 257.

CRITERIA FOR DISCERNING

These two, then, the idol and the demon, describe fundamental conditions of the spiritual derailment that affects the church-community on either side of the spectrum of its two captivities. One amounts to a self-elevation in an alien projection to which the gaze is drawn and bound, and the other to a defilement of the self that afflicts it from the outside; it is exogenously originated but permeates an entity into its innermost core.

The criteria for discerning these spiritual manifestations are formally framed by the symptoms of the phenomena just described. In the first place, if we are talking about spiritual powers, the discernment of spirits is not something that we can do outside of spiritual presence itself. The idol must be revealed, disclosed for what it is; the demon must be named: a labor of the spirit. We can discern these spirits only by being ourselves in the life of the Spirit. This is what the tradition calls faith, the gift of the Spirit through which witness (criteria for discernment) is given to or with (*symmartyrein*, Rom. 8:16) our spirit. Now, this criterion is still very formal and abstract. Such spiritual presence in the midst of our ambiguous world takes the shape of that community that is called out of everyday life (*ekklēsia*) to then reenter it, making a difference. This is the church, the *temple of the Spirit* in, with, and under which the discernment of spirits happens (*ubi spiritus, ibi ecclesia*). And the shape of this discerning is framed by the essentially constitutive features (*esse*) of the church.

The first of these features is that the church is a gathering of the *people of God* in the power of the Spirit that is addressed by the Word of God, and which in turn responds to this address in prayer, confession, praise, and witness. This fundamental feature of the church is the one that emphasizes God's transcendence, God's invisible manifestation in the Word. The audible character of this ecclesial element, in its double movement *from God* and *to God*, already indicates its critical relation to idolatry, the cult practice of the gaze arrested in the image. It is in this feature of the church that the question of idolatry ought to be discerned. The idol is crushed when the Word reveals the otherness of a God in whom a gaze cannot rest, a God whose otherness is made manifest only by the power of a strange evanescing Word. It is always a characteristic of idolatry when the word conforms to our own prejudices and no longer confronts, awakens. The prophetic tradition has always been and continues to be defined precisely by its fight against idolatry. Where there is fight against idolatry, there is prophecy. This was certainly the great contribution of the theology of the Word in the first part of the twentieth century. It was, even if still one-sided, a revolt against the idols that the great powers of the Western world had erected. *Protest* is the word that best describes this function of the church's struggle against idolatry; and it does so in two of the denotations of the word: it means not just an active objection to a situation, but also an act of professing a faith, a fundamental conviction. Protest is the proper attitude of a community that has been addressed by the word of the Other, by the promise of an other world.

The second fundamental feature is that the church is a communion modeled by the *body of Christ.* In the practice of the church this modeling is represented by the sacramental function of the church, traditionally by baptism as the entrance rite in the communion and then by the renewal of the community's bonds in the sharing of the bread and the cup. Again there is a double movement that characterizes this feature of the church. One movement is that the community gathers as a healing community, calling people out of their quotidian existence. The body of Christ restores the organism, strengthening its weak members by virtue of its bonds of solidarity.

Properly understood, this feature of the church pertains to immanence and not to a transcendent reality magically descending upon us. The community that gathers in this spirit is the body of Christ insofar as this body has become thoroughly flesh (*logos ensarkos*) and still is among us totally in the finitude of embodiment. This is what Luther and the Confessions call the "second mode of Christ's presence." (There is always some idolatry in sacramentalism.) The New Testament notion of *koinōnia* as it is presented in Gal. 2:1-10 stresses this sense of the communion and, in fact, dismisses all but the "remembrance of the poor" as the basic criterion for fellowship.[43] The second, converse movement manifests itself in the community's reentering everyday life, making in it a difference. It is the difference in the one who, having turned away from everyday life, comes back to it restored. This is what *con-version* (*metanoia*) means. This return, in the words of Jan Patočka, comes with the message that "the everyday, its life and its 'peace,' have an end."[44] This has been traditionally called the diaconal function of the church. The body that is healed is a body that heals. But this healing is neither an adjustment nor an adaptation; its trust is utterly eschatological. In this gathering/serving dynamic (*koinōnia/diakonia*), demons are exorcized and people are free to be themselves again. Released from the demonic grip, the community can be there for others, to use Bonhoeffer's apt expression—which he himself practiced. The communal and diaconal practice of solidarity is the church's response to the challenge of demonry, as its emphasis on the otherness of the Word addresses the phenomenon of idolatry.

I believe that the ecclesiology of Juan Luis Segundo, in the first volume of his *Theology for the Artisans of a New Humanity*, more than three decades after

---

43. For an excellent interpretation of this passage, see Barbara Rossing, "Models of *Koinōnia* in the New Testament and Early Church," in *The Church as Communion: Lutheran Contributions to Ecclesiology* (ed. Heinrich Holze; Geneva: LWF, 1997), 65–80.

44. Patočka, *Heretical Essays*, 134.

its publication, needs to be revisited.[45] There he defines the church as the community of "those who know." Although such an affirmation can suggest a lurking Gnosticism, Segundo could not have been more faithful to the gospel. The church is composed of the followers of Jesus who, unlike those represented by the parable of the Great Judgment in Matthew 25 who thought they knew him and thus could recognize him, will not be surprised to know that Christ is to be met among those who in this world are lowly, excluded, and shaken. But this knowledge, as much as it is a promise, is also the acknowledgment of the transience of the church, the consciousness that its end does not belong to itself, as the "end" of Jesus did not belong to those faithful women. What the church knows and understands is embedded in the practice of those women, who buy oil and spices and go to the tomb to anoint a dead and decaying body; it is the belief against all evidence that no gesture of love will ever be lost.

This brings us again to the words of Czech philosopher Jan Patočka, the main author of the Carta 77, which represented the voice of protest against the political regime in Czechoslovakia (which included then the playwright and later elected president of the Czech Republic, Václav Havel), who later died while under police "interrogation." Though not a theologian, Patočka, in his posthumously published *Heretical Essays in the Philosophy of History*, gives expression to an image that could not be more apt to define the church: the community of those who are moved and shaken, but those who also understand. Patočka has called this the "solidarity of the shaken," which is, he continues,

> the solidarity of those who are capable of understanding what life and death are all about. That history is the conflict of *mere life*, barren and chained to fear, with *life at its peak*, life that does not plan for the ordinary days of a future but sees clearly that the everyday, its life and its "peace," have an end. Only one who is able to grasp this, who is capable of conversion, of *metanoia*, is a spiritual person. A spiritual person, however, always understands, and that understanding is no mere observation of facts, it is not "objective knowledge." . . . The solidarity of the shaken is built up in persecution and uncertainty.[46]

In the transit between house and street and in this *cross*-ing of the divide between globalization and exclusion, in this crucible ("in persecution and uncertainty") the church of the crucified God finds and founds itself.

---

45. Juan Luis Segundo, *The Community Called Church* (Maryknoll, N.Y.: Orbis, 1973). The original Spanish publication is from 1968.
46. Patočka, *Heretical Essays*, 134 (emphases in the original).

ECCLESIAL ENDS
ON THE RELATION
OF CHURCH AND SOCIETY

7

Has the Church failed mankind, or has mankind failed the Church?
When the Church is no longer regarded, not even opposed, and men have forgotten
All gods except Usury, Lust and Power.
T. S. Eliot[1]

CHURCH AND SOCIETY

Over the last one hundred years or so, the relationship between social crisis
and religious allegiance has received considerable attention in sociological literature. Max Weber, a name that cannot be bypassed in this discussion, has
a classic text in which the contours of such a relation are closely defined. His
argument is encapsulated in the following quotation:

> [S]trata with high social and economic privilege will scarcely be prone
> to evolve the idea of salvation. Rather, they assign to religion the pri-
> mary function of *legitimizing* their own life pattern and situation in the
> world. . . . Correspondingly different is the situation of the disprivileged.
> Their particular need is for release from suffering.[2]

Weber's analysis of the relationship between religious needs and social structure
is blunt and perceptive, suggesting a direct link between a socioeconomic position and the articulation of religious needs. For him social stratification presents

---

1. T. S. Eliot, "Choruses from the Rock," *The Complete Poems and Plays: 1909–1950* (New
York: Harcourt Brace, 1952), 108–9.
2. Max Weber, *Economy and Society: An Outline of Interpretative Sociology* (Berkeley: University of California Press, 1978), 491–92.

different challenges for religion and the church. Pierre Bourdieu, commenting on Weber's thesis, draws the logical conclusion that

> religious demands tend to organize themselves along two broad types of social situations, namely, the demands of legitimization of the established order for the privileged classes, and the demands of compensation proper to the disadvantaged classes.[3]

I have argued that a direct link between social stratum and the articulation of religious beliefs cannot be ascertained in the strict way that Weber suggests. On the part of the churches, a doctrinal defense of the bourgeois order or of the global economic system in order to fit the interests of its privileged membership is not evident. Neither is there a direct correlation between deliverance from suffering and the theological expression of the faith among the marginalized. In extreme cases we do find apologetic appeals to doctrines in support of a political regime, of which Nazi Germany, South Africa's apartheid, and Pinochet's Chile are but a few examples. We also find the message of liberation being proclaimed among the disenfranchised (as the theological reflections in base Christian communities exemplify), but these are rather exceptions and do not turn church confessions in general into articulated ideological systems in the strict sense of the term. In fact, when explicit ideological elements (as a defense of the worldview of the dominant class) are doctrinally framed, they are most often denounced as false and inconsistent. Establishing this inconsistency was, for example, the strength of the Barmen Declaration (particularly thesis 3).[4]

Pedro A. R. de Oliveira has demonstrated in the case of Brazilian Roman Catholicism that "the content of religious representations is always conditioned by the religious system in which they are born, which imposes structural limits to innovations." A religious system, he continues, has only a relative capability of making "adaptations of the religious representations to the concrete demands of the functioning of the social formation in which they are inserted. They cannot go beyond given structural limits . . . without losing their religious identity."[5]

For two interrelated reasons Christianity does not function as a direct legitimization of capitalism. First, its symbolic structure emerged in a different mode

---

3. Pierre Bourdieu, *A Economia das Trocas Simbólicas* (São Paulo: Perspectiva, 1974), 87.

4. The "anathema" of the thesis reads: "We reject the false doctrine that the church could have permission to abandon the form of its message and order to its pleasure or to changes in current reigning ideological and political convictions." Rolf Ahlers, *The Barmen Theological Declaration of 1934: The Archeology of a Confessional Text* (Lewiston, N.Y.: Edwin Mellen, 1986), 41.

5. Pedro A. Ribeiro de Oliveira, *Religião e Dominação de Classe* (Petropolis: Vozes, 1985), 325.

of production. Second, capitalism does not require such legitimizing. "The religious representations can be useful for the capitalist mode of production . . . but they are not necessary to its functioning, they do not legitimate either economic or political power."[6] This is not to deny the recognition of a "relative autonomy"[7] of the religious sphere. However, this relative autonomy, while not reducing the role of religion to a legitimizing function, provides for an indirect legitimacy. This indirect legitimizing happens when religion offers a meaningful symbolic superstructure that harmonizes the structural conflicts of society like a coat of varnish over a rough surface.

What unites Christians is stronger than what divides them; this is one of the presuppositions with which the ecumenical movement works. Reflecting about this, Juan Luis Segundo offered a very enlightening suggestion that allows for the connection between the present, articulated and globalized economic system, on the one hand, and the evolution of the ecumenical movement, on the other. This connection presents the reverse side of the Reformation that split the Western church in the initial phase of the capitalist system ("financial capitalism"), when plurality was required to overcome the objective moral and doctrinal unity of the Middle Ages. Using a concept of ideology that defines a veil that covers up contradictions, Segundo writes:

> The so much championed "unity of the Christians," with its pastoral consequences, constitutes a clear ideological element. The ideal of the unity for liberation turned into the ideal of the unity to cover up conflicts, to minimize them in face of something more important and thus to serve, in an indirect way, to maintain the status quo . . . the ideology that places the [ideological] superstructure at the service of the existing order is, in most cases, not a conscious maneuver: it is an unconscious sliding of ideas through furrows that will prevent them from clashing with that order.[8]

The real doctrinal conflict, as far as economic and social injustice is concerned, is not among confessional systems, creeds, or religious organizations; the latter might at most be a cipher that indicates different socioeconomic interests. Antonio Gramsci's remarks on the ludicrousness of looking at either the European East or the West for clarity on the procession of the Holy Spirit is a pointer to

---

6. Ibid., 319.

7. Otto Maduro, *Religião e Luta de Classe* (Petropolis: Vozes, 1981), 113–49.

8. Juan Luis Segundo, "As Elites Latino-Americanas," in *Fé Cristã e Transformação Social na América Latina* (ed. Instituto Fe y Secularidad; Petropolis: Vozes, 1977), 186.

this.[9] Banners do not explain the conflicts, though they might symbolize them or serve as emblems. To take the symbols for the reality to which they point is religious idolatry; to explain the reality in which they emerge sans societal context is philosophical idealism. Symbols or emblems enlighten participation in reality and acquire their meanings out of this participation, and these meanings can be varied.

Studies of the symbols of "popular religiosity" in Latin America, for example, have shown their ambivalence. They can function within a religious system to enhance the meaning of the symbolic structure without their particular contextualization. The rereading of these symbols from a contextual standpoint allows their meanings to be unfolded in metaphors, which produce semantic dissonance. Such unfolding of symbols is a very common experience in the rereading of the Bible or in popular religious traditions. Biblical or popular images that have become symbolic ensigns of common religious representations give rise to an array of metaphors that allow language to transcend the common limits imposed on it and thus to name a world that is being rediscovered. The metaphorical clash of categories disturbs the system of representations by introducing into it meanings of practical and particular experiences. The social conflicts, by the very presuppositions of their dynamics, will be regarded as anomic; to name them is to allow particularity to shake harmony.

Social conflicts and the content of unjust relations in a socioeconomic system will only appear in the doctrinal tension between the universal and the particular, between the religious symbolic system (with its creeds, dogmas, and confessions) and the contextual insurgence of images particular to it. These particular images, working as metaphors, are endowed with a new and unexpected contextual meaning, which can sustain many different ideological intentions. These particular images are the result of the transformation of the symbols into metaphors; that is, they are applied to describe a new reality. For example, the biblical Exodus was claimed in defense of the United States' takeover of Mexican territory, in the South African Boer appropriation of native territory, and in Latin America as the symbol of deliverance from socioeconomic oppression. However, the symbolic function of the Exodus in the Jewish-Christian tradition is relatively free from these metaphorical employments. Such examples are legion.[10]

---

9. Antonio Gramsci, *Selections from the Prison Notebooks* (New York: International Publishers, 1971), 409.

10. Ulrich Schoenborn, *Migalhas Exegéticas* (Sao Leopoldo: Sinodal, 1982), 126–30. For an example of how this happens, see Virgilio Elizondo, "La Virgen de Guadalupe como Símbolo Cultural," in *Raíces de la teología latinoamericana* (ed. Pablo Richard; San Jose: Cehila/Dei, 1985), 393–400.

A discussion about social class, however, differs from one about social crisis. A society divided by class, ethnicity, religion, cast, race, and so forth, might be a stable society masking the church's insertion in it and therefore blurring the distinction between being *in* the world and being *of* (in the sense of belonging to) the world, to use Jesus' prayer for the disciples in John 17 (cf. vv. 11 and 14). A crisis is present when a social divide becomes itself the arena, the *agon* on which major social issues are at stake. It is the social moment of severance, judgment, and bewilderment. In such a situation what is *critical* is not society as such with all the divisions it might entail, but the social institutions that become disembedded, ripped from their locales, their "natural" environment.[11] One could therefore define a crisis as a situation in which divisive issues lose their "naturalness," their innocence. This naturalness and rootedness happens by virtue of the conflation of the two fundamental processes by which institutions are engendered and takes place by the encroachment of politics into the economic sphere and vice versa. What results from this double encroachment is a hybrid phenomenon. Landless peasants living in tents on the sides of roads and highways in Brazil and homeless people living in the parks or empty lots of Chicago are examples of such hybridity, or of how the "house" hits the "road." A twin case, revealing the other side of the same phenomenon, is not poverty and destitution but overabundance, such as we find in shopping malls, galleries, or arcades.

Walter Benjamin, in a massive work that was left unfinished at the time of his death in 1940, used the Parisian arcades or passageways as an allegory of late modern societies. He offers the following comment: "Already the inscriptions and signs on the entranceways (one could just as well say 'exits,' since with these particular hybrid forms of house and street, every gate is simultaneously entrance and exit) . . . have about them something enigmatic."[12] And he continues later, "More than anywhere else, the street reveals itself in the arcade as the furnished and familiar interior of the masses."[13] These images of the arcade are dissimulations of social crises. Homeless people manifest the same phenomenon, only in its reverse, as in a mirror. If on one side of the image people are there to see (and to buy), but not to be seen, on the other side the displaced people are there exposed to the gaze (without exchange value), but are equally not seen. On one side products are at disposal; on the other the disposed are without products.

---

11. Anthony Giddens, *Modernity and Self-Identity: Self and Society in Late Modern Age* (Stanford: Stanford University Press, 1991), 17–20.

12. Walter Benjamin, *The Arcades Project* (trans. Howard Eiland and Kevin McLaughlin; Cambridge, Mass.: Harvard University Press, 1999), 871.

13. Ibid., 879.

What needs to be examined is the relation of the church to this phenomenon. I have already mentioned that the church is also defined as a "third space," placing it in the very midst of the hybrid social configurations that reveal and conceal the crises of society. How can the church be faithful to its calling of proclaiming the good news and celebrating the newness of life when it finds itself not only enmeshed *in* this world but also partaking in the same process that creates the crises in society? And crisis means judgment, the judgment of the world.

CRISES IN THE CHURCH AND SOCIETY

A crisis in a sharply divided society, be it by class or otherwise, might imply a corresponding crisis in ecclesial formations as they are manifested in sects, in messianic movements, and in few cases in church-type organizations.[14] But normally mainstream churches reveal a surprising capability of "inclusivity," a tolerance, a serenity in absorbing and stabilizing social conflict within their own ranks, creating a rather complex interaction between church and society in which there is no mirroring effect.[15]

The reverse also seems to be true. Divisions among churches and the schisms within them most often cannot be directly correlated to those of society. Antonio Gramsci, in his studies on the philosophy of praxis, gives us this insightful observation:

> In the discussion between Rome and Byzantium on the Procession of the Holy Spirit, it would be ridiculous to look in the structure of the European East for the claim that it proceeds only from the Father, and in that of the West for the claim that it proceeds from the Father and the Son.[16]

Gramsci suggests that the problem in finding the relationship between social crises and the crises of the church can be interpreted as a problem of translation between two sets of languages, the social-historical inquiry and the theological discourse. It is not that they are unrelated but that they do not stand in direct correlation to each other. How should we then speak about the relationship between social crisis and the church, provided that we take for granted that

---

14. For example, the Confessing Movement in Germany during Nazism, the schism in the Evangelical Lutheran Church in Chile, some churches in South Africa during apartheid, etc. This phenomenon was also observed by Ernst Troeltsch.

15. Ernst Troeltsch, *The Social Teaching of the Christian Churches* (2 vols.; Chicago: University of Chicago Press, 1981), 2:997–98.

16. Gramsci, *Prison Notebooks*, 408–9.

the church is part of society and is therefore implicated in its social fabric and dynamics? Which language should we use? Do we go to the social sciences with the hope that they will provide us with the categories that can be applied to the examination both of social systems and of ecclesial formations (in the tradition of Troeltsch and H. Richard Niebuhr)? What do we gain and what is lost in such an approach?

This problem has received a provocative treatment by John Milbank in his book *Theology and Social Theory.*[17] Milbank argues that the problem we are dealing with emerged in the modern West when theology exited the *saeculum* and confined its own language to a religious sphere no longer competent to unfold from its "irenic" ontology—an "ontology of peace"—a social theory of its own to counter and conquer the dominant "ontology of violence" supposed by "secular" social theorists and incongruent with what he regards to be the irenic principle of the Christian faith. In this exit lies modern western theology's problem, its "false humility," the surrendering of its intellectual responsibility, qua theology, toward the social. With acute attention to avoid the demonic captivity, he flirts with idolatry.

Gramsci, however, goes in another direction and hints at a solution for bridging the translation gap, focusing on the historical experience of conflict and cohesion in the context of the experiences of the Eastern and the Western church:

> The two Churches, whose existence and whose conflict is dependent on the structure and the whole of history, posed questions which are principles of distinction and internal cohesion for each side . . . and it is this problem of distinction and conflict that constitutes the historical problem.[18]

He argues that while theological language functions as a tool for building this internal cohesion and distinctiveness within historical realities of conflict that reach to the heart of the social crises, these can be better articulated and analyzed by "secular" theory than by the theological banners that signalize them.

THE THEOLOGICAL LOSS OF THE *SAECULUM*

Between the irenic theology of the belligerent Milbank and the militant social theory of the gentle-hearted Gramsci, the divide for understanding the

17. John Milbank, *Theology and Social Theory: Beyond Secular Reason* (Oxford: Blackwell, 1990).

18. Gramsci, *Prison Notebooks*, 409.

relationship between social crises and the church looms large. Where to now? *Tertium non datur?* Is there not a third option? I do not think so. Milbank's proposal is forceful in the programmatic suggestion that theology should regain its capability of tackling social theory from within its own domain, instead of hiding itself in a false humility by appealing to the wisdom of social theory. Nevertheless, it was not the capability of extending the "ontology of peace" into the social domain that was lost but rather the ability to think in precise theological terms about the nature of social conflict and social crisis, that is, the ability to articulate theologically the significance or implication of the difference between the two proposals as it manifests itself in social existence.

This loss, I argue, started to take shape at a moment in the early Constantinian church when a crisis in society became a fundamental crisis for the church. The year was 410 when Alaric sacked Rome, and Augustine set himself to write *The City of God* as an explicit response to the crisis that affected the church, which was being held responsible for Rome's calamity because it had displaced the old pagan deities. Augustine's celebrated solution in the differentiation of the two cities introduces a distinction qualified by two sets of categories that will function as catalysts for the way the West thinks of itself. The worldly city is described as the space of aimless wanderings, of going in circles, while the heavenly city is connected with the image of a pilgrimage, a progression (*procursus*) toward the divine end.[19] The distinction leads to a growing separation between *topos* and *chronos*, between space and time, in which space imagery dominates the *saeculum*, while time and history have been endowed with a set of qualities that if not explicitly theological are implicitly so.[20]

What is the loss I suggest we are experiencing, which has impoverished our theological imagination and language and disabled them to address social crises *theologically*? As Milbank correctly argues, the distinction introduced by Augustine is in itself not responsible for the creation of the *saeculum* as a realm beyond the reach of the theological discourse. Augustine thinks of both cities theologically, yet only one is related to God's end, only one ends in blessedness; the other is condemned. Only in one can we reach the divine presence (*parousia*). In one, crisis (*krisis* in its etymological sense) marks the possibility of novelty and of presence through repentance and renewal; in the other it is just an expression of decay and annihilation (Augustine, we are reminded, equates

---

19. Karl Löwith, *Meaning in History: The Theological Implications of the Philosophy of History* (Chicago: University of Chicago Press, 1949), 169.

20. On this separation and for further literature on the subject, see also my article "Re(li)gion: The Lord of History and the Illusory Space," in *Region and Religion: Land Territory and Nation from a Theological Perspective* (ed. Viggo Mortensen; Geneva: LWF/DTS, 1994), 79–95.

evil and nonbeing, as a *privatio boni*). *Pax mundi non speranda*: there is no hope in worldly peace. Karl Löwith summarizes this point with precision:

> To a man like Augustine all our talk about progress, crisis, and world order would have seemed insignificant; for, from the Christian point of view, there is only one progress: the advance toward an ever sharper distinction between faith and unbelief, Christ and Antichrist; there are only two crises of real significance: Eden and Calvary; and there is only one world order: the divine dispensation, whereas the history of empires "runs riot in an endless variety of sottish pleasures."[21]

Augustine's move, while avoiding a "detheologization" of the *saeculum*, produced instead a "de-eschatologizing" of the secular space that continued through the ages and reached its culmination in modern times. Secular space and the images that it evokes were confined to the earthly city, whose *telos* lies outside of itself; in itself it is aimless, endless in the very sense that its end (if there is one for Augustine)[22] can only be brought about from outside. Anthony Giddens has called attention to this process that he calls "separation of time and space" as a peculiar characteristic of modern social life that emptied out time and space by pulling "space away from place."[23] If this is definitely a characteristic of modernity, the descent of this severance can be traced as far back as Augustine's *City of God*, in which time kept an eschatological frame but secular space was devoid of any eschatological significance, disqualified as a realm of presence, and homogenized.

This separation of eschatological time as *Heilsgeschichte*, or salvation history, and secular space receives theological significance when we realize that in talking about crisis we move into a linguistic register in which questions of the divine manifestation or presence (*parousia*) or questions about the end, about

---

21. Löwith, *Meaning in History*, 172.

22. The only argument Augustine provides for dismissing the theory of eternal cyclic recurrence is a supernatural one and admittedly not supported by his otherwise careful rational argumentation and rebuttal. See Löwith, *Meaning in History*, 165.

23. Giddens, *Modernity and Self-Identity*, 16. An example to illustrate this process is the development of mechanical clocks, which allowed for a time reckoning that could be totally isolated from a locale, apart even from the solar movement it attempted to imitate. In the recent development of digital clocks, even the analogical connection to the heliotrope disappears. Simultaneously we have also the development of cartography that follows a parallel path in which space is universalized in map projections that no longer give privilege to any location, as used to be the case with the previous use of itineraries. Geographies have become homogeneous media of quantifiable extensions; they do not entail ends or qualitative locations. Henri Lefebvre, *The Production of Space* (trans. D. N. Smith; Oxford: Blackwell, 1991), argues that a qualification of space is now emerging in late modern societies. See particularly pp. 410–18.

the *eschaton*, are not entertained. It is rather difficult for us to understand how profoundly these three concepts—*krisis, parousia*, and *eschata*—are intertwined in biblical literature[24] and in early Patristic thought.[25] This is the loss implied by Augustine's separation of eschatological time and secular space. The limit of our language might not be exactly the limit of our world, for in this world there is silence and the experience of the ineffable, but it indeed indicates our incapability of thinking its other, that which lies beyond its limit.

THE ENDS OF THE WORLD

The *eschata*, as the concept is used in the New Testament, is conceived as a "pocket-experience,"[26] an event that is situated and refers to a concrete and localizable situation. It can connote the last in a temporal succession, as well as the last in rank, the ultimate in place, the outer limit, the borderline, or the lowest. As such—and this is the point of its theological significance—it becomes the turning point, a place of conversion, *metanoia* (a transmutation of the mind to beyond its own confines). The *eschatoi* (those who inhabit the end) become *protoi* (those to whom a new beginning is granted), and the other way around. *Eschata* signals the points of qualitative change, the point at which grace and judgment meet each other, the critical point of simultaneous presence (*parousia*) and absence (*apousia*), a limit-to and a limit-of.[27] Crises in society, if they are to be theologically analyzed, ought then to be eschatologized; they ought to be analyzed as events of divine absence and presence, as expressions of an agonic experience of reaching the end or an end in the midst of the *saeculum*.

But are they recognizable if they are by definition the closure of a reality, the margin of our experience and of our world? Can we avoid committing them to sheer silence since they represent the impossible, the limit beyond which there is only nonsense, the mystical, as the early Wittgenstein has argued?[28] Can we be housed in or cross the limit itself and endure its annihilating power

---

24. See Jacob Tesfai, "This Is My Resting Place: An Inquiry into the Role of Time and Space in the Old Testament" (Ph.D. diss., Lutheran School of Theology at Chicago, 1975); W. D. Davies, *The Gospel and the Land* (Berkeley: University of California Press, 1974); Katherine Elena Wolff, *Geh in das Land, das ich dir zeigen werde: Das Land Israel in der frühen rabbinischen Tradition und im Neuen Testament* (Frankfurt: Peter Lang, 1989).

25. I am thinking here particularly of Irenaeus of Lyon with the profusion of spatial imagery he employed, which would not leave us far from accuracy to speak about a geography of grace as well as a geography of apostasy. See his language in *Against Heresies* 5.1.1.

26. The expression is borrowed from Tesfai, "This Is My Resting Place."

27. See David Tracy, *Blessed Rage for Order: The New Pluralism in Theology* (New York: Seabury, 1975), 92–94.

28. Ludwig Wittgenstein, *Tractatus logico-philosophicus: Logisch-philosophische Abhandlung* (Frankfurt: Suhrkamp, 1978), 7, 115.

and experience the utter awe of a novelty made present there? Or can we avoid hiding the margins for the power they have to reveal the fragility of the system, as Mary Douglas reminds us?[29]

Theology has to do with revelation. Revelation is the disclosure of a reality beyond that which is familiar; it breaks with the quotidian. It is that which breaks through the margins; it is difference irrupting into identity, otherness into sameness. However, two conditions need to be met for any talk about revelation to proceed. First, we need to ask whether there is an adequate method of exploring the margins; second, we need a language to express it in which crises are not reduced to intra-systemic anomalies, as is so often the case when the term loses its theological association with the *eschata* and also with *parousia*.

Insofar as methodology is concerned, I can only point to directions we could follow, leading us to the name of the most eschatological of all modern thinkers, Michel Foucault.[30] Genealogy is what Foucault, after Nietzsche, calls this method. While he uses the notion of "genealogy," it might not be the most appropriate term to express the method. As Foucault defines it, it is not an attempt to go to the origins in order to "capture the exact essence of things," but a concerted effort to find in a historical beginning "the dissension of other things, . . . disparity. . . . The origin lies in a place of inevitable loss . . . [it is] the site of a fleeting articulation that discourse has obscured and finally lost . . . because knowledge was not made for understanding; it is made for cutting."[31] And in the cutting is the crisis left as a margin not to be seen, not to be explored, for there the gates of error are opened, while the truth the *saeculum* relies upon is the history of an error "that cannot be refuted because it was hardened into an unalterable form in the long baking process of history."[32] It is an attempt of raising the other, suppressed, question that was left behind as the untruth, the irrelevant, the deviant, the excluded, that which subsists in the "underside of history," to use Gustavo Gutiérrez's felicitous expression. This is what I have been engaged in in the very attempt to bring to the surface the now almost unthinkable social and spatial connotations of eschatology. Foucault is asking for the question of liminality, which we have defined as the eschatological question par excellence. The genealogical method when assessed theologically is in fact

---

29. "[A]ll margins are dangerous. If they are pulled this way or that the shape of fundamental experience is altered. Any structure of ideas is vulnerable at its margins." Mary Douglas, *Purity and Danger: An Analysis of Concepts of Pollution and Taboo* (New York: Routledge, 2002), 149.

30. For a further elaboration of this method, I refer the reader to my article "Scientific Facts and Embodied Knowledges: Social Circumstances in Science and Theology," *Modern Theology* 11, no. 3 (July 1995): 341–61.

31. Michel Foucault, *The Foucault Reader* (ed. Paul Rabinow; New York: Pantheon, 1984), 78–79, 88.

32. Ibid., 79.

an eschatological method. It is a way of going about establishing the crises, the points of rupture, discontinuities, and differences–beyond which we most often don't venture to gaze–and then understanding these limits as markers of divine presence/absence, local manifestations of a revelation hidden in its opposite (*abscondita sub contraria specie*).

The method is not only pertinent to noetic questions, questions that pertain to the conditions of the possibility of acquiring knowledge. It can be applied to other forms of exclusion and marginalization, be they psychological (the exclusion of the "mentally ill" from the canons of rationality), economic (the exclusion of masses from the new global economic market), ethnic, biological, cultural, and so on.

Can we think of the poor, migrants, people of color, women, the terminally ill, the insane, the delinquents as those indwelling an *eschaton*? Can we make their crises our own to the point of inhabiting their own marginality? Are we able to make sense of their questions when they seem so strange and outside of the realm of the acceptable, that which evades reasonableness as it is canonically defined by our secular theoreticians? Or are we ourselves at an *eschaton*? And if we are there, do we recognize it, or are we in denial for the sake of being acceptable and adjusted to the *saeculum*? But, further and most importantly, theologically, can we see in the process of exclusion also that which makes the *eschatoi* the *protoi*, in which we experience presence in absence, in which the difference is itself the point? Do we have a church language that can even entertain these questions?

IN CRISIS, THERE THE CHURCH IS

This brings me to the beginning of the quest, and to the second qualification mentioned earlier–the need for an adequate language. What kind of language are we to use in describing this eschatalogical limit? Where is this vocabulary housed? Cornelius Castoriadis suggests a clue in his elegant definition of religion:

> Religion offers a name for the unnamable, a representation of that which cannot be represented, a place to that which cannot be located. Realizes and satisfies, at the same time, the experience of abyss and the refusal to accept it, circumscribing it–pretending to circumscribe it–giving to it one or many figures, designating the places where it dwells, the moments to which it gives privilege, the persons that embody it, the words and texts that reveal it. Religion is, *par excellence*, the presentation/concealment of Chaos. It constitutes itself a compromise solution that prepares, at the same time, the impossibility for the humans to lock themselves in the

here-and-now of their "real existence," and the almost equal impossibility
of accepting the experience of abyss.[33]

Castoriadis's general definition is defective only in that he does not realize how
much he is really indebted to a Judeo-Christian eschatological vision while
trying to provide a universal definition of religion.[34] It is within this vision that
an ecclesiology can be meaningfully formulated as a space inserted in between
severed spaces, in the location of the breach, the crisis. In other words, the
church, as the space of grace, as the conduit of the Spirit that is at the *eschata*, the
places of risk, of condemnation, but so also the place of healing and salvation, is
a community of those who in the margin barely hanging on to life are sustained
as a body by their faith and by one another, and are there in the midst of the
unutterable turmoil able to name and be named by their relationship to God
and to one another. Could this communion be expressed in the image of the
body of the one who was lacerated in the eschatological moment of Calvary,
and whose resurrected corpus retains the scars as a testimony of that *eschaton*?
Could not this be the true meaning of the *extra ecclesia nulla salus*, that there is
no salvation outside the church, the place in which liberation and healing (salvation) are a practice through proclamation (as denunciation and annunciation)
and the celebration of communion, to paraphrase Augsburg Confession 7?

In her essay "Models of *Koinōnia* in the New Testament and Early Church,"[35]
Barbara Rossing calls attention to the diversity of models of *koinōnia* in the
New Testament and finds its power in "its capacity to bridge spheres of life
we often view as quite separate." Although her own reading does not make
explicit the eschatological implications of communion, her conclusion that,
within all the diversity that the concept of *koinōnia* makes allowance for, it is
the remembrance of the poor (Gal. 2:10) that remains as the ultimate criterion
is a definite pointer. This remembrance of the poor suggests the remembrance
of margins, which therefore calls for an eschatological reading. In this reading
the bridges she refers to are to be understood as attempts of crossing the *eschata*;
this crossing itself being the unifying condition within all theological diversity
that in the Pauline text is acknowledged. If this solidarity with the poor establishes the ecclesiological basis of a communion, it is precisely because of the
place of the poor, the marginal space they inhabit or, to put it more succinctly,

---

33. Cornelius Castoriadis, *Os Destinos do Totalitarismo e Outros Escritos* (Porto Alegre: MPM,
1985), 113.

34. Although he does not trace his own sources, Castoriadis inserts himself in a tradition
for defining religion in eschatological terms that can be traced back to Bloch, Hölderlin,
and Luther.

35. Barbara Rossing, "Models of *Koinōnia* in the New Testament and Early Church," in
The Church as Communion: Lutheran Contributions to Ecclesiology (ed. Heinrich Holze; Geneva:
LWF/DTS, 1997), 65–80.

the eschatological place they are in. It is there one meets one's end, there one meets one's beginning. In the crises of society, there the church is. In this we follow Bonhoeffer's insight. He did not say where the church *should* be, but that it is there where it *already* is: "Revelation becomes the accident of a substance already there."[36]

Czech philosopher Jan Patočka gives language to the experience of communion as that which happens at the very point of the crossing. He starts with a long meditation on a text of Teilhard de Chardin in which he reflects on the war experience of being on the front. He quotes Teilhard:

> The front is not simply a flaming line where the accumulated energies of hostile masses are released and mutually neutralized. It is also the locus of a distinct Life . . . that bears the world of humans toward its new destiny. . . . [T]here one finds oneself at the extreme limit of what has happened and what is to be done.[37]

Being on the front is described as an eschatological experience that at the same time reveals the dreariness of the crisis and the reality of community and a future. Patočka adds that in the front "[t]here is not only struggle but also solidarity, there is not only society, but also community, and community has other bonds besides a common enemy."[38] And he describes these bonds that hold the community in the powerful language of "the solidarity of the shaken."[39]

A COPERNICAN REVOLUTION

The perspective of seeing the church's location as being on the divide, in the "front-line experience" of Teilhard and Patočka, precisely emerging and making itself manifest in the moments of crisis, in the eschatological momentum and locus, calls us to rethink the marks of the church as to its location in time and space, and function within them. The church dares to celebrate that which it does not possess, to "represent" that which it does not own, and to proclaim a word that is not of this world.

It is *revolutionary* in the sense in which the word was employed originally by Copernicus's famous work on the revolution of the planets that changed our

---

36. Dietrich Bonhoeffer, *Christ the Center* (trans. Edwin H. Robertson; San Francisco: Harper, 1978), 56.

37. Jan Patočka, *Heretical Essays in the Philosophy of History* (trans. Erazim Kohák; Chicago: Open Court, 1996), 125.

38. Ibid., 149.

39. Ibid., 134. For the complete quotation see the penultimate paragraph of chap. 6, p. 105.

view from a geocentric to a heliocentric planetary system.[40] The church has its gravitational center outside its own ways of representing itself in the two senses of representation we have examined. Dietrich Bonhoeffer is here of help again. In his lectures on Christology, translated in English as *Christ the Center*, he offers an explanation of what the "center" means when talking about Christ and his existing as church-community:

> That Christ is the centre of our existence does not mean that he is central in our personality, our thinking and our feeling. Christ is also the centre when he stands, in terms of our consciousness, on our periphery, also when Christian piety is displaced to the periphery of our being. The statement made about his centrality . . . has the character of an ontological and theological statement. It does not refer to our personality, but to our being a person before God. The centre of the person cannot be demonstrated.[41]

To paraphrase, the center of Christ existing as church-community, the identity of the church, cannot be represented either by the product of its labor or by the modes of interaction of its members. This is a revolutionary move (analogous to Copernicus's) that changes the gravitational basis for the existence of the church: the margins become the center, the periphery the axis of the church's own being.

From its original astronomic usage, the word *revolution* has been synonymous with radical social change, and so it became also a trope to describe fundamental changes and even reversals in the way we understand a given subject matter, from science[42] to religion.[43]

The term in this epistemological sense, suggesting a radical change in the orientation of one's thinking, which in biblical terms is called a *metanoia*, a conversion, was initially used by none other than Walter Benjamin. For him a Copernican-like revolution happens when we understand the present as an awakening. He writes:

> The Copernican revolution in historical perception is as follows. Formerly it was thought that a fixed point had been found in "what has

---

40. The groundbreaking work of Copernicus was entitled *De revolutionibus orbium coelestium* (On the Revolution of Heavenly Spheres). It was published in 1543 in Nurenberg under the editorial responsibility of the famed Lutheran theologian Andreas Osiander, who wrote an anonymous preface for the controversial book, calling it a "hypothesis."

41. Bonhoeffer, *Christ the Center*, 60f.

42. Thomas Kuhn, *The Structure of Scientific Revolutions* (Chicago: University of Chicago Press, 1962), 111.

43. John Hicks, *God Has Many Names* (Philadelphia: Westminster, 1980), 35–39, 69–70.

happened," and one saw the present engaged in tentatively concentrat-
ing the forces of knowledge on this ground. Now the relation has to be
overturned, and what has been is to become the dialectical reversion—the
flash of awakened consciousness.[44]

Instead of falling into the slumbering dreams of a future that evades the present
and neglects the past, Benjamin moves in the same direction as his contemporary compatriot and companion in the struggle against fascism, Bonhoeffer.
It is now and here, awakening from the dream called past, that we bring it to
bear upon our present.

> The new, dialectical method of doing history presents itself as the art of
> experiencing the present as waking world, a world to which the dream we
> name the past refers in truth. To pass through and carry out *what has been*
> in remembering the dream!—Therefore: remembering and awakening are
> most intimately related. Awakening is namely the dialectical, Copernican
> turn of remembrance.[45]

Benjamin's Copernican turn of awakening and remembrance allows us to com-
prehend the church as the community in the present that does what it does "in
remembrance of." This remembrance, this *anamnesis* (1 Cor. 11:24-25), signals a
community that lives awake in the present. This community celebrates the past
not as a forgone "what-has-been" but as that which is awakened in the prayers
that bring to remembrance the "cloud of witness" that surrounds it (Heb. 12:1).
It is stirred by the words of old proclaimed anew, and celebrates the presence
in communion by the work of the Spirit. Remembering and awakening correspond precisely to the two fundamental components of the Eucharistic celebration, the *anamnetic* act of doing it in remembrance as the words of institution
prescribe, and the *epicletic* prayer for the presence of the Holy Spirit, which
opens up a new and hopeful future. Rubem Alves in describing the task of a
historian finds precisely this sacramental connection between the past remembered, the present awakened, and the future that is promised. Thus he writes:

> The historian is someone who recovers forgotten memories and dissemi-
> nates them as a sacrament to those who have lost the memory. Indeed,
> what finer community sacrament is there than the memories of a com-
> mon past, punctuated by existence of pain, of sacrifice and of hope?

---

44. Benjamin, *Arcades Project*, 388.
45. Ibid., 389. "Remembrance" in this and other texts of the author translates Benjamin's
technical term *Eingedenken*, which has been variously translated as "remembrance," "empa-
thetic memory," or "being mindful of."

To recover in order to disseminate. The historian is not an archaeologist
of memories. He is a sower of visions and hopes.[46]

When Segundo called the church the community of those "who already
know,"[47] he was expressing in other words the same notion of awakening to
which Benjamin refers. It is not a community that *ought* to become, but a community that is already present in the midst of our world where the crises of
society make themselves manifest. Segundo illustrates this with the parable of
the Great Judgment in Matthew 25 (vv. 31-46). The point of the parable for
him is not a moral one but the surprise that both groups, the righteous and
the unrighteous, experience. The righteous did not know that in feeding the
hungry, giving water to the thirsty, welcoming the stranger, clothing the naked,
and visiting the sick and imprisoned, they were doing it for Christ. There was
the church even as they did not know it. However, even more decisive is the
surprise of the unrighteous when they asked, "Lord, when was it that we saw
you hungry or thirsty or a stranger or naked or sick or in prison, and did not
take care of you?" (v. 44). The rhetorical question implies that they thought
they knew the Lord and would take care of him if they encountered him. Yet
they missed the very presence of Jesus there where the least ones are to be
found. But we do not have the excuse of not knowing this anymore; we know
it already. The church is apostolic when it is reminded of the presence of Jesus
and awakened through the Spirit by the witness of those who testified to the
life, passion, death, and resurrection of Jesus the Christ, and where he now is
as the community in its eschatological experience of being on the front, where
there is no *safety*, but the bursting out of *salvation*.

---

46. Rubem Alves, "Las ideas teológicas y sus caminos por los surcos institutucionales
del Protestantismo brasilerio," in *Materiales para una historia de la teologia en América Latina*
(ed. Pablo Richard; San José, Costa Rica: DEI, 1981), 363ff. Cited in José Míguez Bonino,
Faces of Protestantism in Latin America: 1993 Carnahan Lectures (Grand Rapids: Eerdmans,
1997), 107.

47. Juan Luis Segundo, *The Community Called Church* (Maryknoll, N.Y.: Orbis,
1973), 111.

AT EASE

ECCLESIAL ADJACENCIES

8

I was talking about time. It's so hard for me to believe in it. Some things go. Pass on. Some things just stay. I used to think it was my memory. You know. . . . But it is not. Places, places are still there . . . and not just in my memory, but out there in the world. What I remember is a picture floating around out there outside my head. I mean, even if I don't think it, even if I die, the picture of what I did, or knew, or saw is still out there. Right in the place where it happened.

Toni Morrison[1]

THE CHURCH AND THE KINGDOM

The two typical entrapments or captivities of the church discussed earlier–the idols of the house and the demons of the street–point to two distinct ways in which the church finds its relationship to society. On one side, it is related to the realm of the household, of the production and reproduction of life where each individual has an irreducible identity defined by his or her output in the household. On the other, the church is also related to the realm of the street, of interpersonal encounters in a collective context where individuality is predicated on relational exchanges; one is defined by one's perceived public persona. The relationship between church and society will be defined by how the church-community steers its course between the household or the economic realm and the street or the political realm.

These two realities taken as a whole configure what we call society. In the New Testament the concept is often rendered as *kosmos*, the world. As vague and ominous as the concept of society is, its resulting establishment is a combination and conflation of the two processes in which human activity unfolds. In its midst is the church enmeshed in these very social processes; unable to dissociate itself, it is still *in* society and yet prays that it be not *of* it (John 17:16). Church is not confined to the norms of the society. Instead, life in the church is defined and valued according to the two modes of representation it entails.

_____

1. Words of Sethe in Toni Morrison, *Beloved* (New York: Plume, 1987), 35f.

How do we understand this being *in* but not *of*? This is the task of ecclesiology, the study of the church, which therefore is also a study of the relationship between the church and its end, or its ending, that which demarcates its boundaries.

In this context particular communities live the front-line experience. There the gospel of the reign or the kingdom of God, as the eschatological symbol par excellence, finds its expression. It is a gospel embodied in given locations and places where it represents itself in the limits of the "house" and of the "street," and not bound to any. As such, stresses Leonardo Boff, the promise that the kingdom occasions "will no longer be *utopia* . . . but *topia*, the object of happiness for all the people."[2] And it will be this *topos*, because the message of the kingdom has a particular, exclusive, and locatable addressee: the poor, as the specific cradle of the church.[3] Or in the words of Juan Luis Segundo:

> *The kingdom of God is not announced to everyone.* It is not "proclaimed" to all. . . . The kingdom is destined for certain groups. It is theirs. It belongs to them. Only for them it will cause joy. And, according to Jesus, the dividing line between joy and woe produced by the kingdom runs between *the poor* and *the rich.*[4]

This dividing line is both socially and spatially or geographically located; it runs between neighborhoods in our cities, between living quarters in a household dividing the spaces between masters and servants. It separates continents, countries, neighborhoods, and so forth. Yet the kingdom—as well as judgment and condemnation—is not about the side one is on; it is rather about the very divide that, as Segundo says, "runs between" them.

The combination of a particular ecclesiology with the eschatological message of the incoming reign of God created the frame for understanding the church as the total, eschatological presence of Christ. But due to its being *in* the world, it is also a transient institution. This eschatological approach has the impending urgency of apocalyptic tidings, because what is to be expected lies already here, nearby or adjacently, instead of being perennially deferred to an impending future or else already realized in a distant past.

---

2. Leonardo Boff, "Salvation in Jesus Christ and the Process of Liberation," *Concilium* 96 (1974): 81.

3. Jon Sobrino, "Central Position of the Reign of God," in *Mysterium Liberationis* (ed. Ignacio Ellacuría and Jon Sobrino; Maryknoll, N.Y.: Orbis, 1993), 367–71. See also Ignacio Ellacuría, "The Church of the Poor, Historical Sacrament of Liberation," in *Mysterium Liberationis*, 543–64.

4. Juan Luis Segundo, *The Historical Jesus of the Synoptics* (trans. John Drury; Maryknoll, N.Y.: Orbis, 1985), 90.

Under this perspective even the so-called postponement of the *parousia* is read in another light. This postponement is a long-held theory that the announcement of God's reign and its imminent coming was a cause of frustration for the early followers of Jesus who, in the transition from the first to the second generation of followers, were supposedly expecting it to happen in a time soon to arrive (cf. Mark 13:30). But if we look at it as an eschatological reality already present in the boundaries, or on the front line—the divides that mark the crises of society—the announcement of the impending coming of the kingdom looks different. *The advent of the kingdom is lodged in the adjacency of a new reality spatially located and not solely in a deferred future.*

The well-known formula by which Oscar Cullmann defined Jesus' apparently contradictory affirmation about the coming kingdom and its being simultaneously upon us—"already, but not yet"—seems indeed paradoxical. But the paradox fades in the moment when eschatology is interpreted as a spatial reality. The kingdom is topologically nearby, even if people have not fully and resolutely stepped over into it where it already is. The editors of a collection of worldwide representatives of liberation theology phrased it like this:

> Hence, eschatology is no longer "the last things" but "those things in our midst." The stress is on a God acting in history and on the need to discover God's direction for abundant life in the midst of our ambiguous and conflict ridden history. Prophecy, then, so intimately connected to eschatological vision and hope, does not involve predicting the future or mapping out the end times, but discerning God's activity in the world now, the meaning of that activity for the community of faith, and the appropriate response.[5]

The ecclesiological dimension of eschatology is decisively tilted in favor of an argument for the discontinuity rather than an opposition between the church and the kingdom. The often-quoted thesis from the Catholic modernist Alfred Loisy—"Jesus foretold the kingdom, and it was the Church that came"[6]—is read as apparently Loisy intended when he called the church "a provisional institution, a transitional organization . . . the vestibule of . . . the kingdom."[7] To be fair to him, the expression "transitional organization" should not be read

---

5. Mary P. Engel and Susan B. Thistlethwaite, "Introduction: Making Connections among Liberation Theologies around the World," in *Lift Every Voice: Constructing Christian Theologies from the Underside* (rev. ed.; ed. Susan B. Thistlethwaite and Mary P. Engel; Maryknoll, N.Y.: Orbis, 1998), 14–15.

6. Alfred Loisy, *The Gospel and the Church* (trans. Christopher Home; Philadelphia: Fortress Press, 1976), 166.

7. Ibid., 168.

metaphorically as a vessel on a journey over time to be left behind upon arrival, which is a position normally associated with modern Protestantism. But it also does not allow for the church to be identified in its essence with the kingdom as such, lacking only in plenitude. This is a position associated with the Roman Catholic Church where the church (and the history in which it is inserted as salvation history) is essentially connected to the kingdom (*ecclesia triumphans*), as a seed is to the tree, and only incidentally to the world (*ecclesia militans*).[8] In other words, the church is this hybrid entity that is at once sacramental (a means to the kingdom) and a particular human community. Its universality does not refer to the totality of humanity, but to existing in accordance with (*kata-*) the wholeness (*-holos*) of what it means to be human.[9]

The church is the hybrid space of adjacency between the old *aeon* and the new yet topologically already nearby.[10] It is a space between spaces, belonging to neither, yet adjacent to both, which is best expressed by the Greek word *chōra*, which etymologically means to lie open, listen, be attentive, be ready to receive.[11] It defines a space between places or limits, an adjacent ground. The church, therefore, is an eschatological reality that stands in the margins of this present realm and in the *choratic* adjacency of the realm of God, sharing all the ambiguity that adjacency suggests. The margin that defines the adjacency of realms constitutes the church insofar as it is a space for the solidarity of those relegated to the confines of the world, of the marginalized and all those who stand by them and share their plight.[12] In the words of Gustavo Gutiérrez, "If the church wishes to be faithful to the God of Jesus Christ, it must become aware of itself from the underneath, from among the poor of this world, the exploited classes, the despised ethnic groups, the marginalized cultures."[13]

---

8. The most recent example of this position is found in the declaration of the Vatican Sacred Congregation for the Doctrine of Faith, *Dominus Iesus* (2000).

9. See Juan Luis Segundo, *The Community Called Church* (Maryknoll, N.Y.: Orbis, 1973), 3–11.

10. In the Catholic tradition, Leonardo Boff suggests that the doctrine of purgatory might be interpreted as this transitory or ecclesial reality in which the *homo incurvatus* is converted into the *home erectus* who can see God face-to-face. Leonardo Boff, *Hablemos de la otra vida* (Bilbao: Sal Tarrae, 1984), 66.

11. For an excellent discussion of this attitude of reception as *pathos*, see Reinhard Hütter, *Suffering Divine Things: Theology as Church Practice* (trans. Doug Stott; Grand Rapids: Eerdmans, 2000), 29–32.

12. Gayatri C. Spivak, "Can the Subaltern Speak?" in *Colonial Discourse and Postcolonial Theory* (New York: Columbia University Press, 1994), 66–111.

13. Gustavo Gutiérrez, *The Power of the Poor in History: Selected Writings* (London: SCM, 1983), 211.

ADJACENCY

Late in his life, after having converted to Catholicism, French Arabist Louis Massignon founded a religious community. Its unique feature was to have its members live a Christian life in the midst of a Muslim context in Turkey. The purpose was not to convert the neighbor but to live out their Christianity while being hosted by those of another faith. This approach to interfaith engagement also changes one's way of understanding the relation between church and society in general, and so also of mission. The first challenge is not to be hospitable to the other, but to be in their place as a guest, accepting the terms of the other. This is also a front-line experience, an eschatological event: to be in someone else's place. The community Massignon formed was called Badaliya, Arabic for "substitution." But this substitution does not mean surrogacy or replacement. In the words of Italian philosopher Giorgio Agamben, discussing Massignon's community, it means "*exiling oneself to the other as he or she is.*"[14]

This "exiling oneself to the other" subverts the two basic forms of representation by which identity is construed; it is being housed where one's "house" is not one's own (the realm of one's production), and it is being exposed on the "street" (the realm of interpersonal relations), instead of shielding oneself with protective masks.

ZACCHAEUS: A MEDITATION ON ADJACENCY

This dialectical dynamics of being exiled, which means outside (*ex-*) of one's own ground (*-solum*) and exposed, can be elucidated by the story of Zacchaeus (Luke 19:1-10), the chief tax collector from Jericho, a town situated about twenty miles northeast of Jerusalem. While it does not seem to be a story about the church, it is precisely a story that illustrates how church happens in its transitioning between house and street, yet confined to neither.

Not very often are rich and powerful people named in the New Testament—except those who persecuted Jesus. But the one in this passage has a name: Zacchaeus, which means "pure" or "innocent" (from the Hebrew *zakai*). The New Testament is full of these ironic twists. The one who was named to be pure and innocent was a chief tax collector, and we know that tax collectors ranked atop the list of sinners as corrupt and guilty people. But as in the baptismal promise that makes us righteous, a righteousness and innocence return to us through repentance, which means a return to baptism. In the ceremony of his

---

14. Giorgio Agamben, *The Coming Community* (trans. Michael Hardt; Minneapolis: University of Minnesota Press, 2007), 23 (emphasis in the original).

naming, Zacchaeus also was given this promise.[15] And the story is about how Zacchaeus became *zakai*, how he became what he was promised to be.

Tax collectors, let alone chief tax collectors, were considered a special class of sinners for a number of reasons. They were, like Zacchaeus, fellow Judeans but working for the Roman occupiers. What we know of them, which should also apply to Zacchaeus, is that they not only got rich by impoverishing others but reportedly would send troops to invade the homes of those who allegedly were withholding unreported goods and proceed to ransack them on account of presumably unpaid taxes. Simply put, Zacchaeus and his cronies invaded homes of common people and plundered them of what they had, and the more they could get, the richer they would become. That was their goal, and Zacchaeus reached it. He was a rich man, as the text tells us.

What made Zacchaeus unique and brought him to this story that we cherish in the Gospel of Luke is that he somehow knew that he needed something that all his wealth could not afford: he had wealth but not health; he was safe but not saved.

The text tells us he was a *zeteios*, someone who inquires, searches, and seeks. Seekers are people who search for something they miss. And Zacchaeus not only knew that he missed something. Zacchaeus learned that there was a healer coming to town by the name of Jesus. Somehow he was not in denial. He was in search of a cure for the malady that afflicted him. He realized that he needed some sort of healing, but more important, he knew he needed liberation. He needed to live by the promise of his name.

The text tells us that he was of short stature. But the word for stature (*hēlikia*) can also be translated as maturity or, metaphorically, character. This would mean that he had a small or micro (*micros*) character, a poor or not well-developed character. In other words, he lacked integrity. Though rich in terms of money and goods, Zacchaeus was of a failing and debased stature. He was a man held in low esteem. And he knew that about himself, no matter his actual physical height, be it four or six feet. It does not take much guessing to know what people like him do to compensate for their actual state and low character (for their lack of stature and character). They climb! They will do whatever it takes to be above the common folk who they know, even if they will not admit it, have a greater character and higher stature and integrity. So they climb political ladders, corporate ladders; they climb whatever it takes to achieve the

---

15. The giving of the name in contemporaneous Judaism meant something similar in the Christian sacrament of baptism. This is what we do, often unaware, when we celebrate the beginning of a new year on the first day of January, which in early Christianity was celebrated as the day Jesus was named. See Hermann Brandt, "Was feiern Christen am 1. Januar? Zur Wiedergewinnung eines Christuszeugnisses älterer Gesangbücher und Zinzendorfs," *Lutherische Kirche in der Welt: Jahrbuch des Martin-Luther-Bundes* 54 (2007): 79–106.

superiority they claim for themselves by the wealth they have accumulated. Zacchaeus thus climbed a sycamore tree that was nearby. He clambered high enough to raise himself above the common folk (*ochlos*). So Zacchaeus went up in the hope that he would see this acclaimed healer and that the man of Nazareth, respected as he was by the common folk whom Zacchaeus preyed upon, would eventually see him and affirm the stature he earned by climbing, though not by character. Maybe all his ego was waiting for was to hear Jesus say: "Zacchaeus, you climbed that tree to see me. That is what makes you greater than this entire crowd." And that, he hoped, would restore his ego and boost his character and give him the stature he lacked.

The man from Nazareth, however, looks at the man in the tree, way above the common folk, and even above Jesus himself, for Jesus needs to look up to him, as the text says. But then he orders him to come down immediately. How does one translate those words of Jesus as they are rendered in Greek: *Zakchaie, speusas katabēthi sēmeron gar en tō oikō sou dei me meinai* (v. 5b)? These words have been translated in several ways,[16] most of which miss the sharpness of the saying. The language is very strong. *Dei me meinai* is not a self-invitation to be a guest, a gesture of etiquette. It is an imperative; it is a demand, even a threat. The Greek *dei* is an impersonal verb that expresses a commanding or divine imperative. My best attempt is to render it like this: "Zacchaeus, get down at once; today I must definitely be a squatter in your house." To paraphrase it for its contextual nuance: "Zacchaeus, get down from there and face your own low and debased stature and know yourself for what you truly are. And today I must get into your luxurious and secured home as you have invaded and plundered the poor houses of this people."

Very harsh grace conveyed by Jesus, but grace indeed! Zacchaeus humbly tumbles down from his tree, which means literally that he repents, meets his true stature, exposes his character for what it is. Zacchaeus, of course, is a bit embarrassed but relieved, as is someone who admits to a long-hidden wrongdoing. And he happily welcomes Jesus into his house. And before Jesus says anything, it is Zacchaeus who hastens to tell him that half of what he has will go to the poor, and to any persons he had defrauded he will provide fourfold restitution. In doing so he is surpassing the law that prescribes that one-fifth of the defrauded amount should be added to the restitution. The words he receives from Jesus are nothing short of what he was looking for. "Today healing/liberation/salvation (*sōtēria*) has come to this house." Salvation was not promised to him in heaven. It was given; it happened and continued to be valid (*egeneto*–the verb is in aorist, a verbal inflection that denotes an action without signaling

---

16. NRSV has it as: "Zacchaeus, hurry and come down; for I must stay at your house today."

its completion or duration) in the very gesture of the rich man's act of vulnerability. Zacchaeus became again *zakai*, innocent, like someone brought back to and out of his baptismal font, with the integrity of a child of Abraham. His repentance brought him back to the day of his naming.

AT EASE: PEACE BE WITH YOU

In the transition between the street and the house, Zacchaeus found the liberation he was longing for. His house became the place of salvation not because of what it held within it but because it was open to the street and pouring into the "street" its own wealth. The house was transformed from a stronghold to a place of adjacency, a vulnerable space that became accessible to the other. *Adjacency* is the word that describes where church happens, the space that is not produced or represented. The word *adjacency* has an interesting etymology, which Agamben describes in such a way as to offer a definition of the church, the place and event in which one can be *at ease* in the face of threatening and radical difference.

> Ease is the proper name of this unrepresentable space. The term "ease" in fact designates, according to its etymology, the space adjacent (*ad-jacens, adjacentia*), the . . . place where each can move freely, in a semantic constellation where spatial proximity borders on the opportune time (*ad-agio, moving at ease*) and convenience borders on the correct relation.[17]

Adjacency means "lying by," "being at ease" in the encounter with otherness that can be threatening, but equally offers a place of salvation, health, and liberation. However, this adjacent character of the church is not a blending of differences. Differences remain and so they must. The other is still irreducibly the other.

A simple illustration is a medicine or a drug one takes to heal an illness. In Greek, the word for "drug" is *pharmakon*, which can be both a poison and a medicine. The medicine invades the body like a poison to fight the disease. But at the same time it brings the possibility of a cure. Analogies are always limited ways of expressing a concept, but in this case it helps in explaining the relationship between danger and healing. This is best expressed in the words of poet Friedrich Hölderlin:

> Near is
> And difficult to grasp, the God.

---

17. Agamben, *Coming Community*, 24.

But where danger threatens
That which saves from it also grows.[18]

Being at ease militates against defensiveness. Being at ease, however, is not condescending tolerance or simple indolence. It involves risk as well as its awareness, and therefore it is definitely not intolerance either. It is not about protecting one's heritage, the esteemed liturgy, the confessional documents, ecclesial polity and offices, or even the Bible; it is about honoring them, aware that they are *exposed* to challenges whose impacts are unforeseeable. Yet it is in the crossing and in the touching, in the adjacent field between one and the other, in the risky zone of enmity where people are exposed to each other, where love abides and life blossoms.[19]

This brings us to the opposite example, showing how the church does not happen when it enshrines itself in the idolatry of its own household.

In John 20 we have the story of Jesus' first appearance to the gathered disciples on the evening of the day of his resurrection. The disciples were gathered in a house with doors locked for fear of the people who would persecute them. But Jesus came into the house and said unto them, "Peace be with you." The disciples rejoiced in seeing him; all now was cozy and relaxed. Their tense demeanor was happily exchanged for snug comfort. Jesus' words in wishing them peace, however, did not allude to anything even close to their cozy and relaxed feeling. The text says that Jesus repeated the same words, "Peace be with you." The repetition is intriguing. If Jesus said it once, it should be good enough. The clue to understanding this repetition is offered some verses earlier (v. 16) when Jesus appeared to Mary Magdalene. She addressed him as "Rabbouni," which means "teacher." And wouldn't teachers know the old Latin saying, *Repetitio est mater studiorum*, "Repetition is the mother of learning"? Peace did not mean: "Settle back and relax." "Peace" or "being at ease"–the two are the same–meant something else. As the exemplary teacher he was, Jesus then explained what peace really implies: "As the Father sent me, so I send you" (v. 21). Peace meant: "Get out of here," or "Open these doors and fear not." While the disciples apparently took the wish as equivalent to being relaxed and

---

18. Friedrich Hölderlin, *Poems and Fragments* (trans. Michael Hamburger; London: Anvil Press Poetry, 2004), 551.

19. Deanna Thompson, in her book *Crossing the Divide: Luther, Feminism, and the Cross* (Minneapolis: Fortress Press, 2004), offers a sustained reflection on the connection between the perils of the cross and the experience of friendship and love. For another perspective on what "being at ease" means, see John F. Hoffmeyer, "Desire in Consumer Culture: Trinitarian Transformations," in *Being the Church in the Midst of Empire: Trinitarian Reflections* (ed. Karen L. Bloomquist; Minneapolis: Lutheran University Press, 2007), 149–62, where he talks of encountering Christ in the vulnerability of human persons.

happy, Jesus meant it in the sense of adjacency. The disciples were summoned to face the adjacency of the world that they were so afraid of.

CHRYSOSTOM

In sermon 45 of "Homilies on the Acts,"[20] Chrysostom illustrates what I am trying to explain here. The church, Chrysostom recognizes, has plenty of "lands, has money, and revenues." This was, after all, the early Constantinian church that thrived under imperial protection. Institutions for the care of the poor and strangers were created by the church for its diaconal work to be carried out. They were called *Xenodoxeion*, which means a place to host strangers. It seems a great thing for the church to do, and indeed it was. But to readers today as well as to his hearers when he delivered the sermon, there is a surprise in wait: to the chagrin of his listeners as well as today's readers, Chrysostom launches an attack on them. They were not commended for their works of charity but admonished for being putty in the hands of well-off Christians. These hospices were being used to keep the poor and the strangers out of sight, out of the houses of the very members of the church. These charitable places became instruments to prevent exposure and to avoid the face of the poor. In doing so, argues Chrysostom, they were keeping Christ and angels at bay. They were not heeding the warning of Hebrews 13:2, "Do not neglect to show hospitality to strangers, for by doing that some have entertained angels without knowing it," or the judging words of Christ, "Truly I tell you, just as you did not do it to one of the least of these, you did not do it to me" (Matt. 25:45). As was the case in the story of Zacchaeus, the message here is also clear. Without exposure there is no repentance; without repentance, no grace; without grace, no transformation! And church fails to happen.

Chrysostom criticizes his fellow Christians because they were excusing themselves from meeting Christ in the spaces of their own adjacency, because church charities were doing it for them. So he asks rhetorically: "Do not the priests pray? then why should I pray?" If the church cares for the little ones, does it mean that you need not care and receive Christ in your own home? Chrysostom offers the reversal of the Zacchaeus story, making precisely the same point. His acknowledged shame about the attitude of fellow Christians is a revealing acclamation of what his church was doing in receiving the poor and the stranger into its premises, the hosting room for the strangers. But the irony of his indictment is that while the church was doing the right and charitable thing, many of its wealthy members were themselves not being church. By

---

20. *The Nicene and Post-Nicene Fathers*, 2nd ser., vol. 11 (ed. Philip Schaff; repr., Peabody, Mass.: Hendrickson, 1995), 272–77.

virtue of their membership, they were indeed associated with the church, but were they not using the church to mask their very inability to *be* church?

Chrysostom offers an example that connects to the story of Jesus' coming to the disciples in the locked room:

> For is it not absurd, that whereas, if soldiers should come, you have rooms set apart for them, and show much care for them, and furnish them with everything, because they keep off from you the visible war of this world, yet strangers have no place where they might abide?[21]

The renowned preacher of the early church was intimating that the "peace" that people believed they had was a cover-up of denial, a way of keeping off the "visible war of this world." But that was not the true peace for Chrysostom, and it also was not what Jesus meant when he said, "Peace be with you." This peace, in the words of Patočka, can only be found in a life that is no longer "chained by fear," life that "sees clearly that the everyday, its life and its 'peace,' have an end."[22] As the disciples locked themselves in that room, Christians in Chrysostom's time (and, needless to say, ours as well) protected themselves with well-armored gates from being exposed to the front-line experience where the "visible war" is being fought in the social divides then and now.

Adjacency defines the place of the church as there where freedom and danger are experienced next to each other. It is left to us to define this place that I have described by the metaphors of house and street in their transitional and transformational relations.

---

21. Ibid., 277.

22. Jan Patočka, *Heretical Essays in the Philosophy of History* (trans. Erazim Kohák; Chicago: Open Court, 1996), 134.

THE PLACE
OF THE CHURCH

9

*If the theory is correct that feeling is not located in the head, that we sentiently experience a
window, a cloud, a tree not in our brains but, rather, in the place where we see it, then we
are, in looking at our beloved, too, outside ourselves. But in a torment of tension
and ravishment. Our feeling dazzled, flutters like a flock of birds. . . .
And as the birds seek refuge in the leafy recesses of a tree . . . feelings escape into . . .
where they can lie low in safety. And no passer-by would guess that it is just here,
in what is defective and censurable, that the fleeting darts of adoration nestle.*
Walter Benjamin[1]

The metaphors of house and street, embedded in the "economic" and "political" paradigms, have so far been a useful tool in discussing the location as well
as the captivities of the church. As helpful as they may be, and they are, they
are still vague in providing an assessment for placing the church where it actually is. House and street have been used by and large as negative criteria to say
what the church is not, while containing elements of both. But a more detailed
discussion about our understanding of place and space is called for to provide
some clearer contours to locate where and when church happens. And to this
end I use yet another metaphor: tapestry.

TAPESTRY: A METAPHOR

The biblical narrative is a story that moves from creation to consummation,
which is symbolized by two places: the Garden of Eden in the beginning of
Genesis and the New Jerusalem at the end of Revelation. Like all the rest of
God's creation, these two places are gifts but also represent sites, locations
where life flourishes and the divine donor is present and in neither is there a
need for a demarcated sacred space. But in between these two sites there is a
pilgrimage, what Augustine called *procursus*, a journey through an ensemble

---

1. Walter Benjamin, *Reflections: Essays, Aphorisms, Autobiographical Writings* (New York:
Schocken, 1986), 68.

of places that frame the narrative: fields, houses, deserts, and so forth. In the ambiguous experience of these places, divine presence (*parousia*) and absence (*apousia*) cross each other. And, of course, in the midst of it all is a place called Golgotha, the site where God surrendered Godself to the very gift that was given, for God so loved spaces and places as to fill them with divine presence (John 3:16). The Giver gave herself in the gift as the Gift itself; God became spacious in surrendering Godself up to the emptiness of a space. Is not the narrative of the faith, then, the creation and fulfillment of space and, in the midst of it, the experience of being exiled from it? Between spaces of belonging (which means being present by desire) and exile (being uprooted), between houses and streets, we live our lives and shape our places, or else are by them displaced. Between houses and streets we also find the unique placing of the church. However, what needs to be examined is the very uniqueness of this place or space that we call church.

In search of a metaphor to anchor this examination of the place of the church, let us consider this poem by Christian Morgenstern:

> One time there was a picket fence
> with spaces to gaze from hence to thence.
>
> An architect who saw this sight
> approached it suddenly one night,
>
> removed the spaces from the fence
> and built of them a residence.[2]

The poem offers a trope of how spaces are malleable and can be transformed. Its rococo style and the motif of taking the empty spaces in a picket fence to build a hosting place are indeed suggestive. But the notion of a picket fence does not go together with the notion of the gift. Licensed by some poetic freedom, I will slightly change the root metaphor and instead of a picket fence I will suggest another metaphor: a tapestry—and the rest might remain the same, for it allows us to think also about an interlocking set of laces that are spaces out of which we build places. Thus, instead of a fence, a tapestry sustains our spatial existence by its interwoven threads of woofs and warps. The longitudinal threads, the woofs, are, as it were, the Edens of our existence. The transversal warps that the weaver keeps threading are the New Jerusalems that cross the paths of our lives and hold them together as the weaving continues.

---

2. Cited by Michel de Certeaux, *The Practice of Everyday Life* (Berkeley: University of California Press, 1988), 127.

In the loops, hanging in faith to the entwined threads, we keep on creating and re-creating those spaces, sustaining ourselves by holding on to those threads, and not rarely losing our grip. We do not inhabit the threads; we are by their interwoven patterns sustained in the loops. Starting then with this metaphor, we might proceed with the weaving in search of a pattern that might locate the place of the church.

METABOLISM: SPACE AS GIFT AND TASK

We create spaces and we also destroy them, as much as spaces shape, build, and threaten our existence. But above all, space is something given. What we do with spaces is what we do with a gift, and, as any gift, it comes with an intention. Whatever construction we put into the doctrine of the creation out of nothing, the bottom line is that the spaces we live our lives in, our vital spaces, are ultimately this gift, a *donum* and not a neutral ground that is simply there apart from God's creative and redemptive purposes. Whatever one does with and in space is done upon a divine gift. After all, the body, whose resurrection Christians confess, is the minimum space we are all endowed with, and so it is also with the New Jerusalem, the city we constantly fail to build, but which still is the warp that sustains the tapestry. But once we assert this, the question is what this gift of the tapestry of our existence does to us, and what we do to and with it.[3]

Space is a category so vast that it demands an initial categorical delimitation, attempting to stay as close as possible to the way that we as embodied beings experience embodiment. As much as our biological organism is constantly reproducing itself through a process called metabolism, an analogous process *takes place* with our surroundings–a room, a park, a street, a chapel, a library, a cell, with which there is a constant give-and-take (i.e., metabolism)–which shape us as much as we constantly shape them. Our bodies and their surroundings are embedded in this metabolism through which they create an identity and leave a mark that generates a morphology, or a differential space, a space that distinguishes itself from other spaces. When we say that something "takes place," it means that in a given space a differential sign is

---

3. The theological relevance of space is not an issue to be approached without recognizing its perils. Paul Tillich warned that space is pagan and that only time, with which space is at battle, is spiritual and Christian. Paul Tillich, *Der Widerstreit von Raum und Zeit* (Stuttgart: Evangelische Verlagswerk, 1963), 140–48. I have argued elsewhere that this very divorce of time from space is a peculiar Western and modern feature. "Re(li)gion: The Lord of History and the Illusory Space," in *Region and Religion* (ed. Viggo Mortensen; Geneva: LWF, 1994). I will leave this discussion about the relation of time and space aside and restrict my remarks to our experience of *physical* space as locales and places that are extensions that embody us and that we embody, that we build and by which we are built.

left, but this is always a struggle. The struggle to create a unique identity or a signature is what Henri Lefebvre has called "trial by space," which happens in the confrontation between our finite freedom and destiny.[4] We want to create a marked space that defines our identity, our body, our social position, our home, church, employment, vacation site, that which is proper to who we are or who we would like to be.

THE SPECTRUM OF SPATIAL EXPERIENCES: BANQUET ROOMS AND DESERTS

This struggle in spatial encounters, this trial by space–be it travel to outer space, the crossing of a street in our neighborhood, the touch of another person, or even the intake of some food into our body–is always an experience of otherness, an encounter with another space. Michel Foucault called it "heterotopia,"[5] suggesting that the other place is always the place of an *other*. Taking a clue from a text of Paul Tillich, this meeting of an other can be of two kinds. We can meet an other when the encounter is complementary, as a discovery of ourselves, or the encounter can be of a confrontational nature, where we meet the other as a stranger, exposing us to what we are not, which can come as a promise or then as the threat of annihilation. In short, the difference is between the *estranged* and the *stranger*.[6] These two forms of encounter are opposed poles in a vast spectrum of experiences we go through in our everyday lives.

In the first case, the experience of otherness is one of belonging, of being recognized. The biblical parables of banquets are exemplars of such encounters. (The prodigal son is given back an identity he had lost in displacement. Displaced people are invited in. The host recognizes the guest and asks him to move closer.) But such encounters with expectations of recognition can turn also into displacement. (A guest is put in "his place" because he has pretended to be more than he is; or, worse, is sent away for not being properly attired for the occasion.) If one pretends to be what one is not in the social fabric of a "banquet," one is put in one's proper place. In this case one does not take place, and experiences what Kafka called a "non-person."

In the second case–in the encounter of the other as a stranger–the desert, the place from which one does not take much or leave a significant trace behind, often represents the experience of sheer otherness. The reason why desert experiences are often associated with trial and, indeed, trial by space is because little metabolism takes place. Therefore, it is in the desert experiences

---

4. Henry Lefebvre, *The Production of Space* (Oxford: Blackwell, 1991), 416–18.
5. Michel Foucault, *The Foucault Reader* (ed. Paul Rabinow; New York: Pantheon, 1984), 252.
6. Paul Tillich, *Theology of Culture* (New York: Oxford University Press, 1959), 10.

that we are often confronted with epiphanies or mirages, for in the absence of metabolism we become susceptible to sheer otherness, to that which we cannot process or metabolize, be it the devil or the unutterable presence of the divine.[7] When we move into a heterotopia, as the strange place, it is not only because we do not recognize it; a strange place does not carry our imprint. The estrangement is double. The other place or the place of the other also does not recognize us. When Job describes the experience of being in Sheol, it is for him a radical condition of being *dis*-placed. So we read: "Those who go down to Sheol do not come up; they return no more to their houses, nor do their places know them any more" (Job 7:9-10; also Ps. 103:16). This is the reason Job attributes subjectivity to places: because they embody intentions that invite or exclude us. A desert knows one as little as a building inaccessible to a physically challenged person knows that person.

Spaces are not a neutral reality we can dispose of or simply use. This is an abstract view of spaces. Such abstraction removes from spaces the fact that they embody purpose and meaning; they do something to us as we interact with them. We take place; we make it our own, we give it a shape, generating morphology and leaving an ink, an insignia.[8]

Between these two experiences, deserts and banquets, we negotiate our "taking-place" in and through the laces of the tapestry that I have suggested here. However, deserts and banquets are often not part of our everyday life, but they typify experiences akin to them. Like deserts, there are some spaces we encounter whose primary intent is to move us beyond them; they are shaped to keep us moving into other spaces. Others, akin to banquets, are designed to entail the purpose of our existence within them; we are grafted into their texture. I will call the first locales, and the second places.

TYPES OF SPACE: LOCALES AND PLACES

Locales are positions we are in that indicate and locate us within a trajectory. Locales interplay between centrifugal and centripetal forces. They send us somewhere else, as much as they are designed to attract us. They are not functions of rest but of motion and transit; they are points in the transition from place to place. If a store is in a location, that is, in a locale, it means that it is

---

7. Starvation and the discipline of fasting create a similar condition. They are forms of estrangement, one imposed and the other chosen. This phenomenon accounts also for the way hunger strikes are effective; they make the participants in the strike to be the uncomfortable strangers in the social fabric in which they are inserted.

8. Even pristine nature is charged with these intentions, if by nothing else, by the very fact of being represented, by observation, photography, or painting. The intention they carry comes from the gaze of the observer/photographer/painter who intentionally chooses, frames, and demarcates what is conveyed.

in a given place of transit where it can attract business or customers, but after we buy our merchandise we should move on. We are always in a locale for the sake of something else. Take, for example, an airport, a bus station, a street, an airplane, a bus, or a train. They are spaces in which we find ourselves in the expectation of meeting otherness. No matter how comfortable the facilities in a locale might be, there is no limit to the annoyance that, for example, a delayed or canceled flight can cause. Locales are given stations where we might find ourselves in a given moment of transition from place to place. Locales are best described by itineraries. They are like looking at a subway chart that tells the point we are at and the destination we are heading to, but reveals little if anything at all of the surrounding territory. Itineraries do not place us; they locate us.

The architecture of locales is designed to be open and public with very little private room available. Their decoration will be posters, murals, advertisements, simulacra, outdoors—all that can catch the eye in a glance but does not hold the gaze, for one is moving and must be invited to move. One does not inhabit a locale; one just happens to be there. Locales simultaneously invite us in and also send us off. They are rather impervious to our shaping of them. One does not rearrange the furniture in an airport. One does not sit in a first-class coach if the train ticket is for a second-class seat. The case of Rosa Parks, who in Montgomery, Alabama, refused to give her seat to a white man in a segregated bus, shows how incredibly costly but creatively disturbing it is to shape a locale apart from the original intent with which it was designed or endowed.

Different are places. Their invested intent is not in being provisory spaces of transition; their function is to be catalysts. They gather for the sake of providing refuge, shelter, or intimacy. Houses or homes are the names we often give to inclusive places. Their intent is to release one from the transitory experiences of everyday life, from locales we move through. Within limits and according to financial resources, these places, unlike locales, are moldable to one's own intention. One makes a house or an apartment one's own by designing, decorating, redesigning, or furnishing it. Home, the old saying goes, is the place where one's heart is. (Or as Jacques Derrida nicely rephrases it, "The correct location of the heart is the place that is best placed.")[9] You know the intent of a place when you hear the welcoming salutation: *Mi casa es tu casa* (My house is your house). If locales are represented by itineraries, maps, then blueprints or photographs represent places. These two forms of representation follow precisely those of the "political" and the "economic" paradigms discussed in previous chapters.

---

9. Jacques Derrida, *The Gift of Death* (trans. David Wills; Chicago: University of Chicago Press, 1995), 97.

Our everyday life is a negotiation between these two experiences in an alternating and pendulous movement. One of these experiences is marked by the spaces of transit, which are not ends in themselves, and the other experience is the space of rest and shelter, or even seclusion. But what counts here is the dynamic relation between locales and places, how we transit through the tapestry. Inability to move among these different spaces is what defines displacement. Displacement is thus not a vacuum, but the state of being immobilized in a given space. This incapability to leave a place, to transit, is to be shut in, in a prison, a hospice, or even a home (as the experience of many women around the world to this day attests; a place called home has doors and windows that open also from the inside). Displacement also means having a *locale* as the only *place* one has. Homeless people, landless peasants, are those condemned to live in and make a place out of locales meant for transit. These are the mirror images of those who are shut in; they share the same displacement or exclusion by being secluded to a space of transit. The expression "doing time" conveys this sense of immobility, of being stuck between locales and places. There is life and hope as long as there is movement and as long as this tapestry keeps being woven.

HYBRID SPACES: THIN AND THICK

Between locales and places there is a third type of physical space. They are hybrid spaces. Offices, arcades, classrooms, assembly lines, church buildings, hospitals, commuter apartments, sweatshops, cafés, halfway houses, parks, town squares, and theaters are typical hybrid spaces, which are places both of transition and of dwelling, but not exactly either of them. Hybrid spaces are not like locales, simply transitions between one space and another. Neither are they like places that center our sense of belonging. They are spaces between places and locales. Accessibility to hybrid spaces is what grants us a possibility to move around between locales and places, yet inhabit neither. Postcolonial studies call this spatial condition of those who are territorially, culturally, or politically neither insiders nor outsiders, and yet both, hybridity. Flanked by locales and places, being both and neither, hybrid space best describes a way of taking-place that allows for further reflection. Take two different examples of hybrid spaces: a sweatshop and a café. The opposing experiences that they convey are real, but both share the commonality of being neither spaces of transition nor spaces of shelter or dwelling, yet having features of both; and they are, for better or worse, places that indicate neither that one is displaced nor that one necessarily belongs.[10]

---

10. Sociologists also describe displacement as exclusion, a condition to which increasing armies of desolate people are being added daily in this global economy.

Hybrid spaces are further divided into thick and thin. Thick hybrid spaces are thick in the sense that they leave in us an imprint of their inherent purpose: due to the memorable impressions of their grandeur, or impressions of memories that they symbolize, or still by the way they alter our circumstances, they shape our perception of space more significantly than we endow them with our spatial construction. However, thick spaces are also catalysts of our intentions. They are thick because they hold our attention and entail an enduring intention. Thin spaces do neither. Thin spaces are either so moldable to our purposes as to be innocuous (like a cubicle office that one can "decorate" to the extreme, only to empty it all in a box the day one leaves the job), or else they are so impermeable that they soon become equally insignificant (like assembly lines in a car factory).

MONUMENTAL AND ARCHIVAL SPACES

My intent in this discussion of types of spaces is to locate when and where church happens and to understand the uniqueness of the space where church happens. If I am to succeed, even partially, it is imperative to look into how this hybrid space of church operates. One can distinguish three types of hybrid spaces that can bring locales and places to a new level of significance, and these can be called *monumental, archival,* and *epiphanic* spaces. I will make brief comments about the first two as to their uniqueness, and keep the rest of my remarks for the third and last, which is often confused with the other two but is quite distinct and will offer the configuration of the space called church.

First, monumental spaces are a thick result of the hybridity of locales and places that function like a relief in a flat surface. They are appealing because of their majestic and imposing features. They do not need to tell a story; they are the story in themselves. They stand as symbolic representations of their surroundings. They do not need to be defined, for they are themselves the definition; they have a synthetic quality. The Empire State Building, Christ the Redeemer at Corcovado in Rio, the John Hancock Building, Mount Kilimanjaro, Central Park in New York, Saint Peter's Square in Rome, the Alhambra in Granada, Big Ben in London, and the Great Wall of China are magnificent examples of such monumental spaces. Their symbolic meaning ensues from the fact that in their design they are conduits of meanings broader than themselves by their irresistible capacity for arresting the gaze. They fascinate us as a gift to be preserved in the traces that they leave in our memories, photo albums, and mementos. Monumental spaces are memorable.

Second, archival spaces are similar, but their main characteristic is not the turgid appearance and plastic imprint of the shapes, sounds, and colors they leave for long in our minds and the sensuous attention they summon. Archival spaces are not the synthesized story of a place, as monumental spaces are; instead, they contain stories, they are a registry of memorable events. Monumental spaces are memorable; archival spaces are repositories of memories. While monumental spaces connect a locale to a place, archival spaces are locales that connect us to a history and to stories of other places. Their fascination is not in themselves but in the memories they evoke. Take for example the Water Tower in Chicago, Ground Zero in New York, the church door in Wittenberg. There is not much to be seen in the spaces themselves, but one hardly misses the stories they tell. Cemeteries, museums, libraries, and historic sites and buildings are archival places par excellence.

Although spaces can be both monumental and archival, the basic intention in each is distinct; either the monumental or the archival prevails. But the one that prevails often depends on who invests it with a certain gaze, which in turn determines its meaning. A familiar example would be Mount Rushmore. For some who make the pilgrimage, it might be dominantly a monumental space when its ponderous features prevail, while for others it is an archival space of the memory of what has made the United States the nation it is.

EPIPHANIC SPACES: A NOTE OF CAUTION

The third form of thick hybrid spaces can, for want of a better word, be called epiphanic. I am trying initially to avoid the use of the notion of "sacred spaces" or even "holy places," because these suggest a fundamental distinction from any other space as being profane (even though eventually I am going to use these notions). The problem with these expressions is that they tend to be essentialist, as if something of an ontological quality is embedded in their being. Such essentialism, then, turns profane spaces into sites that are released from any constraint as to their exchangeability and exploitation. The necessary other side of sacred essentialism is the unrestricted exploitation of the profane. In other words, the unrestricted exploitation of space is the counterpart to the institution of "sacred" spaces and sanctuaries. And the reverse is also true: when essentialized, the institution of "sacred" spaces and sanctuaries is a function of the exploitation of other spaces. The preservation or institution of designated places as "sacred" can be also the moral and religious sanction for exploitation of all other spaces.[11]

The move from epiphanic spaces to the institution of "sacred places" as spaces endowed with a different ontic quality is what may be properly called idolatry, which I discussed in detail in chapter 6. The idol arrests the gaze; its

---

11. See my article "The Way the World Ends: An Essay in Cross and Eschatology," *CTM* 27, no. 2 (2000): 85–97.

nature is opaque. One is fixated by it in a representation, taking it for what it presumably stands for. In the Solid Declaration 10 of the Formula of Concord,[12] the Lutheran Reformation has maintained that idolatry is defined by turning something that is—or might be—good into something that is essential, defining something as of the essence when it is actually an *adiaphoron*, something indifferent. Therefore, it is important to recognize monumental and archival spaces for their specific qualities and, undoubtedly, their greatness, for they often are taken to be holy for the wrong reason, that is, for either their monumental or their archival features. Due to the endurance that monumental and archival spaces have, it is tempting to attribute the long-lasting quality of their magnificence to an ontological difference that would put them qualitatively apart from the rest of creation.

Epiphanic spaces do not have an ontological quality. It is the event that accounts for its uniqueness as a space, the event in which the divine is made manifest. Epiphany can be a burning bush in the desert or a stable in which a displaced mother gives birth to a child. Like monumental and archival spaces, epiphanic spaces are also thick spaces in the sense that they leave a lasting imprint in the mind and the emotions. They call for attention and embody enduring intentions. But unlike other thick spaces, epiphanic spaces have their own specific traits. First, like monumental spaces, they are memorable. However, they are memorable not for their imposing shapes and designs (which they could also have, yet without seizing the gaze), but for their quality of transparency, of sending the gaze beyond the space itself, something that monumental spaces do not do. Second, epiphanic spaces, like archival spaces, are storages of memories. However, they are a registry of memories in and through which a future is unveiled—a promise is also entailed. Their intent as spaces endowed with subjectivity is eschatological, while archival spaces are genealogical. The memory in them is the memory of a future, anticipated (as a prolepsis) in stories of the past remembered.

Moreover, epiphanic spaces are places of *parousia*, places where the divine presence is embodied in the very stuff of the world as wrappings of the divine gift. And this could be anywhere, from the mundane to the majestic: in a building, in music, in preaching, in paintings, in a meal, in statues, in the pages of a book, or in the embrace of a friend or even a stranger. All these may be wrappings of the divine gift of epiphanic presence. As with a gift offered, the wrapping both conceals it and announces and anticipates its presence.

This presence has three forms of manifestations, as most persons in the Christian tradition recognize. The first manifestation is the man Jesus of

---

12. *The Book of Concord* (ed. Robert Kolb and Timothy J. Wengert; Minneapolis: Fortress Press, 2000), 635–40.

Nazareth, whose history and stories are housed by epiphanic spaces. The second is the communion of those who follow and confess him throughout history, by the preaching of the Word and the administration of the sacraments that epiphanic spaces celebrate. And the third mode of presence comes in a disguised or anonymous way anywhere in the whole of creation, which makes *any* space potentially epiphanic.[13]

THE CHURCH AS EPIPHANIC SPACE

Churches are hybrid spaces of the epiphanic type. As memorable sites entailing stories, keeping the past and opening the present to messianic possibilities, their hybridity resides in the fact that they mark stations of transition and also places of rest, shelter, and healing but are not exactly either of them. How can this hybridity be expressed in the particular case of churches?

Certain formal features can be lifted up, which have implications for the way we recognize, design, experience, and interact with these hybrid spaces. First, there is a poetics of space construction, which resembles the creation of an icon. Second, there is a practice that distinguishes hybrid spaces and is inscribed in its very texture, a practice of adjacency. Third, there is a given doxological posture that demarcates and identifies a space as a contemplative and healing place. To these I now turn, trying to show how they function.

AN ICONIC POETRY

Holy spaces are poetic. The poetics of space designates what the Greek word *poiesis* conveys; it refers to the "creation," to the making or production of a space in the very sense of the economic paradigm or the house metaphor discussed earlier. Any space definable as an entity—a building, a reservation, a park, a church, a train, and many others, including human sexual reproduction—once demarcated and given an identity, is, as we have seen, the result of a metabolic relationship between natural elements and human labor.[14] There is no *creatio ex nihilo*, no creation out of nothing: *ex nihilo nihil*, except for God's own creation (which we see only in faith, and will see with our own eyes when and where the tapestry of God's providence enfolds us). But in the midst of the unfolding of

---

13. I am here following in particular Luther's articulation of the three modes of Christ's presence in his *Confession concerning Christ's Supper* (1528), *LW* 37:222–24. The Western Enlightenment tradition, with its hesitant attitude toward apophatic and mystical aspects of the faith, often obliterated this third mode of presence, and this is a further reason for essentializing sacred spaces.

14. For the use of the biological metaphor of metabolism in connection with human labor, see my article "Labor: A Suggestion for Rethinking the Way of the Christian," *WW* 4, no. 2 (1986): 194–206.

this weaving, all we have is *poiesis* or labor in metabolic exchange. An epiphanic space is always a space demarcated over against other spaces by the fact that there is an intention in its construction and in the delineation of its boundaries. Its intention is not defined by utility. Unlike office buildings, houses, gyms, streets, hotels, or cars, a church belongs to a different economy. Its end is not a return to an investment but lies in its divestiture. The idolatrous temptation of the church is to think of itself as its own production, as if out of nothing. This inevitably results in the worship of the wrapping and not the gift it contains.

But this does not mean that the church is not a space that, while it divests and shares, also provides and nurtures. In both its divestment and its nurturing, the *poetic* labor is the one of presenting the Gift. The attitude of the "poet" who builds, designs, furnishes, and decorates it with colors, shapes, and sounds should be as the attitude of one who is wrapping a gift. The wrapping communicates the endearment with which the Gift is given. However, the wrapping is not the reason for the Gift, neither does it summon it; the wrapping conveys, carries, and holds the Gift–it gives it a visible tactile shape for the senses to feel.[15] The poetic vocation of the church might leave a signature, but it will finally be underwritten *soli Deo gloria*, "to God alone the glory," as was done by that great poet of musical ornamentation, Johann Sebastian Bach, in signing the scores to his compositions.

The following illustration will help expound the point I am trying to convey. In the twelfth century the Notre Dame Cathedral in Chartres, France, was struck by lightning and burned to the ground. The legend has it that thousands of people from all over came to rebuild it: masons, burghers, artisans, carpenters, clowns, master builders, peasants, noblemen, nuns and monks, women and men. And the now famous pilgrimage site stands there and no one to this day knows who built it. It was an anonymous act of divestment for the sake of creating a space for the glory of God. While the idol looms in its presence, beauty can yet be transparent! This old legend is a classic illustration of what true art is, and yet it also is a reminder of what we have lost. This is vividly expressed in the words of Ingmar Bergman, the Swedish film director. Today, he bemoans, art has been

> separated from worship. It severed an umbilical cord and now lives its
> own sterile life, generating and degenerating itself. . . . Today . . . we stand
> and bleat about our loneliness without listening to each other and without
> realizing that we are smothering each other to death . . . [We] stare into
> each other's eyes and yet deny the existence of each other.[16]

---

15. For Luther space is described as a mask (*larva*), wrapping (*involucrum*), or the dress (*vestitus*) God wears. See *LW* 26:95–96.

16. Ingmar Bergman, *The Seventh Seal* (New York: Simon & Schuster, 1960), 8–9.

When such dissociation happens in connection with a consecrated place, like a church, chapel, temple, mosque, or synagogue; when art and architecture turn into an end of the subjective whim of designers, architects, artists, committees, or donors, then the idol lurks behind.

This is then the first characteristic of the church as an epiphanic space. It is the result of a creative, *poietic* labor that stands for its end, its objective, as the wrapping stands for the gift; it gives to the gift a provisional shape, a culturally determined shape that aims at enhancing the meaning of the content for the senses. The wrapping is the result of a labor that exists neither for its own sake nor for the sake of the laborer but for the gift it wraps. The distinction between being an aim in itself obfuscating the invisible and being an attempt to be a visible cipher referring the beholder not to itself but to that which cannot be seen, is the very difference between the idol and the icon.[17]

A PRACTICE OF ADJACENCY

The second formal feature of a holy place is that it allows for a release, a space in which a practice of engagement and of letting-go takes place. An epiphanic place is welcoming but ends not in itself; it sends people forward. Such are the places in which experiences of healing do not arrest the soul (they are not addictive). Instead they release people to go forth, encouraged and strengthened. The mount of transfiguration is not a dwelling place; one needs to go down the mountain to everyday life. And according to the Gospel of John, chapter 20, not even the safety of the upper room—where the disciples were gathered, afraid of the people outside—can be an end in itself, even while Jesus was there, even when there was presence (*parousia*). Jesus, whose real presence sanctified the place, sent them out!

A holy place, as much as it gathers, nurtures, and fills with joy, also releases and sends people to the midst of life, to the heart of the world. But those who are sent have already been transformed; they leave these spaces renewed and changed. Holy places are places of *metanoia*. And *metanoia* does not transform people out of the world; it changes people for the world. This is at the very root meaning of the word *ekklēsia*, which was borrowed by New Testament authors from the civic arena. It originally meant a gathering or assembly of citizens to decide or legislate on issues concerning public life. After the assembly was over, the people were sent back to the *polis* with the charge of implementing the decisions taken. The features of such a place of assembly, that is, the church, therefore need to convey adjacency to the places where people live

---

17. Jean-Luc Marion, *God without Being* (trans. Thomas A. Carlson; Chicago: University of Chicago Press, 1991), 17–18.

their everyday life, so that they can temporarily exit that life to be healed and transformed in order to return to it. This is the reason the church is a place of turning around, of *metanoia*. Hence it also has features of a locale, a space of transition, without denying its homely features. The Shabbat, which Luther took to be the symbolic institution of the church, is precisely this: a time and place of rest and nurturing, a home inserted in the midst of everyday life. Adjacency, lying by, simultaneously suggests a moment, a state and space of rest, as well as the impending accountability for the demands that lie near. The wrapping is, finally, what one needs to leave behind after the gift has been received.

How does one imagine such a space? How does one build a place that has at the same time the features of protected enclosure and those of adjacency? Different contexts and sites pose different challenges and demand creative, that is, *poietic*, solutions.

Another legend illustrates the point that is made here. It tells the story of a design that combines the architectural features of a place of safety and a space of adjacency. In the old town of Munich stands Frauenkirche, a majestic Gothic church. It was built in the fifteenth century in the heart of Marienplatz, at the time a very busy marketplace. As one enters the nave of the church, there is a paving stone on which one can see the imprint of a foot in low relief. Legend has it that when the construction was under way, the master builder was approached by the devil, who demanded that the church be consecrated to him. Upon the master builder's refusal, the devil issued a challenge: the master builder could have his way of being faithful to God if he could build a church that was at the same time filled with natural light but without any windows visible to sight. If the place turned out to be dark with little light from the outside coming in, the devil would win. And so it would also be, if there were visible windows that would not only be distracting but directly expose people to the busy market outside. The master builder, with the limited technological resources of the fifteenth century, designed a church that from the entry of the nave is filled with natural light but without any windows to be seen. After it was completed, the devil came to see the church and collect his spoils, expecting either an utterly dark place or windows exposed to the gaze. Yet it had the light of adjacency and the warmth of a haven for the weary soul. On seeing the place and realizing that he had lost the bet, the devil out of rage trampled on the paving stone. And his footprint is there to this day for all to see!

As in this legend the demonic temptation of the church is to lock itself in and cut itself off from society, hiding its light (Matt. 5:15). Or else the church loses itself in the world and its distinct voice is not heard, and thus it ceases to be the salt of the earth (Matt. 5:13). In one case we have insulation and in the other acculturation. In one the church's voice is just the monotonous repetition of its own litanies; in the other its voice is co-opted by the ideology of the day.

A ROOM FOR DOXOLOGY

A third sign of a holy space is that it be a place of healing and safety, where people can trust that God is with them, sustaining, nurturing, and comforting them. These are spaces where people can gather and sense an ambience of grace in which any and all words might be uttered without fear and without appeal to the dissimulation that is required by semantic protocols that govern other spaces. From the deepest lament to the loudest doxology, these are the places where one is drawn to silence, to meditation, or to intoning and shouting without reserve. The significance of these spaces is poignantly expressed by John Coltrane in the introduction to his album *A Love Supreme.* Epiphanic spaces are where "all praise be to God to whom all praise is due."

An epiphanic space is a product of a community that gives it spirit, that breathes life into it: a *poeitic* work that gives without reserve because of the nature of the Gift. God surrendering Godself to space and time, to an hour and a place, was itself the Gift without reserve. And so it remains holy as long as this breath is alive, as long as it goes on breathing. Quite simply put, a holy place, as a place in which an epiphanic event happens, is holy insofar as the breath or Spirit that gives witness to our spirit is there to consecrate it–and we call it "spiritual presence." There is no gift without a receiver. The monumental or archival value of a site might be an occasion, but only an occasion, for the Spirit to "con-spire" (*symmartyrein*, "bearing witness with," Rom. 8:16) with our spirit in the gathering of the faithful, unable by themselves to induce the epiphany. Spaces of monumental and archival thickness do not have the *vertical* or doxological quality of a space built for the praise to whom all glory is due. Their thickness does not have the *horizontal* or communal quality of a space built for the people to commune and look into each other's faces and find the Other, as Bergman expressed it. And in every other there is always the Other.

There is a biblical story that conveys the meaning of such a doxological space. In the Gospel according to Luke, Jesus went to visit his friends Martha and Mary. Martha, the text tells us, is extremely busy taking care of the house and being a dedicated host, while Mary sits at Jesus' feet and listens to him. The story's main point is well taken when, upon Martha's complaint that Mary is not helping her, Jesus tells her that she is too busy with the tasks of the house, while Mary has chosen the most important thing. However, the other side of the story is equally worth paying attention to. Although Martha's house was not the *most* important thing, it was indeed *very* important, for it provided the space that framed the encounter of Jesus and Mary. Martha's house was the wrapping, the cover, the shield of the Gift, a space of safety and intimacy; it was a sanctuary, and the Holy One was there hosted. A holy space is the frame in which healing takes place and is celebrated. It does not belong to the ultimate, nor is it of the essence, but it provides for a preliminary experience of salvation, which is what healing ultimately means. Holy places are *loci salutis*, places of salvation, places of shelter, places of nurturing. A holy place is the space where people gather, celebrate, nurture, and support each other in the real presence of divine mystery. The wrapping *presents* the Gift but covers, conceals, and protects it for the sake of the receiver. In receiving the Gift, one is also wrapped in it and by it enfolded.

Paul Robeson, in his autobiography entitled *Here I Stand* (which is not about Luther at the Diet of Worms in 1521!), presents us with a similar doxology. These are the words with which he opens his book. Envisage a proper architecture, a design, a building that would dignify and also shelter:

> I am a Negro. The house I live in is in Harlem. . . . Not far away is the house where my brother Ben lives: the parsonage of Mother A.M.E. Zion Church of which Ben has been pastor for many years. Next door to the parsonage is the church where on Sunday mornings I am united with the fellowship of thousands of my people, singing with them their songs, feeling the warmth of their handshakes and smiles. . . . Yes, I've got a home in that rock! I feel here the embrace of love. *Hello, Paul—it's good to see you! It's good to have you back!* And it's good to be back. For this is my community. . . . Here I stand.[18]

An epiphanic space is the space where you can say boldly, "Here I stand; here I belong."

ENVISIONING

An epiphanic *location* is a place in which church finds its vocation. However, and uniquely so, it is a space of *con*-vocation, *ad*-vocation, and *pro*-vocation. A place that calls us to (con-vocation), holds us by one another (ad-vocation), and sends us forth (pro-vocation).

This, then, is the task before us when we set ourselves to design and create a wrapping for the Gift. Envision, imagine a spatial design—a physical construction down to its ornaments, its music, its shapes and colors—that is fit to host the following scene: Two, three, maybe more women were witnesses to the most devastating experience of their lives; the beloved one was tortured and executed in an excruciatingly painful and shameful death (*mors turpissima*, "the vilest death," Origen called it). They were there and saw it all, as they were also eyewitnesses to the place where his body was laid. After that they went to the adjacent market to buy oil and herbs to prepare a balm to anoint

---

18. Paul Robeson, *Here I Stand* (New York: Othelo, 1958), 9–10.

a body in putrescence. But Shabbat came and they left all chores for a day of rest, lament, prayers, and remembrance. Early the next day they went back to the streets toward the tomb to wrap with ointment the Gift presumed to have been lost. Those women were heading for the most marvelous, albeit terrifying, surprise.

An epiphanic space is one in which people who experience it will say: "I have seen and been in a place others imagined." Such space is not a desideratum, a place yet to be built according to some ideal plans. It is already among us where and when I can speak boldly but, even more, listen attentively; this is where and when church takes place.

CHURCH HAPPENING

SPEAKING THE TRUTH
AND LIBERATION

10

The darkness drops again; but now I know
That twenty centuries of stony sleep
Were vexed to nightmare by a rocking cradle.
William Butler Yeats[1]

Where truth is spoken, there is the church;
and where church is, truth is spoken.
Where the church is, captives are set free;
and where captives are set free, there is the church.

These propositions about truth and church are worthy of further examination, and I herewith present my defense of them. The following discussion does not bring the conversation about the church to a conclusion, but it suggests that it is in the offing. It is not a closure but an opening for the truth lying beyond this text or in its interstices to come forth as a flaming power. This is what in the Rabbinic tradition of reading the Torah is called the "white fire." The white fire goes beyond the interpretations of the black letters of the text; it entails possibilities that are ever growing or, in other words, makes it possible for church to happen, not without the texts that inform it, but also not because of them. The church does not happen in the text but in its interstices.

SPEAKING THE TRUTH

Regardless of whether we practice what we preach, there is an intrinsic connection between truth speaking and the church, and it is certainly not self-evident. In our eager efforts to find ways to portray church, the truth eludes us in the very attempt of trying to represent it within either a political or an economic paradigm (or both). It eludes us, because the truth is an event and can only

---

1. From the poem "Second Coming," in William Butler Yeats, *"Michael Robartes and the Dancer": Manuscript Materials* (ed. Thomas Parkinson and Anne Brannen; Ithaca, N.Y.: Cornell University Press, 1994).

be approximated by principles through which we build relatively stable institutions that we call church in the sociological and institutional sense. These institutions represent the truth for which they stand, but in this representation they simultaneously conceal it. At the same time, they are also conduits that point to the truth for which they stand. But perhaps even more decisively, these institutions are a protective shield against the full exposure to the truth of which only evanescent glimpses irrupt and break through, destabilizing the very representations that purportedly are the truth's proxy or its outward construction. In other words, ecclesial institutions, built according to either of the paradigms mentioned, are never in themselves the church that happens. In her novel *The Color Purple*, Alice Walker conveys this idea through the words of her character Celie:

> She say, Celie, tell the truth, have you ever found God in Church? I never did. I just found a bunch of folks hoping for him to show. Any God I ever felt in church I brought with me. And I think all other folks did too. They come to church to *share* God, not to find God.[2]

The representation that provides stability to the church is at the same time that which conceals the truth for which it stands. The sociology of the church's economic or political mode of representation only detects this ambiguity between the ideal it puts forward and the failure to live it out. But this is not because it will eventually and progressively get there but because the very nature of "representation" entails concealment; the truth it claims is the very veil through which it is put forward.

Sociological analyses, theological typologies, and taxonomies developed by prominent thinkers like Max Weber, Ernst Troeltsch, and H. Richard Niebuhr or more recent attempts by Avery Dulles, Peter Paris, or Leonardo Boff[3] (mentioned in chapter 1, above), have presented various models of the church or ecclesial formations. These models, which have the function of being explanatory or exploratory, are to be either emulated or avoided. While the explanatory function of the model relies on the sociological observation of ecclesial formations, the exploratory function expresses a theological desideratum, an ideal to be achieved or else something to be averted. The methodological

---

2. Alice Walker, *The Color Purple* (New York: Pocket Books, 1982), 200–201. A similar observation is made by British author Monica Furlong, *Contemplating Now* (Cambridge, Mass.: Cowley, 1983), 36.

3. See chap. 1 for references to Weber, Troeltsch, and Dulles. Leonardo Boff, *Ecclesiogenesis: The Base Communities Reinvent the Church* (Maryknoll, N.Y.: Orbis, 1986). See also Richard J. Perry Jr., "A Critical and Comparative Analysis of 'Ideal Types' in the Ethics of Ernst Troeltsch, H. Richard Niebuhr, Eldin Villafañe, and Peter Paris" (Ph.D. diss., Lutheran School of Theology at Chicago, 1996).

approach these studies adopt is to present the sociological expressions of institutions called church or ecclesial communities and then to make a theological
move and draw ideals for what the church *ought* to be. This means that they
all assume that under certain sociological conditions some models or types of
church formation get closer than others in expressing what true church should
or should not be. This is what I referred to earlier and what Max Weber calls
"ideal types."[4] By "ideal" he does not necessarily mean something to be desired;
it could also be something to be obviated. The point is that the "ideal" that
the type presents is not to be found as such in actuality but expresses features
that *if* fully realized would then match the ideal. Ideal types are similar to
caricatures; they are not a picture, yet in broad strokes they present the most
characteristic features of that which is depicted. Between the ideal and the real
there is a hiatus that announces what is to be either filled or avoided. There
is a methodological assumption that underscores most of these analyses: the
sociological and institutional reality of the church finds its theological expression in an ideal not yet concretely or fully embodied. This method is at once
sociologically realist and theologically idealistic.

In ecclesiology this is the approach most often taken. It presents the option
of a road to be traveled versus the one to be avoided to achieve the desired end.
The argument for the road taken goes as follows: The church is still in need of
improvement; its truthfulness is not fully embodied. Time and again this has
become a truism, something that is self-evident without need of justification in
both Roman Catholic and Protestant thinking. Protestants have given expression to such truisms in the famous motto *Ecclesia reformata semper reformanda est,*
"The reformed church is always a reforming church." The Roman Catholic
Church, with its high ecclesiology, recently (in two documents of the Sacred
Congregation for the Doctrine of the Faith)[5] has denied the title "church" to
Protestant communions. But even this church, which claims to possess the truth,
will affirm, as it does in the Second Vatican Council (in *Lumen Gentium*), that the
church is holy but always in need of being further purified: *Ecclesia . . . sancta
simul et semper purificanda.*[6]

The common supposition, therefore, be it among Protestants or Roman
Catholics, is that the challenge is to get the "ought" out of a deficient "is." The
church "ought to be more inclusive," it "ought to be purpose driven," it "ought
to grow," it "ought to do outreach," it "ought to be more public in its witness," it
"ought to reencounter its roots," and one might add one's own "oughts" as well.

---

4. See chap. 1 under "Profiles of Church and Ministry."
5. *Dominus Iesus* (2000) and "Response to Certain Questions 2007," saying that their
truthfulness is seriously deficient, since they lack the historic episcopate and the valid
Eucharist.
6. Constitutio Dogmatica De Ecclesia: Lumen Gentium, 8.

The point is that it is not yet what it is supposed to be, or at least needs constant tending of its garden to pull the weeds out. When this does not happen, one looks over the fence, where the grass seems greener, and changes denomination in order to find a purer or more reforming expression of the ideal. How is this church, which is constantly in need of recycling, going to speak the truth if it is tainted with imperfections?

A look into the already referenced *Sanctorum Communio,* Bonhoeffer's dissertation, offers a very different approach to ecclesiology, which does not start with the "is-ought" pattern. The subtitle of the book, *A Theological [dogmatische,* in German] *Study of the Sociology of the Church,* suggests a reversal of the methodological approach mentioned earlier.[7] As opposed to Troeltsch, Niebuhr, and others, Bonhoeffer's modus operandi is not to study the social sources of an ecclesiology that will then be construed ideally with theological doctrines. For him, the sociological reality of the community ought to be there where the church, theologically speaking, already is in its plenitude. And where would that be?

While an in-depth exposition of Bonhoeffer's ecclesiology cannot be made here, his main point is not difficult to convey. Of the essence is his reliance on a basic Christological conviction, in which, following Luther's Christology, he affirms that Christ is in our midst, even according to his human nature;[8] he is among us concretely now and here. And he is among us "existing as church-community."[9] If one follows through the consequences of his argument, what Bonhoeffer proposes is not what the church ought to be, or how it can bail itself out of the frailty of its institutional reality. His proposal presents a different question. *Where* is the church-community as the existing Christ present? This means that sociology does not tell theology what the church is; sociology and the other sciences can instead offer instruments through which the true church can be detected.

---

7. Dietrich Bonhoeffer, *Sanctorum Communio: A Theological Study of the Sociology of the Church* (DBWE; trans. Richard Krauss and Nancy Lukens; Minneapolis: Fortress Press, 1998). The German edition is entitled *Sanctorum Communio: Eine dogmatische Untersuchung zur Soziologie der Kirche* (Munich: Chr. Kaiser, 1986).

8. Martin Luther, "Confession concerning Christ's Supper (1528)," *LW* 37, *Word and Sacrament* 3 (ed. and trans. Robert H. Fischer; Philadelphia: Fortress Press, 1961), 151–372. See also Neal James Anthony, "A Redeeming Presence within My Tomb, O Lord: Martin Luther's Radical Interpretation of the *Communicatio Idiomatum* and the Location of Complete 'Within Redemption' according to *Theologie Crucie*" (Ph.D. diss., Lutheran School of Theology at Chicago, 2008).

9. Bonhoeffer, *Sanctorum Communio,* 139. The expression in German, "Christus als Gemeinde existierend," is inspired by Hegel's notion of a collective personhood; Bonhoeffer, *Sanctorum Communio,* 133. For the reference to Hegel, see the long quotation on pp. 130ff., n. 68.

To know the whereabouts of the church, one needs to listen for where the truth is being uttered, to look for where the embodied Word exists, which is not only to be found in Jesus of Nazareth but how and where it is embodied today. This embodied *logos* as church-community is the truth in its plenitude (John 14:6). This is the theology of the social reality of the church. But how do we know where this truth can be found embodied today, and what its criterion is?

In Greek and in the whole of the New Testament, the word for truth is *alētheia.* The prefix *a-* denotes a negation. The etymology of *-lētheia* is obscure, but it possibly comes from the word *lēthē*, which means forgetfulness, oblivion, or concealment. The word *alētheia*, therefore, would mean the rejection of oblivion, which thus also connotes "manifestation" or "revelation" and implies that it is also about "remembrance." This chain of denotations entailed in the likely etymological meaning of the word for "truth" is important for a number of reasons, not the least of which is that it means to keep something out of oblivion. When in the words of institution we hear the anamnetic injunction, "Do this in remembrance of me" (1 Cor. 11:24), it is nothing but an aid to memory. By it we pray: "Remind us of where you are." And conversely: "Remind us of who we are." The Romantic motto "Be who you are" can only be interpreted in the sense that who we are is not something to be attained but something to be owned from what in memory has been suppressed. Selective memory is a contraption or a device of an individual or an institutional faculty of representation by which the truth is dissembled in the name of "reinventing" oneself.

To say that the church is the *logos* existing among us embodied (or as Luther said, referring to the Council of Chalcedon, "according to his *humanity*")[10] is to pronounce that he is there where the unconcealed truth manifests itself. This is indeed a disturbing affirmation. We don't like it because our societies are built upon one premise that is very reasonable: never disclose everything. Full disclosure is normally a rhetorical device to hide what should never come to light. However, both selective disclosure and selective memory are mechanisms of protective adaptation. It is reasonable because it is the question of survival that is at stake. The truth—a total exposure, unveiling, and disclosure—can only be an apocalyptic event in which salvation and condemnation are equally and immediately at hand. We must opt out of facing this alternative and, instead, settle for being safe. If in taking care of my health what my doctor and I myself (not to mention the insurance company) are concerned with is my safety, not my salvation, my preservation, not my liberation, then something about me and my condition must be kept from being exposed, either in the paperwork that describes my condition or in the medicines that fence my body from the

---

10. Luther, "Confession concerning Christ's Supper (1528)," *LW* 37:151–372.

invasive effects of bacteria. In order to be safe, one needs to be protected. To be protected means to be concealed, covered by a layer that veils and prevents exposure, as the skin is to the body, or as a shelter to the one who is exposed to the inclemency of the elements. The layers of protection that we require to be safe are ways in which we deflect the truth; they are "lies" without which we would not survive.

Often it is the function of the church to enforce these "lies." These are lies of deception aimed at protection; they are lies of the house, of the "economy." They are different from the lies of pretension, lies perpetrated in the public sphere, in the *polis*: in short, lies of the "political." Both have a function in the church, but they are not what makes church happen.

In a perceptive, albeit embarrassing, observation about the role of the church, British writer and biographer of religious personalities Monica Furlong wrote:

> It is customary to talk as if the purpose of the Church has been to put people in touch with God, or to keep them in touch with God. . . . [A]lthough in face of it [the Church] seems to exist to help its adherents into relationship with God, it equally, and perhaps essentially, plays the opposite role of trying to filter out an experience of transcendence which might be overwhelming.[11]

Indeed, the Bible itself has plenty of stories in which truth is dissimulated; revelation is averted, for it might be deadly overwhelming. Veils are necessary in the midst of ambiguity. The creation story is a fitting example, where God is portrayed in the role of an accomplice. When our mythic forebears Adam and Eve, who live in any and all of us (because a myth is a story that never took place but always happens), broke the basic commandment, they were ashamed of revealing themselves, ashamed of their nudity, of their truth (Gen. 3:8-10). And what did God do? God provided them with garments of skin to cover that which had to be revealed (Gen. 3:21). God covered up the truth of Eve and Adam. God provided them with their first "lie." And then humans came to be what we know we have become, and so we tend to forget who we are.

This story of "the Fall" is ultimately the story of each one of us. In order to step out of the closet and into the world, we need some "garments" to conceal and even render into oblivion who we really are. But to proclaim in faith that Christ is real and present even today, according to the flesh, means that the truth, which he is, is also real and present. Even when it is hidden from our sight, it is made manifest through faith. We have just got to believe the truth.

---

11. Monica Furlong, *Contemplating Now* (Cambridge, Mass.: Cowley, 1983), 36.

We cannot see it because all of us wear spectacles, the scales implanted in us by the common condition we share as sinners. But the fact that we don't see it, or the extent to which it is hidden, doesn't mean it is unreal and is not the truth; it means that it does eventually shine through, even while resisting a stable mode of representation.

Mary Douglas's often-quoted remark that the margins are the fragile part of a society[12] conveys that margins represent the fragility not of themselves but of the center of our society, where power is allocated. It calls the center into question. That is the reason we hide the margins. They are inconvenient. Indeed, the truth is inconvenient. People are kept away from our sight, in jails, in hospices, in ghettos, or sleeping in a park near our home when the night falls. They are the invisible people, as Ralph Ellison and Manuel Scorza call them, or non-persons, as Franz Kafka and Gustavo Gutiérrez call them.

The invisible were also the least ones in Matthew 25. They were invisible precisely to those who presumed to know Jesus, who would be none other than the so-called Christians. That seems to be the point of the parable of the Great Judgment. That they presumed to know Jesus is implicit in their claim when they say that they did not see him: "Lord, when was it that we *saw* you hungry or thirsty or a stranger or naked or sick or in prison . . . ?" (Matt. 25:44). They were confident that they would recognize Christ. This is why Paul, who registered the words of institution for celebrating the Lord's Supper in remembrance of Christ ("Do this in remembrance of me," 1 Cor. 11:24), uses the same words in the letter to the Galatians when he heeds the request of the community in Jerusalem: "Remember the poor" (Gal. 2:10). This story is Paul's account of the Council of Jerusalem as he recalled and registered it in his letter to the Galatians (2:1-10). The church as communion, *koinōnia*, is here affirmed as an event in which remembrance of those whom society forgets is the sole foundation on which church is grounded; it is grounded on what has been rendered to oblivion.

Again, Bonhoeffer's words are helpful here when he employs Luther's doctrine of Christ's ubiquity: "The doctrine of ubiquity teaches a Christ *outside* revelation." And then he adds, "[R]evelation becomes the *accident* of a substance *already* there."[13] The Christ who exists embodied today in the stuff of this

---

12. "[A]ll margins are dangerous. If they are pulled this way or that the shape of fundamental experience is altered. Any structure of ideas is vulnerable at its margins." Mary Douglas, *Purity and Danger: An Analysis of Concepts of Pollution and Taboo* (New York: Routledge, 2002), 149. See also Mary Philip, "Majestic at the Margins," in *Still at the Margins: Biblical Scholarship Fifteen Years after the Voices from the Margin* (ed. R. S. Sugirtharajah; London: T&T Clark, 2008), 104–13.

13. Dietrich Bonhoeffer, *Christ the Center* (New York: Harper & Row, 1966), 56 (emphasis added).

world becomes visible when church-community happens, when Christ who is already here among us is revealed to us.

The truth has the power of manifesting itself, the power of revelation, the power of disclosure and exposure. But this revelation, as Luther put it eloquently, is hidden in its opposite (*abscondita sub contraria specie*) and manifested in what is already existing in our midst. It is even more aptly expressed when Luther says again, "If you want to meet Christ don't stare at heaven; in the alleys, at your doorstep there you find Christ."[14] It is there that Christ exists as church-community. In the words of Bonhoeffer, this Christ existing as community is "the center of our existence . . . when he stands . . . on our periphery."[15] Revelation is an "accident" in the life of God existing among us, an accident in both the philosophical sense of the term (an attribute that is not substantial to the entity, as in "This house is blue," where blue is the accident of the house) and the common use of the term (as in a mishap). This is why Christians call the cross of Christ the decisive revelation; it was an "accident" in the life of God, by which God becomes manifest. So the church as Christ existing as community is hidden to our sight and hides itself in the deception of its "economy" and in the pretension of its "politics." However, *accidentally* it becomes manifest when we see church happening where we least expect it, where the truth shines through. Allow me to quote Bonhoeffer once more: this church "is the center of our existence . . . when Christian piety is displaced to the periphery of our being,"[16] and, we may add, of our society and our institutions (including the institutions called "church").

Hence the truth spoken is the manifestation of that which was rendered invisible, whether we say it in words or gaze at it in catatonic stupor. And this can happen anywhere, even in the institutional church! Church happens, sometimes even in churches when the truth crashes in on us as in an accident.

Where truth is spoken, there the church is, and vice versa. The vice versa makes it an even more daring thesis, but it is definitely coherent if the church is grounded and has its true existence as the ubiquitous presence of Christ in our midst (but more precisely *ubivolic*, that is, where he wants to be). What Luther said of Christ can, therefore, also be said about the church:

> You must place this existence of Christ which constitutes him as one
> person with God, far, far beyond created things, as far as God transcends
> them; and, on the other hand, place it as deep in and as near to all created
> things as God is in them.[17]

---

14. WA 20:514, 27f.
15. Bonhoeffer, *Christ the Center*, 60.
16. Ibid.
17. *LW* 37:223f.

Transcendence and immanence meet themselves in adjacent spaces, in the epidermal rubbing of encountering otherness.[18] It is in this adjacency that church happens; it is an event.

FREEING THE CAPTIVES

How liberating is it to say the truth? This is what moves us to my second proposition. If the church is where the truth is spoken, and vice versa, what is the form that this truth takes?

The Nazareth manifesto in Luke 4 is a text worth consulting to help us understand how truth telling and liberation, revelation and event are related in a paradigmatic way. The text refers to Jesus reading in the synagogue. Jesus is reading out of a scroll of the book of the prophet Isaiah (61:1-2). Jesus is reading out of a prophet's book. He is not himself prophesying. He is not denouncing or announcing a pending event bringing salvation or condemnation. And so he ends his reading with these intriguing words: "Today this scripture has been fulfilled in your hearing" (Luke 4:21). People were indeed intrigued—as we still are—by those words. They wanted to *see* something and not just hear it and believe. But then he adds the truth that in spite of the prophets' words of deliverance, not all is well. When severe famine hit the land, Elijah was sent to none but the widow at Zeraphath; Elisha, living among many lepers in his own land, cured only a Syrian high army official. If the church can be *seen* where the truth is uttered, liberation comes when it is heard. And hearing is much more than the physiological effects that a sound wave has on our tympanum. When Jesus was done with his speech, all in the synagogue were filled with rage and tried to throw him down a cliff on the hill on which the town of Nazareth was built. They could listen to the words of a prophet from far away, who was removed in time and space, but could not hear one of their own who spoke the truth; they would not listen. Jesus, though often taken as a prophet, a rabbi, or a teacher, was something else. Prophetic speech always addresses a situation from the outside. Prophetic indictments and announcements are *delivered* but not necessarily lived out. There is a word in the New Testament for bold statements that are made without reserve: *parrhesia*. *Parrhesia* means to say it (*rēsis*) all (*pan*); it can be translated as boldness of speech. To use the celebrated expression of Luther's Heidelberg Disputation, it means "to call the thing what it is."

---

18. Mary Philip in an essay explores the same theme with an insightfully different metaphor. She describes these adjacent spaces as if they were estuaries. See Mary Philip, "The Space in between Spaces: The Church as Prophetic Pest/Parasite," in *Being the Church in the Midst of Empire: Trinitarian Reflections* (ed. Karen L. Bloomquist; Minneapolis: Lutheran University Press, 2007), 91–106.

The late French philosopher, historian, and cultural critic Michel Foucault, in the last couple of years of his life and work, dedicated a considerable amount of time and energy to the exploration of *parrhesia* in classical Greek literature.[19] He defined it as a unique form of discourse, distinctly different from other forms. The term does not apply, for example, to the discourse of the sage, who in ivory tower detachment explains all things, or to the metaphysicians, the great theoreticians, and so forth. The parrhesiast does something else. For him or her it involves a personal investment with the element of risk, where the individual invests oneself in telling what the case is without generalizing or attempting systematization. Foucault also makes a distinction between the parrhesiast and the prophet. The prophet, like the sage, makes broad claims from a detached position. The prophet comes from outside. But unlike the sage, the prophet does it to denounce the present and announce a future. The parrhesiast, however, just says what the thing really is. It is a form of speech bound to the present. *Parrhesia* is an event that is unrepresentable; it cannot be reproduced.

Parrhesia is the riskiest form of discourse because, unlike prophecy, it does not defer anything to be eventually verified. To exercise *parrhesia* is to give up any and all bargaining power; there is no negotiation. One does not say something to get something in return. Therefore, *parrhesia* can seldom be exercised, for it involves investing oneself, one's very life, in what is being said; the enunciation is itself a deed. And the authenticity of what is being uttered can free the captives, but it can also bring the death of the one who calls the thing what it is. Jesus knew what that cost was. He paid it with his own life.

M. M. Thomas, one of the greatest Indian theologians of the second half of the twentieth century, used another concept (which he borrowed from Mahatma Gandhi) to convey the same idea: *satyagraha*. It is a Sanskrit word that Gandhi preferred over "nonviolence," which for him sounded too passive. *Satyagraha* means the force or firmness (*agraha*) of truth (*satya*). This is the notion that lies behind the inspiration of Gandhi and Christian theologians who themselves exercised *satyagraha* or the biblical *parrhesia*. In addition to M. M. Thomas in India, Dietrich Bonhoeffer in Europe and Martin Luther King Jr. in America are theologians who were followers of Gandhi and who practiced *satyagraha*, and some, like him, paid for it the ultimate price. However, history will never forget what these parrhesiasts did to free the captives, the ones who heeded their message; and in their hearing, the prophecy was, has been, and is being fulfilled.

---

19. Michel Foucault, *Das Wahrsprechen des Anderen: Zwei Vorlesungen von 1983/84* (ed. Ulrike Reuter et al.; Frankfurt: Materialis, 1988); idem, *Fearless Speech* (ed. Joseph Pearson; Los Angeles: Semiotext[e]), 2001.

Speaking boldly is liberating, even if it is the "free at last" of which Martin Luther King Jr. spoke regarding his own fate. That is where and when church happens.[20]

EVENT

The year was 1987 and the scenario a commonplace at that time: A group of landless peasants was camped on the side of a major highway linking Brazil to Paraguay in the southwest part of the country. The camp was squeezed between the runway and the fence of a well-guarded large farm, close to the city of Cascavel. Nearly 150 people–children, women, and men of all ages–lived under black plastic tents that were like ovens under the burning tropical sun. They had already been there for a number of months after being forcibly expelled from a farm they had occupied. Two of us from the Pastoral Land Commission (CPT), a Capuchin brother and I, were called in to help this group process some internal conflicts in the camp. Dysfunctional communal relations were never surprising under those stressful and dire conditions. Among the activities that took place during the two days we spent with them was a Bible study carried out with the whole camp. Many of those in the group were illiterate or had received little formal education, which meant that the printed text alone was not enough to convey the content of the chosen text. So in addition to using the printed text, we resorted to storytelling, dramatic performance, and artistic portrayals of scenes.

The text chosen was Revelation 13. We selected this text deliberately, for it is a text about naming the evil that surrounds us. In a sense, the text is elusive and intended to be so for the sake of dodging censorship. But for readers who were being persecuted, like the exiled John of Patmos himself, the meaning would come clearly through. It describes the system of this world as the dragon that brings forth two beasts. The first beast represents the oppressive economic system, called in the text the beast that comes from the sea. The second represents the emperor, called in the text the beast of the earth.

All the techniques employed by the author of the book of Revelation cannot be rehearsed here.[21] But the climactic moment of the narrative, for which John has been preparing the reader, is relevant here and so it was for the

---

20. Cynthia Moe-Lobeda gives this truth-speaking a different terminology and talks of it as "the power that frees and sends the church." Cynthia Moe-Lobeda, *Public Church: For the Life of the World* (Minneapolis: Augsburg Fortress, 2004), 50–54. She goes on to say that this power to serve others and resist evil is terribly costly (53).

21. For an interpretation of many nuances of this text, see my essay "Revelation 13: Between the Colonial and the Postcolonial; A Reading from Brazil," in *From Every People and Nation: The Book of Revelation in Intercultural Perspective* (ed. David Rhoads; Minneapolis: Fortress Press, 2005), 183–99 (chap. 13).

landless peasants we were accompanying. This climax is an almost sarcastic moment, in which John teases the readers into admitting for themselves that all the exotic creatures the seer has just displayed are nothing but figments of an idolatrous imagination. After all the supernatural, phantasmal imagery of dragons and beasts, the narrative ends with a riddle. "This calls for wisdom: let anyone with understanding calculate the number of the beast, for it is the number of a person. Its number is six hundred sixty-six" (v. 18). Behold the last surprise: the beast John has been talking about is *human*! Indeed, all too human! The number six symbolizes that which is close to perfection (seven) but not quite. In the words of Psalm 8, the human is made just "a little less than" a god. In addition, creating humans was the work God did on the *sixth* day, just before the closure of holy Shabbat. And a threefold six is very likely an emphatic assertion that it is six, it is six, it is six; that is, it is *wholly human* (symbolized by the emphatic threefold repetition), but nothing more than a human. After awakening his readers with jarring language and the use of cognitive dissonance while dodging the censors with the far-fetched imagery of uncanny creatures, the seer announces in a final ironic move that the incredible beings he has presented are nothing but God's beloved creatures corrupted by power into bestiality!

The seer undoes his own use of extravagant imagery in a surprising twist. He sets it up so that, here at the end, it is now up to the readers to reckon the riddle and own the naming for themselves; it is an invitation to escape from dissimulation.

This is also how the introduction to the Bible study ended, just short of naming the beast. One of the activities that followed was for people to do the naming of the beast for themselves and for their own situation, employing the same tactic John had used. The discussion groups then formed spontaneously, since we gave no directions as to how they should be organized. When the community assembled again late in the afternoon, the groups reported their findings. Some of the naming by the different groups was quite predictable. The beasts they named in their situation included the military, the government, the capitalist system, the rural-based oligarchy, the lumber industry, and so on—those who had deprived them of their land. These were the beasts that had brought them to this place and the beasts with which they as a community still had to contend. However, true as they were, these namings, which indeed have a prophetic tone, involved forces that were all external to the community, and in no way addressed the issues for which we had come to the camp, namely, the internal problems that were plaguing the community itself. To use the seer of Patmos's vision, there was the need not only to name the external beasts oppressing them but also to name the *image(s)* of the beast—those things that the community "worshipped" but which were really of their own making (v. 14): a fetish, an idol.

Then, to our surprise, one of the groups named some of these "images" of the beast. This group was comprised only of women (all the other groups were mixed). Their words cut to the chase. In their report, there was *parrhesia*, the boldness that takes a risk by speaking up. Their naming included three related things: pans (a symbol for the arduous work, normally done by women, of cooking over a small open fire under a hot black plastic tent filled with smoke); alcohol (which mostly men indulged in at night); and the central committee of the camp that was ultimately responsible for administering the camp and which, in this particular camp, unlike others, was comprised of males only). This was the naming that took the courage of a "parrhesiast," a bold speaker. The naming of the beasts by other groups was definitely true and prophetic indeed, and because of their political training, these groups were able to identify those beasts—even without our seer's help. The namings of the women's group point to the fact that we are often blind to the corrupt and destructive reality that is very close and familiar to us, and which we would rather deny because of its consequences. If we name it out loud, we may be able to see it for what it is and dispel its power over us. But in naming it there is risk, and yet, as the poet has said, where risk exists, there grows also that which liberates.[22] And in this liberation church happens, as it happened that afternoon in that improvised tent-camp of landless peasants who were struggling for justice.

That afternoon, amid tears, there was peace, a soothing serenity. It was not a Saturday, but it was Shabbat, and the word that was proclaimed culminated in a Eucharistic celebration in which things left behind, rendered to oblivion, were rescued from selective forgetfulness. But in the very telling of this story, I am stabilizing its figure, even suggesting a representation of what is not able to be represented, much less reproduced. When it happened, it did so with a Roman Catholic priest and a Protestant pastor present to facilitate the event. And yet it did not happen because of them. Neither did it happen because one of them represented the church by its "economy" or the other by its "politics." That afternoon church did not happen because of the complementary thrust of these two modes of church representation. Church happened not because of the Roman Catholic priest or the Lutheran pastor or their adeptness in representing the church, although they were circumstantially instrumental in providing the background conditions that on the occasion hosted the church event. Yet church happened that hot afternoon beside a rural highway in southwest Brazil.

---

22. Friedrich Hölderlin, *Poems and Fragments* (trans. Michael Hamburger; London: Anvil Press Poetry, 2004), 551.

IN THE OFFING

If church happens when the utterance of the truth becomes a liberating event, one needs to pay attention to when truth is spoken. And this occurs, as it were, against the grain. It takes place when the two fundamental paradigms of Western rationality, the "political" and the "economic," are rendered incapable of conveying the truth that manifests itself against the logic of the regimes through which their representation is acknowledged, affirmed, and sustained.

What more can be said here other than to confess that what we normally call church is often not truthful to its theological meaning? And on this account a sociologically based ecclesiology is not wrong, but it does not mean that the true church does not *already* exist embodied in our midst where the truth is spoken and the captives are set free. This is a fundamental ecclesiological affirmation, and it comes without any assurance of a verifiable stable ground by which it can be sustained.

In any given discourse, the phrase "in the offing" does not mean a conclusion or the close of the conversation. It is about a waiting in expectation, a trust in something that seems distant but still in sight and plausible. It is an offer to begin a conversation, a conversation that will evince the fact that church happens not because of, but indeed in the midst of–and in spite of–our sustained attempts to represent church. Church when it happens is not representable. Church is aroused and inflamed by the white fire in the interstices of our ecclesial discourses, offering hope, a hopeful anticipation of the promise of something nearby or at hand, adjacently both ready and *at ease.*

ACKNOWLEDGMENTS

This book had its inception in 2001 in the preparation and delivery of lectures at the fiftieth anniversary of the *Cátedra Carnahan* at Instituto Universitario ISEDET in Buenos Aires, Argentina. Since then it has taken shape thanks to numerous seminars, consultations, and conversations with friends, colleagues, and students near and far. The basic insights and inspirations for this work, however, were garnered during the years (1985–1992) I worked in Brazil with the Ecumenical Commission on Land (Comissão Pastoral da Terra–CPT) in its ministry with landless and displaced peasants in whose midst I saw and experienced church happening.

Though many and varied friends, mentors, and comrades helped shape my reflections on the church, I owe much to the late Juan Luis Segundo, S.J. Conversations with colleagues and friends, be they at a dinner table or across a seminar hall, and even when they had opposing views, played an invaluable role in determining the contours and trajectories of the book. To that end I would like to acknowledge the mentorship and collegial support offered to me by Philip Hefner, Carl Braaten, Reinhard Hütter, Antje Jackelén, Kadi Billman, Barbara Rossing, and Guillermo Hansen, among many others.

Three chapters have been revised and reconstrued from previously published articles. An earlier edition of chapter 4, "On the Authority of the Scriptures: More Than Enough," appeared in *Lutheran Quarterly* 19, no. 4 (Winter 2005): 373–91. Part of chapter 8, "At Ease: Ecclesial Adjacencies," was published in *Christian Century* 123, no. 22 (October 2006): 27–31, and most of the ninth chapter, "The Place of the Church," appeared in *Currents in Theology and Mission* 31, no. 5 (October 2004): 368–80.

I am indebted to Fortress Press and express my deep appreciation to Michael West, editor in chief, for signing up the book as one of its 2010 spring releases; to Susan Johnson, acquisitions editor; and to the staff of Fortress Press for their support and encouragement in this endeavor.

The research for this book was enhanced and made possible by funds from the Lilly Theological Research Grant from the Association of Theological Schools. My sincere gratitude goes to Stephen Graham, Director of Faculty Development and Initiatives in Theological Education, and to Frances

Pacienza, Coordinator, Faculty Programs and Organizational Evaluation, for the timely administering of the same.

The Lutheran School of Theology at Chicago granted me a sabbatical leave in the spring of 2008, during which most of the manuscript was drafted. To the school and its administration, to its many students and the network of contemporaries, goes my heartfelt gratefulness.

I would also like to express my gratitude to Dr. Dagny Bloland and Mathew C. Abraham for their invaluable time in helping me navigate through the nuances of language and making the manuscript more accessible to readers than it otherwise would be. Robert Saler read part of the manuscript and offered insightful suggestions for which I am thankful. To no one am I more obliged for the development and editing of this book than to Dr. Mary Philip (Joy), who accompanied me, "at ease" and with efficient care, through the entire process, from conception to publishing, of making this, my writ, available to a larger public.

Finally, I owe my deepest thanks to my family, especially Christiane, for surviving endless hours of grumpy moods (typical of me while writing) and yet graciously giving serene support.

INDEX

A

abrahamic minority, 94
abscondita sub contraria specie, 118
accident, 120, 161–62
actio, 33
adiaphora, 93, 146
adjacency, *ad-jacens, adjacentia*, vii, 2, 10
ad-vocation, 152
Agamben, Giorgio, 129, 132
agraha, 164
alētheia, 80, 83, 159
Alves, Rubem, 82, 122, 123
anamnesis, anamnetic, 122, 159
antinomianism, vi, 70, 73, 74
apostolic, v, 3, 15, 40, 44, 47, 49, 50, 52, 54, 61, 62, 63, 66, 70, 78, 81, 84, 123
apousia, 94, 116, 138
Arbeit, 33
archē, 77, 79
archival, 144–46, 151. *See also* monumental
Aristotle, 32, 32n4, 33, 36, 37n16, 39, 42
art, 32, 61, 67, 68, 122, 148, 149
Augustine, 39n24, 79n17, 89, 89n2, 100, 114–15, 115n22, 116, 137
authority, vi, 23n38, 25, 27, 35, 36, 43, 49, 50, 51n16, 54, 55, 59, 61–62, 63n9, 89n2, 90, 169
autopoietic, 43, 43n35, 44n37
awakening, 24, 121–23, 166
Azzi, Riolando, 15n10

B

Badaliya, 129
banquet, vii, 140, 141
Barmen Declaration, 108, 108n4
Barth, Karl, 3n4, 97
Barthes, Roland, 99
Basil, 33, 33n5, 50, 50n11, 51–54, 62, 62n5
Bayer, Oswald, 17–18, 39n24, 63, 63n10, 94n14
beast, 2, 165–67
Bedford, Nancy, 41n29
belonging, 4, 5, 43, 70, 90, 99, 111, 128, 138, 140, 143

J

Jenkins, Philip, 16n12
Jinkins, Michael, 96n23
John of Patmos, 165
Jonas, Hans, 101n35
justice, 1, 14, 70, 73, 86; civil justice, 71; social justice, 14; struggle for justice, 13, 167; injustice, 72–73; social injustice, 12, 109

K

Kafka, Franz, 47, 102, 140, 161
kairos, 10
Karkkainen, Veli-Matti, 15n11
Käsemann, Ernst, 75, 76n3, 82, 83n26
kerygma, 62, 76
Kierkegaard, Søren, 47, 49, 50, 50n10, 101
kingdom, 3–4, 54, 125–128; kingdom of heaven, 74; kingdom of God, 126
koinōnia, vi, 34, 89, 104, 119, 161
kosmos, 125
krisis, 114, 116
Kuhn, Thomas, 121n42
Küppers, Jürgen, 37n18

L

labor, 9, 32, 32n4, 33, 34n9, 36–37, 39, 42, 103, 121, 147–49, 147n14; *poietic* labor, 149; laborer, 39, 148–49. *See also* work
Lefebvre, Henri, 115n23, 140
Lessing, Gotthold Ephraim, 17n15, 60–61
Lewis, Sinclair, 23, 23n37, 24–26, 35, 98
liberation, 25, 28, 108–9, 119, 127, 130–32, 155, 159, 163, 167
liminal, 2; liminality, 117
Lindbeck, George, 17, 18
locale, vii, 111, 115n23, 139n3, 141–145, 150. *See also* space
locus salutis, 92
logos, 78, 159; *logos ensarkos*, 104
Loisy, Alfred, 127
Löwith, Karl, 114n19, 115
Lukács, Georg, 22, 23, 95, 98–99
Luther, Martin, vi, 6–9, 22, 37–38, 38n21, 39–41, 53–54, 56, 60, 62–63, 65–74, 83–87, 94, 101, 104, 147n13, 148n15, 150, 152, 158–59, 161–64

M

Machado, António, 90
magisterium, 2, 47n3; *magisterium episcoporum*, 24, 55; *magisterium theologorum*, 55
Manichaeanism, 100
margins, 4–5, 8–9, 34n11, 83, 116–17, 119, 121, 128, 161; marginal, 9, 16, 81, 119; marginality, 118; marginalization, 85, 118; marginalized, 5, 108, 128
Marion, Jean-Luc, 42m31, 95n19, 96, 149n17